Longaberger

Dave Longaberger

Longaberger

An American Success Story

HarperBusiness • *An Imprint of* HarperCollins*Publishers*

HarperCollins books may be purchased for educational, business,
or sales promotional use. For information please write: Special
Markets Department, HarperCollins Publishers, Inc., 10 East 53rd
Street, New York, NY 10022.

FIRST EDITION

Designed by Fritz Metsch

Library of Congress Cataloging-in-Publication Data

Longaberger, Dave.
    Longaberger : an American success story / Dave Longaberger
with Robert L. Shook.—1st ed.
        p. cm.
    ISBN 0-06-662105-4
        1. Longaberger Company—History.   2. Longaberger, Dave.
    3. Basket making—Ohio—History.   4. Basket makers—
    Ohio—Biography.   I. Shook, Robert L., 1938–   II. Title.

TS910.L66 2001
338.7'61746412'092—dc 21   00–047289

01   02   03   04   05   RRD   10   9   8   7   6   5   4

CONTENTS

by Tami Longaberger

Writing this foreword is a very humbling experience and may be one of the most difficult tasks I've faced in many years. The reason is that I'm trying to reflect not only my personal views but also those of all members of the Longaberger family. These views are about a man who gave us so much and who did so much not just for us but for countless others. Of course, I'll never be able fully to capture everyone's views because Dave Longaberger was such an incredible person to each of us in very different and individual ways. Events and emotions throughout the day of my father's funeral were overwhelming for everyone involved. This was a day, I would later realize, that spoke volumes about his relationships with me and with the entire Longaberger Company.

Dad had asked that I talk at the service, but I had resisted. Speaking at a parent's funeral has to be one of the hardest things for a son or daughter to do. Grieving over my loss, I wondered if I might not make it through the remarks. Even if I did, how was I to convey the worth of my dad's life in a few brief minutes? What could I say that would be meaningful to an audience that already knew him so well in so many ways? Some eight thousand people attended his memorial service, which lasted two days. This was a diverse group whose lives had been transformed by the company he had created and, in hundreds if not thousands of instances, by personal moments shared with Dad himself. It seemed that all of them wanted to tell me their own stories about my dad, about how he had touched them, changed them, pushed them, and rewarded them.

My attention was being pulled in a hundred different directions, and for one long, scary moment I didn't know how to go about fulfilling my dad's wish. Then it hit me. I remembered that, deep in his heart, Dad had always found more faith in people and their abilities than they had in themselves. At the office and on the shop floor, he'd constantly challenge us to do something that we might have thought impossible. Then we'd go out and get it done, report back to him, and he'd just smile and say, "See, I knew I hired the right people." When employees saw the unwavering confidence that Dave Longaberger had in them, they weren't going to let him down. Over time, his confidence built a strength within the company that was pervasive and incredibly powerful.

With this in mind, I found myself standing in the pulpit. I looked out at the mourners and realized that something amazing had happened. Once again, even in death, he was pushing me to stretch, to try new things, to meet the next challenge. That is his legacy to me and to his business, and that is why The Longaberger Company can confidently approach the future even though he's gone. Dad set it up that way.

I think it's important to say that my dad was involved with the creation of this book for all but the final editing. You'll learn a lot about him in these pages. Yet, because he was humble, you won't find certain special acts and qualities that are well known to all of us who were closest to him. He wouldn't detail all the sacrifices he made in order to get the business started, nor describe what it was like when he came home after making some tough decisions, nor the absolute agony he went through when he had to lay people off. You won't read about the many people he lent money to in the form of a fifty here and a hundred there, or that some took advantage of him and never paid him back. Only somebody who was with him each day saw these things and knew that his love for his company and its people had no boundaries. His employees were his family. He was constantly looking to help our people, his family, to grow and do things differently and to improve what they did on the job. That remains a hallmark of our company today.

You also won't read what it was like to encounter his sense of humor first hand. Both on and off the job, my dad saw himself as a comic. He loved jokes and pranks and having fun. To get a laugh, he used rubber chickens, disappearing ink, and pepper gum that tasted awful. He'd tie a knot in your drinking straw or slip fudge into your coffee. One time, when I was in high school, we had been dining at a restaurant. When I returned to our table from the rest room, he had everyone in the place stand up and applaud. I was so embarrassed that I went back into the rest room and crawled out the window.

Growing up, I never imagined going to work for my father, let alone following him as the Longaberger CEO. In 1984 I graduated from The Ohio State University with a degree in marketing. At that time the company had 350 employees and no college graduates on the payroll. It wasn't looking to hire college grads and probably wouldn't have brought in its first one if she hadn't been Dave Longaberger's daughter.

My father had had a difficult time in school because of his stuttering and other problems. Never sold on formal education, he had advised me against attending college. I think a lot of his motivation in life came from wanting to prove to himself and others that he could do things beyond what people expected of someone without a lot of schooling. So you can imagine how impressed he was with my degree! Happy for me, yes. Impressed? Let's just say he had his own ideas about business. When I was twenty-one, he asked me to work for him and I said, "Yes, but only until I get a real job." He must have loved that one, knowing right there that my real business education was about to begin. I spent the next fifteen years watching him follow his intuitions, issue his challenges, express his vision, and make the decisions that needed to be made. Some of those decisions were about me, and even in the early days we always had a good working relationship. In the heat of business, I may have quit, or he may have fired me once or twice, but only for an hour or so.

Without my knowing it, he was constantly imparting values that will be illustrated in this book, values that have been central to the company's success in moving from 350 employees and $8 million in revenues in 1973 to some 8,000 employees and $1 billion by the end of the year 2000. Dad was constantly reinventing The Longaberger Company, and his concept and view of constant and positive change are still embraced today. Anyone who knew him recognized his familiar phrase "subject to change."

Here is one example of my dad's approach to people and things. About a decade ago, he came to me and said, "Tami, we ought to start selling pottery. Get your marketing team on this and get it developed." I wasn't convinced that this was a good idea, so I didn't immediately follow through. Then, at our 1990 convention, without letting me know what was coming, he stood up and announced to our sales force that we'd have a pottery line within six months. He'd just made a public commitment to this plan, and we now had no choice but to get it done. Our pottery line is now a $200 million business. What he did with pottery he also did with cloth liners for our baskets and several other innovative products.

Most famously (depending on whom you talk to!), he single-handedly envisioned our new and much-needed corporate headquarters in the precise form of our classic Market Basket. This was the craziest notion anyone had ever heard. It made our finance people cringe not only because the unique design cost an extra $2 million but also because, in the words of one group of bankers, "If things go bad, you won't be able to sell it."

"If things go bad," my dad said, "I won't care."

Once again, Dad was right. We've already earned back $2 million and more because of the publicity generated by his design.

I know now that I went through the same process with him that many others did. I originally resisted some of his ideas, as realtors, bankers, architects, and others had done. Only gradually did I learn that he was a visionary with the gifts and the will to make his vision not just real but a unique and fantastic success. He was never focused just on the present. With our vendors, for instance, he would always challenge them to do more with less, and they responded. This partnership with our vendors, with the objective of doing things better for less and bringing our customers more value, remains a pillar of Longaberger today. Often, to a comment that such and such a project will look great when completed, he'd say, "It's there already. I've seen it."

Today, in my role as CEO, I sometimes tell others in the company that we need to move in a certain direction, and they don't instantly respond. I think back to my father's conviction that if you instinctively know something is right for the business, then you must "follow your gut," as he would have put it, by finding in yourself a way to get others involved, motivating them to find a way. Those times that Dad "fired" me from Longaberger, he wanted me to stay. He wanted to teach me, and that's exactly what he did through his actions and his relentless devotion.

Another of his lessons was that the workers doing a particular job were always the best source of information about their own areas or departments. The weavers know what is happening in that vast, amazing section, including where the problems are and how to fix them. Get down on the manufacturing floor, he would tell me, and talk to the people there and get some answers. One of my fondest images is of my dad walking on that floor, which was his haven inside the business. He loved to speak with employees, joke with them, and draw strength from them. This was never more true than after he became ill. His greatest asset was his relationship with the people at the company. Those connections have not been severed, not even in death.

In June 1997, Dad was diagnosed with cancer. I remember leaving the hospital after learning this and knowing that my life had changed forever. I was already thinking about everything that had to be done and all the people I needed to contact. The magnitude of the shift in responsibility hit me, and I began putting together my list of things to do. I wasn't going to be able to be the daughter who took care of her father now, because Dad was counting on me to take care of the business. That was the biggest burden I could lift from him. He'd been consciously preparing me for this day for fifteen years. I couldn't imagine letting him down because, inside, I knew that what he saw for all his people, including me, was success. This was my dad's gift.

For months, I struggled to understand why he'd gotten cancer. My greatest comfort came in thinking of this period as Dad's ultimate sacrifice. Since starting the company, in 1973, he'd sacrificed for it over and over. Now, rather than lie down and take it, he would tough his way through two years of this devastating disease. Why? To give everyone at Longaberger the time to adjust to the idea that he wouldn't always be around. This wasn't the best thing for Dad, but it was the best thing for the transition of the company—financially, legally, emotionally, and organizationally. If he'd just given up, we wouldn't have been able to handle things nearly as well.

During those two years, my relationship with my father, which had had its share of challenges, became complete. I knew that I had his love and his approval to run the company. Unlike a lot of entrepreneurs, he'd been smart enough to groom someone to take over after his death. That's rarely the case in a family- or founder-held company. It is a testament to how much he cared for this business and his absolute commitment that it should outlive him. Before the end, we had many chances to talk, and there was nothing left unsaid.

He didn't hand off the company to me as he was lying on his deathbed. He had already done it by making me earn the job every step of the way. He let me make mistakes, and after I'd really screwed up he'd smile and say, "There, you learned something, didn't you?"

I'd get mad and ask him, "If you knew that already, why did you let me fail?"

"So you could figure out," he would say, "how to reach around and pick yourself up. Because when you need to do this the most, I won't be there to help you."

He was always looking ahead.

Most people in business are concerned about the next quarter or the next six months. In our meetings, Dad would say, "In a hundred years, we'll all be dead, but what will the company look like? What will it be trying to accomplish?" That's an extremely unusual way for a CEO to think. He wanted these questions to be the guiding spirit at Longaberger.

In a hundred years, I hope we're doing business in ways that are new and visionary, but I also hope we have the same values my father always had: integrity, honesty, standing on our word, being respectful of others, treating people right, and understanding our customers and sales associates. The values and business principles he taught us all will sustain our company for generations to come.

This foreword would not be complete without listing all the Longaberger family members who meant so much to my dad.

His father and mother: John Wendell and Bonnie Jean Gist Longaberger.

His second daughter: Rachel Longaberger.

His grandchildren: Kaitlin, Dustin, Claire, Matthew, and Benjamin.

His brothers and sisters: Genevieve, Wendy, Jerry, Larry, Rich, Mary Ann, Judy, Ginny Lou, Gary, Carmen, and Jeff.

PREFACE

by Robert L. Shook

As a business writer and Columbus, Ohio, resident, I have followed the incredible success story of The Longaberger Company for years. Like many central Ohioans, I have marveled at how that little basket company in Dresden has become a major force in the state's economy.

In late 1998, the company's public relations department called me to discuss the possibility of my becoming involved in its founder's autobiography. The book would tell Dave Longaberger's story as well as guide aspiring entrepreneurs. Dave planned to meet with three writers and select one of them to work on his book. At the time I had two book contracts, with final drafts due by late 1999. No matter. I didn't want to pass up the opportunity to meet a man who had become a living legend in the past twenty years. I'd meet him, and if we reached an agreement, I'd get started on Dave's book after finishing my two other manuscripts.

I spent two days researching the company. On October 5, 1998, I met with Dave's daughter Rachel and with Tom Reidy, the company's in-house legal counsel. During dinner at the Hyatt Hotel in Columbus, Rachel and Tom gave me a detailed account of the Longaberger story, and by the end of the meal I was convinced that the book had a lot of potential. They also mentioned that Dave had cancer. He was one of twenty patients in the United States receiving a particular experimental treatment at the M. D. Anderson Cancer Center in Houston. They were cautiously optimistic; but having lost a loved one to cancer, I was quite concerned.

After dinner I was told, "We'll talk to Dave and get back to you within a week."

The next afternoon I received a call from Rachel. "I spoke to my father about you, and he would like to meet you. When are you available to visit us?"

The following morning I met Dave. He was one of those people whom you instantly like. I was impressed that such a successful man would be so humble. I also enjoyed his sense of humor. What a fun person to work with, I thought. Having collaborated on other books, I believe it is important to have the right chemistry with someone you'll be working with. If the chemistry is not right, I walk away. This is a cardinal rule of mine, and I have never deviated from it.

Dave must have liked me, too. At the end of the meeting, he said to Rachel, "It won't be necessary for me to meet with those other writers. If it's agreeable with Bob, I'd like to work with him."

Although Dave was upbeat about his cancer, I wanted to begin the project right away. Later that week, I made arrangements to delay my two other writing projects so Dave and I could get started. In hindsight, after getting to know Dave, I felt sure I was doing exactly what he wanted me to do. It wasn't as if he manipulated me, because he was not like that. It was just that he was so sincere and genuine, it's what I wanted to do. As I would soon find out, Dave was by far the best people person I had ever met. I believe this quality played a major role in his success.

During the next four months, I tape-recorded extensive interviews with Dave, some as long as four hours. I also interviewed Longaberger employees, associates, and family members. It was a great learning experience for me. I have often said that the research, combined with the writing of a manuscript that's several times longer than a thesis, is equivalent to my earning an M.B.A. In the case of this book, I'll make that a Ph.D.! In short, Dave talked to me about principles of working with people that were far superior to anything I'd come across during my forty-year business and writing career. Over the years, I have studied the tactics and techniques of the nation's top management gurus. I've read their books and magazine articles and attended their lectures. I've also interviewed many of the CEOs of leading companies such as General Motors, Ford, Honda, General Electric, AT&T, DuPont, American Express, Prudential, and MCI. And I have conducted lengthy personal interviews with many of America's most successful entrepreneurs. My exposure to these eminent business leaders has given me valuable insight into how America's foremost companies are run.

To articulate the lessons taught by these great leaders, I must fully understand what they are telling me. In spite of all my years of studying and writing about business, the lessons I learned from Dave Longaberger have been the most enlightening of my career. His ability to lead and motivate people is borne of sheer genius. I have never met anyone so admired by employees, nor have I ever come across anyone who has generated so much loyalty. Interestingly, Dave never went to college or took a business-training course. He started with nothing, and in the course of twenty-five years built a $700 million privately owned company. I attribute his incredible success to his excellent people skills.

Again and again, Dave told me, "I don't care what business you're in, your success will ultimately depend on the relationships you build with people." The more I observed The Longaberger Company, the more I realized how right he was. His formula for success seemed so obvious, yet it's a management principle that people rarely apply.

As you read this book, you'll conclude as I did that the world needs more people like Dave Longaberger—individuals of integrity who are not willing to compromise their principles or sacrifice their dreams. And what excites me most is that if readers emulate Dave, there will eventually be a lot more of us out there like him.

In recent years, Dave has become known for his vision. He never hesitated in sharing his dreams with his people. In its infancy, he talked about the future of The Longaberger Company, and in the beginning he had his share of pessimists and naysayers. However, as his visions unfolded, people began to accept Dave's forecasts as gospel. What Dave talked about usually came true.

When I last interviewed Dave, his cancer had advanced, and I felt it was probably the last time we'd meet. By this point, I had become very fond of him. I realized that perhaps Dave's most endearing quality was that he cared so much about you that you automatically felt the same way about him. I clearly knew why the thousands of men and women at The Longaberger Company loved him so much.

I was about halfway through writing the manuscript when I told Dave, "I now have everything I need on tape to write your story."

"Keep up the good work, Bob," he encouraged me.

"I anticipate completing the manuscript within ninety days," I told him. "I'll be anxious to have you read the final draft."

"That won't be necessary," he answered. "I can already visualize the book without having to read it."

On March 17, 1999, Dave succumbed to cancer. Two days later, an estimated eight thousand people attended a memorial service to pay their last respects to a man they dearly loved.

I'll never forget my last meeting with Dave. I'm sure he knew he'd never have the opportunity to read our book. But by sharing his vision of it, he was expressing his faith in me. Like the thousands who worked for Dave, I had been inspired by him to do my best, and I was determined not to let him down.

This is Dave's story as told in his own words.

ACKNOWLEDGMENTS

The Longaberger Company wishes to express sincere appreciation to Executive Editor Dave Conti and the entire staff at HarperCollins, who have been invaluable in showing all of us what goes into the making and marketing of a book; to literary agent Reid Boates for all of his much-needed and appreciated advice; to Stephen Singular for his invaluable editorial assistance; to Tom Reidy and Bob Beam, who took time from their busy schedules to read and edit the original manuscript and to provide guidance along the way; to Marge Shipley, who double-checked the historical facts and worked tirelessly on the pictorial archives; and to Julie Moorehead and Karen Blackstone for developing and implementing a marketing plan to share this book with readers everywhere.

And we want to give special thanks to Robert Shook for his dedicated efforts in helping us tell our story. His work has made this book a true success.

INTRODUCTION

I might be the last guy you'd figure could make it in the business world. I was twenty-one when I finally finished high school. If my class had elected a "least likely to succeed," it would have been me.

Many years have passed since I completed my formal education. But I've learned so much more since then about things they can't teach you in school. You're not going to learn how to deal with people from reading textbooks, and the way I look at it, understanding people is what builds great organizations. The lessons I learned about people are what I attribute to having made The Longaberger Company a $700 million business. That's what our revenues totaled in 1998, and with the management team now in place, you ain't seen nothin' yet!

It's hard to pinpoint exactly when our company made its debut. In 1973, when I owned a restaurant and a grocery store in Dresden, Ohio, I started selling baskets that my father made. For the first five years I was simultaneously running three businesses, so the basket company wasn't getting nearly the attention a start-up enterprise demands. I was spending a good sixty hours a week running my grocery and restaurant businesses, which didn't leave much time to focus on baskets. It wasn't until 1978 that I started to put some serious effort into it. Nonetheless, 1998 was officially our twenty-fifth anniversary.

Just like my grandfather, Dad worked at the Dresden Basket Company, which closed in 1936. Dad went on to work full-time as a back-tender-machine operator at the Dresden Paper Mill, but he kept making baskets in his spare time. As a father of twelve, Dad did his moonlighting at night and on weekends.

When Dad was a boy, basket making was big business throughout east central Ohio. The town of Dresden borders on Appalachian territory, so most people worked in coal mining and farming. By the time I came along, though, coal was starting to fade out, and most of the farmers had gotten factory jobs. Dresden was still a nice little town to live in, but its economy had seen better days.

In 1973, basket making didn't seem like such a bright idea for a start-up company. People thought, "Well, what can you expect from someone who took fifteen years to finish school?" After all, everything you bought at a store came in a cardboard box or a plastic bag. Handmade baskets were relics.

I didn't go to college, and I didn't read books on how to get rich or how to start a new business. Nor did I ever have any formal training with a big company. Everything I know, I learned by listening and watching. I was never a good reader, but I was a great thinker. Without a doubt, sometimes I learned my best lessons by making mistakes. And believe me, I made plenty of mistakes to learn from! I did things my way, which a lot of folks thought was unconventional. But it was my own style, what you could call "thinking outside the box."

Mark Twain once defined a crank as "a man with a new idea—until he succeeds." When I first started selling baskets, I was called a lot worse things than a crank. For a while, I was considered the dumbest man in town when I set up shop in an old woolen mill. When I bought it, it hadn't been in operation for over a quarter of a century. At the time, it had only part of a roof and full-grown trees sprouting through it! People also laughed at me when I told them about my plans to make our area a guest destination. People couldn't imagine why out-of-towners would ever want to visit someplace out in the boondocks. Then there were those people who thought I had really gone off the deep end when I announced our new headquarters would be housed in a seven-story basket-shaped building.

Admittedly, my management style is unorthodox, so I understand why people call me crazy. I'm sure it has to do with the fact that I advocate such things as having fun in the workplace. "Work should be twenty-five percent fun," I tell everyone. For most businesspeople, the word *fun* is not in their vocabulary during office hours.

I also believe that to be at their best, people need their rest. For this reason, I encourage everyone to leave the office by 5 P.M. sharp. Most executives think they are getting "more bang for their buck" by having their people put in a lot of extra hours. I don't see it that way. To me it's counterproductive, so I practically chase people out of the building at closing time. "What's the problem?" I razz them. "Can't you get your work done during regular office hours?"

Another thing that I promote is having employees evaluate their managers. With other companies, it's usually the other way around. At our company, we refer to it as an "upward evaluation." To do this, we have employees fill out detailed questionnaires telling us what they think about their bosses. Makes sense, doesn't it? Who knows more about managers' skills than the people they manage?

As you read this book, I'll let you in on a lot of things you probably never heard about before. You'll read about a different style of management that's often contrary to what they teach you at the business schools. At the very least, much of what you'll read will be different from anything you've come across. But don't be too fast to refute it; everything I tell you in this book has been field-tested. It works! And it's made The Longaberger Company grow far beyond what anyone ever thought was possible.

Now, we're certainly not an "overnight success story." It took us a quarter of a century to get where we are today. We've had some major setbacks along the way. We've also had our share of good luck and blessings. And I never hesitated to hire people who were smarter than me. What's more, I'm blessed with two wonderful daughters, Tami and Rachel, who have been involved in my business activities their whole lives and have contributed mightily to our successes. They have proven to be so capable that in 1998 my older daughter, Tami, replaced me as CEO, and Rachel was named head of The Longaberger Foundation. I stayed on as chairman of the board, but now I can do a lot of things outside the company, with everything in the good hands of Tami and Rachel.

If you remember nothing else about this book, I hope you realize that if a small-town boy like me can make it, anyone in America who's willing to work hard should be able to make a darn good living. Most things in life are not so difficult. You just have to work to keep them simple. If you're truly determined, there is no limit to what you can accomplish. I am writing this book to help some of you discover that, like me, you can trust your gut; and by doing so, there's no limit to what you can achieve. May I suggest that while you're at it, you do something that's good for a lot of people. That way you'll have more fun, and you'll feel good about what you do.

Everything I Know About Business I Learned from My Mom and Dad

If growing up poor in a family of fourteen had its shortcomings, my brothers, sisters, and I didn't know it. Besides, none of the other kids in Dresden, Ohio, ever seemed any better off than we were.

My roots in Dresden go back to 1896. That's when my grandparents, Carrie and John Longaberger, moved here. Shortly thereafter, my grandfather started working at the Dresden Basket Company. In 1919, my dad, John Wendell Longaberger, followed in his father's footsteps. He dropped out of high school at age seventeen to work at the same basket factory. I don't think any man ever loved making baskets more than my dad. It showed in his work, and he became an excellent craftsman.

The six or so weavers who worked at the Dresden Basket Company before it closed during the Great Depression made baskets for local pottery companies, including those in nearby Roseville and Zanesville. The baskets were used to carry materials to and from the kiln, as well as for shipping finished ware. The pottery industry has long since replaced baskets with cardboard boxes and plastic crates.

In 1936 Mom and Dad bought a small frame house for $1,900 that had three bedrooms and one bathroom. Included in the purchase price was a small shop behind the house that had been used by the Dresden Basket Company before it shut down.

Dad found work as a back-tender-machine operator at the Dresden Paper Mill, where he worked the 6 A.M. to 2 P.M. shift. After work he made baskets for pottery companies, and before long he was designing and making baskets for personal use. His line included baskets for everyday shopping, to take on picnics, and so on. The sign in front of our house read THE OHIO WARE BASKET COMPANY.

For me, those were good days. In fact, I don't know how growing up could have been any better! We were a close-knit family. Even though we didn't have much in the way of material possessions, we were blessed to have each other, especially to have Mom and Dad. Although I never gave it much thought as a kid, our parents and the environment where we grow up have a strong influence on who we become as adults. We grew up knowing we had to work hard, be honest, and help others. Yet all of this is determined by the luck of the draw. We must play the hand that life deals us. It was my good fortune to have drawn a winning hand.

■ THE LONGABERGERS OF DRESDEN, OHIO

In a town of fifteen hundred, I doubt if there was anyone in town who didn't know at least one or two Longabergers. Knowing everybody in town has its pros and cons. On the upside, people are friendly. You can go anywhere, and people will call you by name. "Hey, Popeye, how's it going?" I'd hear all over town. "Popeye" was a nickname my grandfather gave me. When he first saw me, just hours after I was born, he thought my eyes popped out. Ever since, that's what my family, my teachers, and my friends have called me.

The downside of everybody knowing everybody in a small town is that if you do anything you're not supposed to, the word spreads like wildfire. Maybe this isn't so bad; in fact, I think it's why kids in small towns don't get into much trouble. When they do, they can't keep their parents from finding out.

In truth, none of us ever got into trouble, at least nothing serious. We had so much love and respect for Mom and Dad, we didn't want to do anything that could hurt or embarrass them. In a family as large as ours, there was a lot of peer pressure from eleven brothers and sisters. Nobody wanted to be the only one who would cause embarrassment to the family. I never would have finished high school except I promised Mom I wouldn't be the only one of her children not to graduate even though it took me so many years.

Growing up in a family of fourteen means you have to do your part.

This is especially true in a small house with a single bathroom! Early on, we learned to share. Nobody tied it up for long. In the morning, there never seemed to be so much traffic that it made anyone late for school. We always took our baths at night, and, fortunately, all my sisters had straight hair so they didn't use curlers. In those days, my sisters rarely put on makeup; besides, it was too expensive. In a pinch, we could always run out the back door and down the alley to use the neighbor's outhouse.

With so many kids, we learned how to get organized. We also learned how to adjust to change. The second floor of our house was one big room with a stairway going up the middle. We slept in rows of single beds—girls on the left side and boys on the right. Richie was born two years after me, and when we were little, we shared a single bed. Around the seventh grade or so, we were too big, and that's when we each got our own bed. There were two bedrooms on the first floor. One was for Mom and Dad, and the other room had bunk beds that belonged to the two oldest girls, Genevieve and Wendy. When they moved out, my two older brothers, Jerry and Larry, inherited that bedroom. Later, it became Richie's and mine.

We had a full house on Eighth Street, but that was our life, and that's all we knew. We didn't have scooters and bicycles, so we took turns playing with the toys we did have. The best part about having all those brothers and sisters was always having someone to play with. Mom and Dad couldn't afford a lot of gifts for Christmas, but each of us did get one present. It was always a toy, and if there was any money left over, we'd get something practical such as a shirt or a pair of shoes. There was never enough money, so we kids didn't exchange gifts. This was Dad's policy, and everyone abided by it. Nevertheless, we got excited about the gift-giving part of Christmas just like other kids. On Christmas Eve, Mom and Dad would place the presents under the tree; we'd open them together the next morning. We enjoyed each other's excitement over the presents.

The one luxury we did have was the television set Dad bought in 1952. It was out of character for him to be one of the first in Dresden to get something. I suppose with fourteen people watching it at the same time, he figured we'd get our money's worth. We couldn't afford for all of us to go to the movies, and we never went to a restaurant. Neither did Mom and Dad ever go out by themselves.

With the help of my older sisters, Mom prepared all the meals, and although she never asked us to, before heading out the door, we'd all pitch in with cleaning up after supper. There were always enough Longaberger kids to form a crowd for group games after supper, and we all had friends who came over to play. Most of the time, we'd go down the street to the school playground. Basketball was my favorite sport.

Growing up in the small town of Dresden was a delight. We may have been poor, but we were showered with love and care. And boy, did we have fun.

■ THE MAN WHO LOVED TO MAKE BASKETS

If Dad could have supported the family only by making baskets, he would have done it day and night. But getting paid as little as fifty cents a basket, this was not possible. When Mom and Dad bought the house on Eighth Street, they already had five children, with number six on the way. As the family kept growing, his moonlighting activities became as much a necessity as a labor of love.

Dad worked long, hard hours. When he first started making baskets in his little shop, he probably gave away more than he sold. In our tiny house, everywhere you turned, you'd see a basket. There was a basket for dirty laundry, one to hold umbrellas, another for flowers. Dad made them for Mom to use for everything.

As Dad's passion grew for weaving baskets, so did his desire for perfection. He'd put in whatever time was necessary, making each one his best possible basket. On weekends, he'd seek out the best trees, cut them down, load them onto his pickup, and drive eighty miles to Marietta, where his splints were made. Later he'd pick up the splints, haul them back to Dresden, and lay them on the lawn to dry. Finally, he'd stack them on racks in his workshop.

We didn't have a family car, but as far as Dad was concerned, we didn't need one. The paper mill was a five-minute walk from the house, and the school was just down the street. Except for his visits to the forest and trips to Marietta, Dad's whole world encompassed less than a square mile. Mom gave birth to eleven of us at home, so Dad only once drove her to the hospital when Jeff, the youngest, was born. I can't remember ever seeing Dad in "downtown" Dresden except on Satur-day when he went to get a haircut. Now when I say downtown, I refer to Main Street, which was all of six blocks long and only three blocks away from our house. That's where Mom did the family shopping. Weather permitting, she'd ride her bike, which naturally had one of Dad's baskets attached to its handlebars.

Dad's life revolved around family and work. His workweek was pre-dictable. Dad came home from the paper mill just a few minutes after two o'clock. He'd have lunch, and within fifteen minutes he'd head for his little shop. When we came home from school, we knew where we could find him. He'd come in for dinner and then head back to the shop to make still more baskets before retiring for the night. Dad rarely stopped, although he did enjoy watching television. Before tele-vision, his main source of recreation was to sit in the living room and listen to our big Philco console radio; surprisingly, he liked the soaps. He was a man of few words, so if any one of us wanted conversation with him, we'd have to start it. Dad didn't talk much, but we knew he was always there for us.

My father didn't have a lazy bone in his body. His strong work ethic must have had a powerful influence on me. Even as a small boy, I had a burning desire to work. I also saw how much pride Dad took in his craft. He was a perfectionist, and this inspired me to do my best at any-thing I did. Dad clearly enjoyed working, so from watching him I asso-ciated work with having fun.

Dad was a world-class craftsman but not much of a businessman. And he might have been the world's worst salesman. He relied on peo-ple coming to our house located on a side street about three short blocks off Main Street. Even Dresden's Main Street didn't get much traffic, so you can imagine how little activity Dad's shop generated on Eighth Street. His marketing efforts were confined to that Ohio Ware Basket Company sign in front of the house. If you wanted to buy a bas-ket, you'd have to come to our front door, knock, and ask whoever was there if you could buy one. Dad's prices were far too low, and he gave away far too many. What's more, he liked to barter.

Of course there's nothing wrong with bartering. It's just that Dad was terrible at it. He might trade a basket for a dozen eggs or a sack of tomatoes. His sales force consisted of some of us kids who would occa-sionally drop off baskets for consignment at local stores.

Larry and Jerry, my two oldest brothers, were permitted to work in Dad's shop. Every now and then, my oldest sister, Genevieve, also did some weaving with Dad. All twelve children couldn't work in the shop; there simply wasn't enough room. As child number five, I had to find odd jobs to earn spending money. This was fine with me because I could make more on my own than what Dad was willing to pay!

■ SCHOOL DAYS, SCHOOL DAZE

At a very young age I concluded that school wasn't for me. I was in the first grade.

I stuttered terribly. When we had to stand and tell our names, the other kids thought it was very funny. It took forever to get out my name, Dave Longaberger. It got worse in first grade when I had to read before the class. The other kids couldn't wait until it was my turn. It made their day. I had to repeat first grade because my reading was so poor. Looking back, it's obvious that I started off on the wrong foot. It hurt to be laughed at. People said that I'd get over my stuttering by putting pebbles in my mouth. So I tried using pebbles, but it didn't make any difference.

The fourth-grade teacher was determined to make a reader out of me. She insisted on having me stand up and read out loud. No matter how much my classmates laughed, she was relentless.

"Let's see, who wants to read next?" she'd ask.

The good readers would raise their hands, calling, "Me, me!" But I sensed she would call on me. I could feel my face flush. I slumped behind my desk, attempting to go unnoticed.

"Popeye, please stand up and read."

Before I could even stand, the snickering began. I'd feel all the more self-conscious, which made me stutter even more. She must hate me, I'd think to myself.

Teachers separated the good readers from the poor readers. Slow readers got tagged as slow students—and the tag usually stuck throughout your school days. Eventually, you came to truly believe that you were a poor student. Take it from me, poor students don't like school. I did notice that the good students enjoyed school. But the weak ones like me dreaded it.

Unlike other accomplishments in my life, I had no pride in my schoolwork. Classwork and homework aren't much fun for poor students.

Eventually kids got tired of making fun of me. By the end of the year, I still stuttered, but there was no more laughing. To me, this seemed like quite an accomplishment.

On top of my stuttering, I had epilepsy. I could never tell when a seizure would come on because there was no pattern. The seizures always happened at inopportune times. Without warning, on the playground or in the classroom, I'd go into a convulsion. This provoked still more teasing.

"Hey, Popeye, I've never seen a seizure," someone would say. "Let me know when you're gonna have one."

As I grew older, the seizures happened less frequently. By the time I was twelve, they had stopped.

In the fifth grade, I was kept back again. This meant my brother Richie, who was two years younger, would be a fifth grader with me. Someone else probably would have been embarrassed to have his kid brother catch up with him. But I suffered so much humiliation in school I was becoming immune to it. Besides, Richie and I were very close, so I actually enjoyed having him in my class. But this lasted only one year.

After our summer vacation, the next school term began. Richie and I walked into the sixth-grade classroom and sat together. About five minutes later, Mr. Bond, who was principal as well as sixth-grade teacher, welcomed everyone back for the new school year.

He looked around the room and spotted me.

"What are you doing here, Popeye?"

I looked at him, not knowing what to say. What did I do this time? I thought to myself.

"Aren't you supposed to be next door?" he asked.

My heart sank. That room was for fifth graders. I was so embarrassed, I didn't say a word. I just left the room with my head down.

Now I was in the same grade with my sister Mary Ann, who was a year younger than Richie.

Back then, I couldn't understand why my teacher, Ruby Adams, made me take fifth grade a third time. Years later, I figured it out. She must have been in love with me.

■ LESSONS LEARNED AFTER SCHOOL

Toward the end of last period, I couldn't wait for the bell to ring. By then, my mind was racing with what I planned for after school. The moment I heard the bell, I jumped out of my seat and ran to Fred Shoemaker's neighborhood grocery store.

Mr. Shoemaker had hired me when I was seven years old. I stuttered so badly when I asked him to hire me, he took pity on me.

"I-I'll d-do anything," I said. And I did. I dusted. I shoveled snow. I cleaned the toilet. I straightened the shelves. Whatever there was to do, I was willing to do, and I loved it.

I loved greeting shoppers. It made me feel as if they were coming into my store. And as far as I was concerned, they were my customers.

The Shoemakers didn't have any children, and Mr. Shoemaker and his wife, Mimi, treated me as if I was their son. They even took me to see my first circus.

Mr. Shoemaker's little store was just three blocks from our house. Even when I wasn't working, I'd go down there to hang out with him. Sometimes when there weren't any customers, we'd sit around the pot-bellied stove and chat. As a special treat, he'd put a pan of water on the stove and cook hot dogs for us.

Like my dad, Mr. Shoemaker was a hardworking, honest man. He, too, served as a good role model. Although I was not motivated in school, I wanted to learn everything about the grocery store. The more responsibility Mr. Shoemaker gave me, the more I loved working there. In the beginning, I did little things like dusting shelves and sweeping floors, but soon I helped to stack the shelves. I took so much pride in how the shelves looked that I couldn't stand to see anything out of its proper place. I walked up and down, inspecting the aisles, constantly straightening cans and jars. Dusty, disorganized shelves would drive me up a wall. I kept inventing ways to make everything look better. Those grocery shelves were my domain, and how they looked was up to me.

I worked at the store after school and on weekends. My favorite day of the week was Wednesday. That's when the C. D. Kenny Wholesale Company truck came from Columbus to make its weekly delivery. I may as well have skipped school on Wednesdays because I was unable to concentrate. I could only daydream about putting the new stock on the shelves.

I may have been a poor student, but no other kid in Dresden could hold a candle to me when it came to working in a grocery store. It wasn't too long before I was creating displays. Mr. Shoemaker put me in charge of organizing what food went where. I was by far the youngest kid in town with such an awesome responsibility. I knew how much Mr. Shoemaker cared about me, and I wanted to do a great job to please him. He believed in me, and I wasn't about to let him down.

There were several grocery stores in Dresden. By the time I was ten, every owner had approached me with job offers.

"If you ever decide to leave where you are, Popeye, there will always be a job for you at my place," they'd say.

When I wasn't working in the grocery store, I'd find all sorts of odd jobs. I was just seven when I earned money hauling garbage. I'd carry it to the city dump in my wagon for twenty-five cents a trip. I loved mowing grass and shoveling snow. In the wintertime, I'd pray for a big snowstorm to hit Dresden on the weekend, because I could make an extra five dollars. That was a lot of money back then. A lot of other kids also shoveled snow, but nobody could do it as well as I did. I'd figure out how to shovel snow faster and neater, always trying to improve my technique. Another kid might shovel snow for three houses in an afternoon. I'd do four or five houses in the same amount of time. Not only was I faster; I also left the cleanest sidewalk in town. I took so much pride in my work, it looked "more professional" than anyone else's. I did the same thing mowing grass, and consequently developed a system that gave my lawns a superior appearance. Over time, certain loyal customers would allow only me to care for their lawns. So while the other kids were out trying to line up work, I had a steady flow of regular income!

The Shoemakers eventually sold their corner grocery store. It actually changed ownership four times during my childhood; each time, I was included as part of the fixtures. This gave me an opportunity to observe how different people ran the business. Not all the other owners had the same integrity as Mimi and Fred Shoemaker. I was amazed to witness some "tricks of the trade," or how a merchant could cheat customers. These ranged from false advertising to putting a heavy thumb on the meat scale. I finally quit the grocery store because one couple constantly bickered with each other, and it really got to me.

I took a job running the projector at the local movie house. I must have been about seventeen or so by then, and I worked there until I finished school. Again, I took my work very seriously, and in time became a good projector operator. I recall only one time when I screwed up, and boy, did I do it royally. As I switched from the first projector to the second during a John Wayne movie, I put in the wrong reel. During an intense scene, much to the audience's surprise, Woody Woodpecker suddenly appeared on the screen. My teacher, DeWitt Ring, happened to be in the audience, and he razzed me about it for weeks.

■ THE SALES CONTEST

My buddies and I had found some old lumber and built a makeshift cabin on top of what we called Machine Gun Hill on the outskirts of town. We always talked about someday having a portable radio to take up there so we could listen to what we called "hillbilly music."

Then one day we learned the school was sponsoring a magazine contest for a fund-raiser. At first I didn't give it much thought. After all, how could I compete with the entire school? The winner would have to be a top salesman to win the contest, and I couldn't sell because I stuttered.

Then the school announced that first prize was a portable radio for whoever sold the most magazine subscriptions in ten days. Boy, I thought, if only I could win the sales contest.

My desire to own the radio was evidently greater than my fear of rejection. Stutter or no stutter, I was determined to sell more magazines than any other kid in the school. That radio is mine, I thought to myself.

Since practically everyone in town knew me, I'd go door-to-door, hitting every house in Dresden. As soon as someone came to the door, I started talking about the wonderful magazines I had to sell. The only problem was, the more excited I got, the more I stuttered! People would stand there and listen, but they couldn't understand what I was saying. It didn't matter one iota to me. I just kept talking, nonstop.

Finally, out of frustration, people would say, "Okay, okay, Popeye, I'll buy a subscription. Just give me those forms so I can sign my name." I'd hand over the form and shut up. I realized I made most of my sales because people felt sorry for me. I had no problem with that. I knew they liked me. I realized I was selling myself instead of the magazines.

After the first few days of the contest, I realized that Marilyn Evans was my only competition. And she was indeed an awesome competitor. She was not only the smartest girl in the seventh grade but also the prettiest. To put it mildly, she was an overachiever who didn't like to lose. Our total sales were so ahead of the rest of the students that it had become a two-person contest for that radio. Every day, I'd turn in my order forms, and Marilyn would turn in hers. Marilyn began to come in with more orders than I had. She was pulling away from me, and I started to think I needed a strategy if I were going to beat her.

I began to think about not turning in my orders every day. It's true that the principal had requested this, but he didn't insist on it. Maybe if I waited until the last day to turn in my orders, Marilyn might ease up a bit, thinking I had stopped making sales.

On the last day of the contest, I turned in several days' worth of orders that totaled around $400. Sure enough, Marilyn had slacked off. As a result, I beat her by $200 and I won the radio. That weekend, my friends and I had the time of our lives, spending half the night up on that hill listening to hillbilly music.

Winning the contest did a lot for my confidence. It also taught me three valuable lessons. First, when you compete, don't focus on the competition; instead, focus on how well you can do. Second, no matter what you sell, you're always selling yourself. Third, don't give up when people don't buy. After all, nobody sells 'em all.

■ GOOD FRIENDS

Few friendships in life ever compare to those we have as kids. I had four wonderful friends who go way back. My best buddies in school were Bob Cassidy, Max Hittle, Warney Powell, and my brother Richie. The five of us used to camp out in our little cabin on Machine Gun Hill, the highest point on the outskirts of Dresden. As far as we were concerned, the hill was as close to heaven as it gets. We could see half the county from up there. At night, we'd sit around a campfire and talk about our dreams.

The five of us did everything together. One of our favorite summer activities was going to the swimming hole just outside town. Sometimes we'd go skinny-dipping, and we called ourselves the Bare Ass Club. We even had rules. Boys could swim for twenty-five cents, and girls were admitted free. Oddly, no girls ever came.

Another rule was that nobody could swim by himself. There always had to be someone on the bank who could swim, serving as a lifeguard. We had heard about too many lone swimmers who drowned, and we didn't want that to happen to one of us.

Our favorite sport was basketball. Bob, Warney, Richie, and I had played in pickup games on the school playground ever since grade school. We'd play year-round, even in the winter. As the experienced snow removal expert, I was usually the one who got assigned to shovel the court. When we were older, we played on the Dresden varsity basketball team. With so many years of playing together, we were a tight unit. Although Richie was two years younger, I stopped growing at five foot ten and by high school, he was taller than me. He kept growing and didn't stop until he hit six foot three. There weren't too many players that tall in those days, so Richie was the star of our team. He was also the top scorer and the one who always got his name in the newspapers. I was so proud of him that I'd just as soon see his name as mine in the papers.

However, as the oldest player, I ran the team. I had a fairly good outside shot, my passing game was strong, and I really hustled on defense. In Richie's senior year, we went 15–7, winning our county tournament, taking the sectional, and finally getting beat in the district.

Basketball taught me two valuable lessons. First, I learned about teamwork. Because Dresden was so small, our school had a small student body. This meant we had fewer tall players. However, my buddies and I had played together for years and thus played better as a team than our competition. This proved to be our edge.

John Hadden, my high school coach, taught me a second lesson. "You've got to be good on defense, Dave," he'd tell me. "The best way to get good is to always look your opponent in the eye. The eyes signal which way a player is going to move."

Coach Hadden said that an opponent would send a similar message with body language. By closely watching him, I could anticipate his moves and then steal the ball or block a shot. I've applied some of the coach's thinking to my business career. Ever since, I have paid close attention to non-verbal communication. I believe people are always sending messages with their facial expressions and body language; we just have to be observant to pick them up.

Occasionally, the team traveled to other schools, and those were the only times Richie and I ever went very far from Dresden. One time we played in a tournament in Marietta, Ohio, about eighty miles away down on the Ohio River. Our big thrill was crossing over the bridge and setting foot in West Virginia. It was my first time outside the state of Ohio. I was nearly twenty years old.

With all my after-school jobs, I was the only one in our gang who ever had some spending money. The other guys loved to say, "If Popeye has a dollar, we all got a dollar. Let's go spend it." Actually, in the fifties, a dollar was enough to buy a soda or a sundae for each of us. And back then, movies cost only ten cents for kids. A dollar went a long way. Nevertheless, if I made three or four dollars by Friday, it was spent by the end of the weekend.

I never minded treating my friends. In fact, I couldn't think of a better way to spend my money.

■ MY MENTORS

When I was a kid, I never heard the word *mentor*. I was much older before I even knew what the word meant. So it was late in life when I realized the only true mentors I ever had were Mom and Dad.

As parents, they were a perfect team. Each worked hard at his or her job, Dad in his workshop and Mom in the home. They worked together toward a single objective—do whatever was best for the family. Their work ethic served as a shining example to all of us. They never told us to work. Instead, they demonstrated the true meaning of the word by their actions.

There was just one steadfast rule in the family: we had a responsibility to make extra money. My brothers and I always worked during the summer, and most of the money we earned went toward buying clothes. After the sixth grade, the boys were expected to pay for their own school clothing. This was an unwritten law in the Longaberger household.

Richie and I would thumb a ride to Zanesville toward the end of summer and do our shopping. I always had a little extra money, so we'd spend it on a pass to the Zanesville swimming pool and then take in a movie.

Another unwritten law was to be home at six o'clock for dinner. If you were late, you didn't get anything to eat except cold cereal. During basketball season, Richie and I practiced past six o'clock and, boy, did we eat a lot of cold cereal. There was no eating between meals. There was always plenty of food for three meals a day. But with fourteen in the family, raiding the fridge was not permitted.

Once a month, Mom let each of us pick his or her favorite meal. I loved pancakes, so when my turn came, Mom would be there flipping pancakes just for me. But everyone else had to eat them, too, whether or not they liked pancakes. I couldn't stand rice, but some of my sisters liked it. Of course, when you're hungry enough, you'll eat whatever is on your plate.

Dad was a strict disciplinarian. He had to say something just once, and sometimes he didn't have to complete his sentence. Dad never had to raise his voice, and there was no discussion. If you asked him for a dime to go to the movies and he said no, you didn't ask twice.

We could, however, negotiate with Mom. She hardly ever disagreed with Dad, but every now and then she would. They'd quietly discuss their differences, and just as often as not, Dad would allow her to over-rule him.

Mom and Dad never fought; at least, we never saw them fight. When I was a young kid, I was cutting the grass at a neighbor's house, and the couple started fighting. It was the first time I had ever heard two adults shout at each other. I got so scared I ran home.

Most of my brothers and sisters have a good sense of humor, and it definitely came from my mother's side of the family. Getting a smile out of Dad was harder than getting him to talk. My mother is ninety-one years old, and to this day she still has a keen sense of humor. I'm sure it came from her father, whom we called Grandpa Dave.

Grandpa Dave had worked for the railroad and lost both his legs when he slipped underneath a rail car. One was off above the knee and the other just below the knee. It was amazing how well he walked with two wooden legs.

Grandpa Dave and I had a standing joke—literally. Whenever I'd take one of my friends to his house for the first time, in the middle of a conversation, Grandpa Dave would say, "Boy, my legs are getting tired. You know, I think I'll take them off."

With that, he'd pull up his pants, take out the bolts, remove both his legs, and lay them on the table. My friend would practically faint, or let out a yelp and run out of the house. Grandpa Dave and I would sit there holding our sides and laughing like crazy. He lived to be ninety-nine.

When I was ten years old, I thought my mother was the most wonderful woman in the whole world. One day I saw a beautiful wooden box of candy in the drugstore, and I decided I had to buy it for her. It cost five dollars, which in those days was a lot of money for even a grown man to spend on a box of candy. I negotiated with the drugstore owner and promised to pay him a dollar a week. Although the store didn't do business on credit, I refused to leave until he agreed to accept my offer. Mom's face lit up when I handed her the box of candy. In our family, candy was an extravagance. Just seeing the expression on her beautiful face made it worth every penny to me!

■ LOOKING BACK

When we're very young, we are not aware that what happens in our lives shapes the person we become. Only as a mature man am I able to look back and understand the influence of my past.

There are many things that we don't appreciate in our youth. Take, for example, growing up in a small town. In most small communities there are many opportunities for kids to get after-school jobs because the school, the town's main street, and their homes are all within a short walking distance. It's not the money that matters, but instead the learning experience these jobs provide. Children who live in big cities aren't as likely to find part-time jobs so close by.

I was fortunate to have a job at the corner grocery. Excelling there helped me feel better about my poor performance in the classroom. Sure, there were times in school when I thought I must be really dumb. But then, I'd find my comfort zone at Mr. Shoemaker's store. So what if I couldn't compete with straight A's? No one could beat me on my turf.

I didn't get many strokes in school, so I found ways to get them elsewhere. My parents were too busy to give each of us a lot of individual attention; there simply were too many of us. Besides, they were careful not to show favoritism. So none of us was ever jealous of a brother or a sister, and we each grew up feeling our parents' love.

I've never sought out recognition, and to this day I shy away from the spotlight. Today, pats on the back and praise aren't what motivate me. Instead, I've always competed with myself to do better—like shoveling snow and cutting grass to perfection or stacking inventory at the grocery store. People hardly noticed or, for that matter, hardly cared.

But I cared, and that's why I did it. Back when I got so much teasing in school, I made up my mind it didn't really matter what people thought about me.

This attitude has carried over to my management philosophy. I'm not one of those people with an ego, so when things go wrong, I'm first to take the blame. And when things go right, I'm the first to give credit to others. What I care about is results. Good results please me. I'm not concerned with how things look to the outside world.

In June 1997, I was diagnosed with cancer. I'm currently taking various cancer therapies. My experience in living with stuttering, epilepsy, and learning disabilities helped me learn to cope with cancer. When I was young, I had to keep moving along and not let my handicaps interfere with my life. Looking back, I figure that if I could accept my handicaps as a child, I can certainly do the same thing as a grown man. I've had adversity throughout my life. Big deal. Anyone who lives long enough is bound to have his share. The secret is to meet adversity head-on. When you survive, it makes you stronger.

2

Earning My Master's Degree

By the time I graduated from high school in 1955, I figured it was time to go to work. Other guys my age were practically graduating from college. In the 1950s, big companies had begun raiding college campuses, recruiting seniors fresh out of school. But nobody was knocking at my door. Nor was anyone coming to Dresden seeking twenty-one-year-old guys who had just finished high school. So while I was excited about finally getting out of school, I was scared and I felt inadequate. By then, I didn't think college was an option for me.

It's a safe bet that I had the dubious honor of being Dresden's oldest graduating senior. This distinction didn't exactly jump-start my confidence. What should I do now? Here I am, reading at a sixth-grade level. What could I expect the world to do for me?

I made a mental list of my accomplishments. I could shovel snow and cut grass better than any other kid in town. A lot of good that would do now. And I didn't see much future in my amazing talent for organizing and stacking cans and jars in a grocery store.

At the time, it didn't seem as though I had a lot of choices, but in life there always are choices. Sometimes those options seem bleak, but they can open windows for future opportunities. At any rate, I was twenty-one years old, and whether I knew it or not, the world was my oyster.

■ YOUR FIRST JOB IS JUST YOUR FIRST JOB

I looked under "Help Wanted" in the newspaper and applied for different jobs, but no one was willing to make an offer. With my school record, I didn't blame them. On top of that, I stuttered when I talked, so job interviews made me uncomfortable. I wouldn't have hired me either!

After several weeks of interviews, I answered an ad in the Zanesville newspaper that had been placed by the Fuller Brush Company. My only experience at door-to-door selling went back to the magazine contest I won in the seventh grade. I told myself that if I could do it then, I'd be even better at it six years later.

The interviewer explained that he hired people to sell the company's complete line of household goods.

"We don't just sell brushes," he emphasized. "We have dozens of other products, ranging from dust mops to laundry soap. All you do is knock on the door. When someone answers, you sell them what they already use, except that our products are better."

I nodded.

"Do you think you could sell our products?" he asked.

"Yes," I said, honestly believing I could.

"Well, I don't normally hire anyone just out of high school, but there's something about you I like," he said.

When I asked him about salary, he said, "We pay straight commission."

"How much is that?" I asked.

"It depends," he replied. "If you're good, you'll get a good paycheck." He paused. "And if you're not good," he continued, "you'll get paid what you're worth. That, Dave, is the beauty of a straight commission sales job."

"It sounds fair to me," I replied, and the job was mine.

He then explained that I would be trained on the job, spending several days with a supervisor in a territory that would then be mine.

"Congratulations, Dave," he said, shaking my hand and pointing to a map of Ohio. "You're now the Fuller Brush man for this area that includes Dresden and over here to the east side of Zanesville."

Of all the things I dreamed of doing when I was a kid, being a salesman had never entered my mind. I had always visualized a good salesman as a person with a great gift of gab. He was the guy who could sell refrigerators to the Eskimos. And the way I stuttered, I wasn't sure I could sell popcorn at a baseball game.

The job was attractive because I would control my own destiny. First, I could work my own hours, which meant I didn't have to punch a time clock, and I could work as many hours as I liked. Second, I wouldn't have a boss breathing down my neck, ordering me around. Selling Fuller brushes offered a certain amount of freedom.

I had become the proud owner of a used car, bought with savings from after-school jobs. Some people might have thought my car was a hazard that shouldn't be permitted on the road. But it was my baby, and I loved it. Now I had a new job, too. I felt as free as a bird. I realized that if I didn't like the sales job, I didn't have to do it for the rest of my life. A lot of young people place too much importance on the first job they get. One stumbling block for so many young people is the lack of experience. I've heard them say, "How am I supposed to get experience if nobody will hire me?" Young people shouldn't get too uptight if they don't land their dream job right off the bat. In the real world, people rarely do.

You have to get some experience under your belt. Keep in mind that few people work their entire lives at their first job. If you don't believe me, ask the next twenty-five people you see who've been working ten years or more. Chances are you won't find two who stayed at their first job!

Don't be discouraged if you start off doing something that doesn't turn you on. Give it a chance. If you're not satisfied, you can go on to a better position. You might be pleasantly surprised and discover that it offers more than you ever imagined. In any event, you can always use it as a stepping-stone to something better.

■ SELLING YOURSELF

I quickly discovered that selling Fuller Brush products was similar to selling magazines in the seventh grade: what it all boiled down to with both sales positions was that I had to sell Dave Longaberger.

But I was no longer in the seventh grade. Back then, people admired a stuttering kid who could be so persistent. And they had compassion for me. At twenty-one it was a different ball game. I could no longer depend on people buying from me out of pity.

Granted, Fuller Brush made high-quality products. But the fact remained I had nothing to sell that couldn't be bought at a local shopping center. When you analyze it, few monopolies exist in the world of selling. You can buy anything, from automobiles to life insurance, from dozens of people. It's the same thing with stocks and real estate. All stockbrokers have access to the same traded securities, and all real estate agents can sell the same listed properties. So it's you, the salesperson, who sets you apart from the rest of the herd. If people don't like you, the odds of making a sale are dramatically reduced.

I believe this is true of all selling. You have the world's best product that nobody else can sell. You have yourself to sell. Once you accept this fact, you're on your way to a successful sales career.

I found out early on that it doesn't take a smooth, slick personality to be a top salesman. Thank heaven it doesn't. If there was anyone who didn't come across as smooth, I was that person. After thinking about that for a while, I realized that this was an asset. When I made my sales calls, I came across as low-key and nonthreatening. It's the salesperson who comes on like gangbusters that puts people on guard. Whatever I had, whether help or hindrance, I used to my advantage.

I worked hard to communicate to people that I cared about them and had their best interest at heart. This was easy because it's what I truly felt. I wanted to help people, and I knew that I could because my only goal was to serve them. This made people feel at ease with me. I made them feel comfortable. Once I felt good about Dave Longaberger, a caring salesman who wanted to help people, I could sell Dave Longaberger to others. The same is true with everyone: you have to first be sold on yourself before you can sell yourself!

It's an amazing thing, but when you truly care for your customers, they know it. It's not something you can fake; it must be genuine. It's not only what you say, but also your tone of voice, body language, and facial expressions.

People who have good listening skills also communicate to others that they care. This may surprise some people because the first image that comes to mind when we think about a salesperson is someone who's doing a lot of talking. In truth, a good salesperson listens more than she talks. She asks a lot of questions and then listens carefully while prospects tell her what they want to buy. Then, once she knows what they want, she sells it to them. They like her because she was thoughtful enough to hear them out. Her listening lets customers know that she respects what they think. Likewise, the salesperson who dominates the conversation and doesn't let the prospect get a word in edgewise is the one who sends a signal: "I'm only interested in my commission. I have no interest in you."

I developed a system for selling door-to-door. Each week I spent my mornings, Monday through Thursday, selling, and on Friday I'd do paperwork such as filling out and mailing in orders. On afternoons and weekends, I'd deliver orders from the previous week. The only problem was that my customers didn't pay until I made my deliveries. As I later found out, because they never really made a firm commitment, I didn't have a firm sale. So there would be times when they saw me coming and wouldn't answer their door. Or they'd let me in but give some excuse about why they couldn't pay for their order. As a result, I spent a lot of extra time selling them a second time. This experience would serve me well when we began direct selling at The Longaberger Company.

■ DON'T TAKE REJECTION PERSONALLY

My Fuller Brush sales manager constantly told me, "Nobody sells 'em all, Popeye."

It didn't take me long to realize how important the law of averages was to a salesman. I quickly learned that if I knocked on enough doors and talked to enough people, I'd have a good day. But then there were always those days when everything went wrong. Some days, I couldn't even give my wares away! But the most important lesson I learned was not to become discouraged when I had a bad day. That's how the law of averages works. If I made enough calls, I'd make some sales. Knowing this, I never allowed myself to feel down when I had a bad day.

We've all heard that popular saying "Sometimes you have to kiss a lot of frogs before you find a prince." I learned that I'd hear the word *no* more often than the word *yes*. There are many reasons why people don't buy—most of which have nothing to do with you. It may be that a prospect didn't need your product. Perhaps he couldn't afford it. It could be that he liked your product, but his wife would throw him out of the house if he didn't buy it from her brother. The point is, you must not feel personally rejected.

I had doors slammed in my face. If I ever did take it personally, I would have been devastated. It wasn't me the customers were reject-ing. They were rejecting my product. I believe the biggest reason why so many salespeople fail is because they can't separate themselves from their product. Whether you sell securities, real estate, insurance, or pots and pans, a prospect usually has no reason to dislike you person-ally. Even if he does, it's no big deal! You can never tell when you're going to meet up with someone who is just plain unhappy with every-thing and everyone. No sweat; you'll get over it.

■ DIFFERENT STROKES FOR DIFFERENT FOLKS

After six months of selling for the Fuller Brush Company, I left to take a factory job in Newark, Ohio. The company was taking an inventory and needed some extra help; the pay was $150 a week, which, back then, was a lot of money.

The work was tedious and boring; two weeks later, I was let go and was actually glad to get out of there. After just two weeks, I knew this job wasn't for me. I thought maybe it was the plant that I couldn't stand, so if I could change plants, I might find a career I could sink my teeth into.

I also wanted a job that offered a steady paycheck. At twenty-two, I was too young to appreciate the advantages of a commissioned sales job. Besides, I wanted to buy a new car, and with a guaranteed pay-check each week, I'd be able to get financing. Within a few weeks, I took a job at a different factory. I worked in the book mold department at the same pay that I received from my previous employer. My work-station was between two large, hot furnaces, and the heat was so intense that for every thirty minutes I worked, I had a thirty-minute break. My shift ended at 3 P.M., and I couldn't wait to get out of there. It reminded me of being back in school when I couldn't wait to hear the bell at the end of the day. Every morning became a struggle because I dreaded getting out of bed and going to work. I disliked it so much, I referred to it as "jail." These two jobs were the only time in my life that I dreaded going to work.

That hot, dingy factory was simply too confining. I was making big bucks, but I had to find a job where I'd have more interaction with people. There were many employees who enjoyed this work, but I sim-ply wasn't cut out for it. Please let me emphasize that how I feel about work in a factory is a matter of personal preference. I have the utmost respect for the workers I met at the plant. Many were hardworking people who were able to motivate themselves and find enjoyment in their jobs. Some indicated to me that they felt a sense of accomplishment because they contributed toward making a good product. Others enjoyed feeling that they were part of a team.

This job taught me to respect other people's work. It is wonderful to see how different people enjoy different jobs. I admire someone who derives pleasure from doing work that I myself would rather not do. From this experience I learned that there are vast differences among individuals, and there are all sorts of jobs available to accommodate these differences. For instance, some people love math, and they may become accountants. Others like the sciences and enjoy work in laboratories. One person feels proud to get up every day and put on a business suit when another would just as soon work outdoors doing landscaping and wearing a T-shirt and jeans.

I also learned what it's like to get out of bed each morning and go to a job I couldn't stand. I never forgot that feeling in the pit of my stomach. Ever since, I've been thankful to be blessed with work I enjoyed. I often think back on my time as a factory worker. As a result, in every business I started, I tried to create an environment where people could enjoy their jobs. Work should be fun, not something people dread doing.

■ DAVE DELIVERS

I heard about an opening for a route man at Cannon's Bakery in Dresden. I asked Mom and Dad what they thought. Always to the point, Dad said, "Find a job you enjoy, Popeye."

"I think I'll like driving a bread truck because I enjoy working with people," I explained. "It pays thirty-five dollars a week, plus commissions. At the factory I made a hundred fifty a week."

"It depends on how many commissions you can make," my father said.

"It will take me some time, but I think I can build up the route and eventually make a hundred fifty and then some," I said.

"It's your life," Mom said. "If you feel it's the right thing, then do it."

I felt as though I was finally going somewhere. It made me proud to become one of Cannon's four route salesmen. My job was selling bread, rolls, buns, and cakes to grocery stores and restaurants. I felt comfortable calling on grocers—after all, I spoke their language. I particularly liked that I'd get to use some of my own ideas. I'd get to set up displays in stores. And I would work hard to get to know the store and restaurant owners.

I spent the first few days on my new job riding shotgun with my supervisor. He showed me the route, and we called on customers.

"This is Dave Longaberger," he'd introduce me.

"It's Popeye," I'd say.

As we made the rounds, he pointed out two stores. Both times he said, "See that store? Don't waste your time on them."

When I asked why, he explained, "We've tried and tried but couldn't make any headway with them. There's not a thing you can do."

Now that was a challenge if I ever heard one, I thought. Once I was out on my own, I stopped in to visit that first store.

"Hi, I'm Dave Longaberger," I said. "I'm the new Cannon guy in this area."

The owner said, "How many times do I have to tell you people that I'm completely satisfied with our present suppliers? There's no point in your coming in here again, young man."

"I just wanted to introduce myself, sir. I'm sorry if I bothered you," I answered. "Thank you for your time."

I had the same experience in the second store. I understood why my supervisor advised me to stay away. Still, I wanted those accounts. There had to be a way.

One day, as I drove by the first store, I had a brainstorm. I approached two women who were in the parking lot and introduced myself.

"Ladies, I'd like to give each of you a free Cannon cake. All I want you to do is take it home and see if your family loves it like all our customers do. If you truly enjoy this cake, the next time you go into this store, I'd like you to ask the owner for Cannon products."

They were delighted with the deal. I did this a few more times with other shoppers and then went back to see the grocer.

"Hi, do you remember me?" I asked. "I'm Dave Longaberger from Cannon Bakery. I just stopped in to say hello."

"Customers have been asking for your products," he said. "What do you say we open an account with your bakery?"

I tried this same approach with the other store, and my supervisor was quite impressed with my two new accounts. One of those stores eventually became a big account.

After three years with Cannon's Bakery, I took a bread route with Nickles Bakery. Nickles had four hundred trucks compared with four at Cannon's. I believed there would be more opportunity for me to grow with a bigger company.

When I first began with Nickles, my route had sixty-four customers. My new supervisor told me, "You'll soon find out some of these customers aren't worth making a stop. Half of your customers generate double the business we get from the other half. Just the same, Popeye, we expect you to call on every customer. You're to give them as much attention as you do the big accounts, even though they're a waste of time."

I didn't say a word, but I couldn't see the point in spending a lot of time with marginal customers when I could use that time to serve my biggest customers. I wanted to take the time to have coffee with them and talk shop, or talk about anything from basketball to the county fair.

By spending extra time in certain stores, I even got to know some of the customers. A shopper would spot me and say, "Hey, Dave, we're having a cookout on Saturday. I'm going to need twelve dozen hot dog buns and ten dozen hamburger buns."

Sometimes, instead of asking for the Nickles brand, a shopper would say, "I want two dozen of Dave's buns." In truth, there wasn't a lot of difference between one bakery's products and another's. And the prices were just about the same. So when a shopper went to the grocery store, he was rarely looking for a particular brand. What often happened was that the customer bought the buns that were most prominently displayed on the shelves. This meant that if a grocery was sold on Dave Longaberger, its customers would buy Nickles baked goods.

Since I spent half my youth working in grocery stores, I was able to walk in my customer's shoes. I was lucky, because not every salesperson gets such firsthand experience. However, you can always put in "apron time" behind your customer's counter. This means rolling up your sleeves and pitching in at a customer's place of business. For instance, on a hectic shopping day I'd help at the checkout counter by sacking groceries. I spent time talking with grocers, suggesting how to set up interesting displays. I'd pass on ideas to them that I saw in other towns. I'd do the same for my restaurant customers. I was always making menu suggestions. And when the kitchen got backed up, I'd help clear tables. It was extra work, and all I got was the owner's gratitude. But that gratitude is like gold.

By the end of five years with Nickles, I had reduced the number of accounts on my route from sixty-four to thirty-four, and at the same time brought in twice as much money. My accounts were built one customer at a time. When you get right down to it, all companies are built one customer at a time.

■ WORKING WITH THE COMPETITION

Working a bread route, it didn't take long to find out I was in a dog-eat-dog business. There were seven bread companies competing for the same shelf space. This was my first exposure to cutthroat business. I never knew adult people could behave like my competitors did.

Every bread man was out to get the other six guys. Sabotage was common. A salesman would poke pinholes in a wrapper, causing the competitor's bread to get stale. Or they would mash the bread. Some went so far as to squirt ink from their fountain pens into the packages. It seemed like no one ever missed an opportunity to push a competitor's products to the back of the shelf. It was a no-win situation for us all because it caused losses and headaches for everyone, including the stores and their shoppers.

I knew I wasn't going to enjoy work under these conditions, so I decided to find a way to make peace with my competition. Instead of sabotaging the other guy, I did the opposite. Whenever I set products in a store, I'd take the time to straighten out the competition's merchandise. Naturally, the grocer was grateful, and passed this along to my competitors, who reacted by keeping their hands off Nickles products.

I'd cross paths with the Wonder Bread salesman, and I always gave him a warm hello. Soon we were on a first-name basis. I invited him to join me for a cup of coffee or a quick lunch, and eventually we became good friends. We formed a pact: I'd look out for Wonder Bread products and he'd do the same for Nickles. When the other guys picked up on our agreement, they wanted in on it, too. All in all, everybody had to make fewer stops to fix little problems, so the routes went smoother and the customers were happier. We all went from no-win to win-win.

Even in a healthy competitive environment, we were still competitors. We were in an industry with close margins. The products we sold were nearly identical in quality, packaging, and price. I always felt my edge was Dave Longaberger. My brand of customer service was a value-added commodity, superior to the competition. I delivered not only what I promised but then some. I was always willing to go that extra mile.

On my Nickles route was a stop in a very small town called Toboso. My village of Dresden was so much bigger, I would tease one customer in particular saying, "Who the hell would want to live in Toboso?" It always got a rise out of her because she loved her beautiful little town near historic Black Hand Gorge. Well, more than twenty-five years after I stopped driving for Nickles, I moved to Toboso. Although I hadn't seen my former customer for years, I rang her doorbell with her favorite Nickles cake in my hand. When she opened the door, I said, "I don't know who the hell would want to live in Toboso, but I'm sorry I'm so late delivering your cake." She could hardly believe it was me, or that I was going to be her neighbor.

■ UNIFORMITY AND CONTROL

I worked long hours on my bread route, but I still managed to find time to see Laura Eschman, a local Dresden girl, whom I had known for years. After a short courtship, I felt my career was off and running, and I asked her to marry me. When she accepted, I became all the more motivated to build my bread route.

Since my high school graduation, I had been serving my military obligation in the army reserves. Then, in the spring of 1961, I was drafted by the army to serve active duty. This was during the cold war, at the start of the Berlin crisis. The United States was building up troops in Germany because a conflict with the Soviet Union was brewing. For a while it appeared as if all hell was going to break loose over there. In June I was sent to Fort Hood, Texas, where I was trained to serve in the military police. As it turned out, the Berlin crisis wasn't a crisis after all. Just the same, I served my country for two years in Texas.

The army taught me a lot about uniformity and control. Believe me, there's no better place to learn about these subjects. Of course, with an organization the size of the military, it would be impossible to operate without uniformity and control. So while my army buddies and I joked about how "this man's army" did things, I saw there was a method to its madness. In spite of the bureaucracy, the army managed to get things done. And in the military I learned that every business must have certain procedures and disciplines in place. Most important, a company must have a central headquarters with definite controls that are consistent and clearly communicated throughout the entire organization. Without consistency, there's bound to be chaos.

Four months after I arrived in Texas, my daughter Tami was born. I was on cloud nine and couldn't wait for the day when I'd finally get to see her. I remember that first Christmas without my family—I was so homesick for them. I tied a small stocking on the foot of my bed and asked my buddies in the barracks to put their small change in it. "It's a fund for my little girl," I told them. I was the happiest guy in the whole state of Texas when Laura and the baby came to the base to be with me during the last six months of my active duty.

After my discharge, we moved back to Dresden and lived in a house on Chestnut Street that Laura's parents gave us.

3

Six Weeks Ago I Couldn't Even Spell "Entrepreneur"—Now I *Is* One!

After my discharge from the army, I got my old job back at Nickles Bakery. In 1963 I was in line for promotion when I heard that Harry's Dairy Bar was for sale. Almost every small town has its favorite hangout, and Harry's was that place in Dresden. I always thought no other restaurant in Ohio could beat its large ham sandwich and thick shakes. Its counter had eight stools, plus there were two booths and two tables, giving it a seating capacity of twenty-four people.

I had eaten at Harry's for many years, so I knew that owning it meant putting in long hours. There were a lot of restaurants on my bread route, so I knew that it was really tough going in the food industry. Some of the owners who stuck it out could hardly make a living. In fact, a lot of them in small towns like Dresden would have swapped places with me in a heartbeat. To them, my bread route seemed like a great job—shorter hours, no payrolls to meet, and far less paperwork. I didn't have to constantly worry whether I'd go under, at least while Nickles Bakery stayed in business. And as a big, established company, Nickles was as solid as the Rock of Gibraltar.

So what urged me to venture out on my own? I suppose it was for the same reasons a lot of people have. For starters, I liked the idea of being my own boss. It meant having a lot of freedom. Second, I was willing to work long hours to make the business succeed. Next, owning a restaurant seemed like it would be a lot of fun. After all, I always had a good time whenever I stopped at Harry's. So if I could buy it, I figured I'd have a ball with it.

My daughter, Tami, was two years old. I could imagine her coming in after school for a snack or a dish of ice cream. Later, she would have a place to hang out. If she wanted to work after school or during the summer, what better job could there be than helping me?

When it came to taking risks, I didn't think about it, mostly because I had so little to lose. In a worst-case scenario, I could always go back to driving a bread truck.

■ NOTHING DOWN

With zero money in the bank, I approached Marge and Harry Lowe about their asking price.

"It's yours for fifteen thousand dollars," Harry said.

"Let me see what the bank will loan me," I answered.

I figured I could use my house as collateral, and that would give me about $6,000. Since the restaurant itself was worth $15,000, the bank would lend me the money right off.

The banker didn't figure it the way I did. "You don't know the first thing about the restaurant business," he told me.

"Well, sir, since I was a kid I've worked in a grocery store," I said, "and for the last eight years, I've been going in and out of all sorts of restaurants. I know more than you think."

I could tell from the way the banker looked at me that he didn't agree. He had known me for years. I was the kid who mowed grass and sacked groceries. I was also the kid who took so long to get out of high school.

"I'm sorry," he replied. "We can't make the loan."

I left his office thinking about who might lend me the money. The more I thought about it, the more frustrated I became. I couldn't ask anyone in my family because they simply didn't have it. I thought about taking someone in as a partner, but on my bread route I had seen the many problems that partnerships created. I didn't want to be one of those guys who told everyone, "I've got to talk to my partner. I'll get back to you next week."

Walking down Main Street, I happened to bump into Kenny Martin, who owned a big dairy. I must have looked down in the dumps because Kenny said, "Hey, Popeye, you don't look so good."

"I don't feel so good," I answered, telling him about how I got turned down by the bank.

"Gosh, Popeye, that's a doggone shame. I remember making deliveries to the grocery store and seeing you there. I never did see a kid work as hard as you. How much money are you talking about?"

"I need fifteen thousand dollars, but if the bank lent me eight . . ."

"What do you say I go back to the bank with you and talk to them."

What good fortune to have bumped into Kenny Martin, I thought to myself. Not only was he one of the bank's best customers; he was also the banker's brother-in-law!

Kenny grabbed my arm and marched me right into the bank. We walked up to the banker's desk, and Kenny said, "This man needs to borrow $8,000. Where do I co-sign so he gets that money?"

"Uh, right here, Kenny," the banker said.

After we left the bank, I thanked Kenny again and again. Then I excused myself, saying I had to get back to the Lowes.

Harry's was eight blocks down the street. I was so excited, I don't think my feet hit the ground twice all the way.

I explained to the Lowes that the bank would lend me $8,000.

"I need you to carry me for the balance," I told them.

"Popeye, we can't think of two people we'd rather have own our restaurant than you and Laura."

"We feel the same way," I told them.

"Why don't you let Marge and me sleep on it," Harry said. "Come back tomorrow, and I'll let you know what we decide."

We met the next day. Harry said, "Popeye, we'll take the second mortgage."

That was it, and I was in business.

■ THE ADVANTAGES OF A SMALL-TOWN BUSINESS

For years, there's been a swarm of small-town people moving out to large city areas. It's mainly young people who head to the big city. They're looking for better jobs, a faster lifestyle and so on.

I understand the attraction, but my personal preference has always been small-town living. There are all kinds of advantages to life in a small town. There are many benefits for a business owner.

In a large city, you're lucky if you know the people who live two doors down the street. One nice thing about a small town is that everyone knows you. This especially works in your favor when you're just starting out. Your friends will go out of their way to support your business. They will come in to test the water, but you can't take for granted they'll come back. You've got to give them great service so they will.

There's also less competition in small towns. Some small towns have more than one dress shop, bakery, or hardware store, but in a community the size of Dresden, you may have the only game in town. Back in the 1960s, my dairy bar was the only one in Dresden.

It's true there's a limited number of customers in a small town, but with low overhead you can maintain decent margins. Everything from the cost of labor to advertising is cheaper. Rent is only a fraction of what you pay in big cities. Naturally, the same is true if you buy property. Even back in 1963, shelling out $15,000 for a restaurant was small potatoes. And if you buy an existing business like I did, you're not competing with a lot of other buyers who will drive up the price. Let's face it, if the Lowes had other bidders, a cash buyer would have beat me out.

What's especially nice about doing business in a small town is the many things you can do that generate publicity. Buying uniforms for the Little League or sponsoring the high school marching band gets your picture in the papers. These good deeds draw customers and make your employees feel good about their company.

Speaking of employees, there's a lot to be said about the wonderful work ethic in small towns. I credit the influence of farming on a rural community. Anyone who grew up on a farm knows what I mean. There are always chores to do on a farm: the cow has to be milked every day, the livestock have to be fed, and, as they say, you've got to make hay while the sun shines. Setting up shop in a small town provides a workforce with a strong work ethic.

Did you ever see how fast news travels in a small community? When small-town kids get into trouble, their parents are likely to find out the same day. I believe this keeps them on the straight and narrow. These same kids with good values become good citizens and trusted employees when they grow up.

Anyone wanting to start a national company such as a franchised business should start it in a small town. First, because the overhead is lower, you take less of a hit if things don't work out. Second, big-city customers are harder to please because there are lots of other places they can go. Better to test the water in a small town, and after you've got all the kinks out, head for the big city. Sam Walton did this with

Wal-Mart. Now Wal-Mart is the world's largest retail store. I rest my case.

■ PROMOTE YOUR NAME

Years before, when the Lowes bought Ace's Dairy Bar, they renamed it Harry's Dairy Bar. Once I became its owner, I made a name change, too. I chose Midway Dairy Bar because Dresden was halfway between Zanesville and Coshocton, sixteen miles in each direction.

Naming it Midway turned out to be a big mistake. Everyone in town called me Popeye, so people said, "I'll meet you at Popeye's" or "Let's go to Popeye's for dinner."

Every time someone would say "Popeye's," I'd correct them and say, "No, it's the Midway."

It didn't matter what I called it. It's what the customers wanted to call it that mattered. So I changed the name to Popeye's.

Later, when I started the basket company, I went with Longaberger. I have become a big believer in promoting your family name. I think employees feel more comfortable working for a family business. People feel like they're working for human beings instead of a bunch of suits. Management has a face. I believe this is a nice personal touch that companies should strive to keep. As companies grow and employees have less contact with management, they often feel far removed.

I once read about how Ford Motor Company employees, in the early years in Detroit, used to say, "I work for the Fords." They felt like they were working for Henry Ford himself, who seemed like a regular guy. For years, when people talked about Ford Motor Company, they thought of Henry Ford. Later when Henry Ford II, his grandson, succeeded him as CEO, company employees could continue to say they worked for the Fords.

■ PEOPLE WILL PAY FOR QUALITY

We were so hard-pressed for money we had only $135 in cash the day Popeye's first opened for business. We had to take an inventory after lunch and go to the grocery store to stock up on everything. We'd do the same thing before closing, getting what we needed for the next day's lunch. This went on for several months before we were able to buy directly from a wholesaler.

Right from day one, I never sacrificed quality. Everything always had to be fresh, including the bread and the coffee.

That fresh cup of coffee at Popeye's became one of our trademarks. We'd brew coffee every half hour, no matter what, and pour out what was left in the old pot. There's nothing worse than being served old coffee. I've gone into restaurants that serve coffee that's old enough to vote. People will gladly wait until a new pot is made. It may seem wasteful to throw out coffee that's only thirty minutes old, but I always thought it was an inexpensive way to develop a reputation for quality. In the restaurant business, freshness means quality.

Another thing I learned in the restaurant business: never cut corners to reduce your prices. Popeye's charged a little more than people normally used to pay in our neck of the woods. However, customers soon came to see that they were getting their money's worth. Our prices were 25 percent higher than what restaurants charged in surrounding towns, but the customers kept pouring in because they knew they'd get quality food and outstanding service.

We were also known as the cleanest restaurant in the area. Believe it or not, I liked to wash the dishes myself. Customers felt good about that. They knew I'd make sure everything was spic and span. Nobody would ever catch anything at Popeye's that they didn't come in with.

Later on, I wanted this same emphasis on detail to be given to selling baskets. I believe it works in every business. There is always somebody out there who can undersell you. I wanted the reputation of being the best, not the cheapest!

It's a funny thing about the food business. If somebody was served a bad meal or got poor service, that customer would complain and wouldn't come back for two years. In the grocery store business, if someone bought spoiled milk or a bad piece of meat, they'd complain, and we'd exchange it for them, but they'd be back the next day. Why the two businesses were different in this respect has always been a mystery to me.

I always wanted my customers to be glad they came to Popeye's. If there were any complaints, I insisted that the meal was on the house. That customer would come back. If a customer has a bad experience in your restaurant, he'll tell everyone he knows. A satisfied customer might tell five people. You have to have many more happy customers than unhappy ones. Unless you have an enormous advertising budget, you've got to bend over backward to keep customers satisfied. Those customers are your advertising!

■ YOU CAN'T BE IN TWO PLACES AT THE SAME TIME

There's an old country expression that says, "You can't chase two rabbits with one stone." I learned this the hard way. I reasoned that if Popeye's could do well in Dresden, we could do even better in places with bigger populations.

My game plan was to open a Popeye's in Coshocton, which was nearly ten times as big as Dresden. It would be just a matter of time before we'd have Popeye's restaurants popping up all over. Boy, was I excited to set up in the big city of Coshocton!

So we opened our second Popeye's. I soon discovered I'd have to spend most of my time getting it started. Later I'd be able to split my time going back and forth, from one restaurant to the other. Do you see what I mean about chasing two rabbits with one stone? I couldn't be in two places at the same time.

It took me six months to find out that it was a mistake to open a second restaurant. With me spending half my time at each restaurant, neither one did well! The revenues at the original Popeye's started to decrease. Even though Popeye's was prospering in Dresden, I lost so much money in Coshocton that it was like starting all over again to recoup our losses.

This setback taught me an invaluable lesson that everyone in a personal service business should know. There is a special relationship between the owner of a small business and the customer. When you build a business that centers around you—as I did at Popeye's—your customers become used to the personal touch they receive from you, and this is very difficult to replace or duplicate. There's something about being at a small restaurant where the owner calls you by name, tells you the special, or brings you a free dessert when you get slow service. And when the proprietor thanks you for your business, it's the whole company saying thank you. A waiter or salesperson can thank you, but it's not the same as hearing it from the owner.

This lesson applies not only to other specialty businesses but also to certain professions. When the owner of a haberdashery recommends a tie, you're flattered that he is taking a personal interest in you. It's the same when you buy a new car. Only the owner of the dealership has the power and authority to negotiate the best deal.

"New models are due in next month," he says, "so I'm going to give you my absolute lowest possible price." You know that nobody else can make the same offer without his permission.

When the senior partner of a law firm advises you, or you get to talk to your doctor instead of her nurse, you feel privileged. Of course, a good businessperson has to delegate responsibility to expand the company. But if you're in a business that's built primarily on personal service, you better figure out how to do it without spreading yourself too thin.

■ NOTHING DOWN AGAIN

Five years after Popeye's opened, the word got out that the A&P Grocery in Dresden was going out of business. I wanted to expand the restaurant, so that four-thousand-square-foot space was just about what I needed. I still had no money, so I worked out another land contract with the owner. He agreed to sell for $9,000, and I'd make monthly payments until it was paid off. With the extra space I planned to set up a buffet, so I approached A&P about buying some of the store's equipment. The A&P agreed to sell all of it to me for $2,800, and again I paid nothing down and had a monthly note for the next five years. For $2,800, I got the cash registers, shelving, carts, the meat block, the meat counter—in fact, everything except the coffee grinders. Looking at all this equipment, I decided I should open a grocery store. Why not? Dresden certainly needed one, and ever since I was a kid, I always thought about someday owning a grocery store. One thing I didn't get was the A&P name; they didn't want me affiliated with their company. That was okay because it wasn't what I wanted anyhow.

I had to come up with $5,000 so I could stock the grocery with some inventory. I didn't think the bank would give me a loan, but a while back Fairmont Dairy had offered to finance some restaurant equipment on the condition that I give them my business at Popeye's. I bought all my dairy products from Martin's. No way would I stop buying from Kenny Martin's company.

I called Fairmont and made a counteroffer. I said that if they would lend me $5,000 toward inventory, they'd get the lion's share of shelf space in the dairy section at the grocery store. I made it clear, though, that I'd also carry Martin's Dairy products. I explained that without Kenny Martin, I wouldn't even be in business. They understood and made me the loan.

While $5,000 didn't buy much inventory, even for a small-town grocery, it was a start. I kept putting money into store improvements and at the same time built up the inventory. When I sold the store in 1983, its inventory was valued at $150,000.

Nine thousand dollars for a four-thousand-square-foot building sounds dirt cheap today. But believe me, in 1968, I was paying top dollar. Downtown Dresden was the pits back then. With cash, I could have bought the building for about $4,500. But I knew I was paying for something that would be far more valuable in the future. I knew what I planned to do with the property—and that was more important than its current market price. Over the years, I've bought a lot of property without trying to bargain for a lower price. It's not that I like to pay top dollar for real estate. Instead, I value the property based on what I believe it will be worth in the future.

■ LEARNING FROM MY PEERS

In just a few months my grocery store qualified to become the Dresden IGA Foodliner. I was proud to be a member of the Independent Grocers Association because people knew that IGA stood for quality food. It also meant that IGA would do my books and provide training for my employees, and we'd be able to carry their famous "specials."

Most important, the IGA people told me, "Dave, keep your labor cost at 7 percent and material cost at 18 percent, and you'll make money."

That was all I needed to know. We kept our costs down, and we were netting around 4 percent. Today's big supermarkets do cartwheels when they net half a percent!

I strongly recommend that if you're an independent business owner, you should join your industry's association. In addition to belonging to IGA, I was also a member of the Ohio Restaurant Association. I made a strong effort to attend all meetings. Afterward, I'd get together with other restaurateurs, and that's where I learned some of my best lessons.

When I first joined the association, I was surprised to see how willing the successful members were to give advice to me. They seemed to thrive on sharing their know-how. These individuals were wonderful role models, and I was so grateful to them. Later, when I had some experience under my belt, I, too, was eager to help new members who came to me for advice. By helping others, I felt it was a small way to pay back those who helped me when I was so green.

■ THE FUN FACTOR

Isn't it a shame most people don't enjoy those eight hours a day they put in on the job? The time spent on the job is 50 percent of the time you're awake! Work should be enjoyed, if for no other reason than because life's too short to be miserable forty hours a week.

Some people think that work and fun don't mix. But they can, and I can assure you that the fun factor adds to the bottom line. Even if it didn't, I'd still work hard at making sure my employees were enjoying their jobs. I like to be around people who are having fun.

It doesn't take a genius to know that when we enjoy our work, we're more productive. Remember how you'd make better grades when you enjoyed being in school? Recently, I was talking to a fifth-grade student about her schoolwork.

"I keep falling asleep in my history class," she told me. "And I don't like English."

"Is there anything you like about school?" I asked her. Her face lit up.

"Oh, yes, Mr. Longaberger! I love geography. When I grow up, I'm going to travel all over the world. My favorite thing on TV is the Discovery Channel."

When I asked about her report card, it didn't come as a surprise that her only A was in geography.

That fifth-grade student is no different than people in the workplace. Find something that turns you on, and it's a safe bet you'll do well at it. I loved working at my restaurant, talking with customers, and seeing them enjoy a good meal. I liked changing the menu, experimenting to see which projects generated more business. Like I said, I even liked washing dishes.

Popeye's was a challenge and exciting, too. I couldn't wait to get up in the morning to go to work. I hate hearing from people who have to force themselves out of bed every day and drag themselves to a job they can't stand. I know they sit and daydream about what they'll do after work. They're constantly looking at the clock, counting the minutes until they can leave. How can anyone do a good job when they feel that way?

One way I bring fun into the workplace is through humor. It's a great way to create a comfortable work environment because it relaxes people. Humor is a wonderful common denominator for managers and workers, regardless of the so-called pecking order. When an employer shares a laugh with an employee, it promotes a friendly feeling. When the boss shares a good joke, he's providing a form of entertainment. When you think about it, isn't this thoughtful? Humor communicates to others that you care about them.

All too often an uptight boss thinks humor in the workplace is inappropriate. That person usually takes himself too seriously and comes across as pompous and boring. Even in a crisis, I rely on humor to put things in perspective. With a touch of humor during a tense situation, you are able to approach problems more calmly. And when you get right down to it, most problems are not as serious as they first appear.

As the owner of a restaurant and grocery store, I tried to create a fun-place-to-be atmosphere, with customers as well as employees. One of my favorite lines when waiting tables was, "How much are you going to tip me?" Of course, I didn't want them to tip me, and if they insisted, I'd say, "Give it to one of the waitresses on your way out."

I loved playing pranks on customers. One of my favorites was my plastic ice cube with a fly inside it. I used to put the ice cube in somebody's water glass and tip off my waitresses and a few other customers. We'd wait patiently until a customer noticed it floating in the glass. Then there would be a sudden shriek that would cause everyone to crack up. And I can't tell you how many times I served a rubber chicken to a customer. I'd put the fake chicken on a plate and serve it with real vegetables, potatoes, and gravy. I did the same thing with a rubber hot dog. I'd put it in a bun and send it out with coney dog sauce. The look on the customer's face was priceless. Some of my customers were so conditioned to my pranks, I swear they were disappointed when I didn't pull one on them.

At the grocery store, I was always putting dog food in a cat lover's cart, and I would do the opposite with a dog owner. Then at the check-out line, I'd say, "Didn't you used to have a cat? Why in the world did you purchase dog food?"

Once a little boy came into the store for a bottle of soda. "Would you put it in a sack?" he politely asked.

"Sure thing," I said, and I removed the lid and poured his soda into a sack.

His eyes got as big as saucers. "No, I wanted the *bottle* of soda in the sack," he said.

I winked at him, and all of a sudden the kid started laughing so hard he could hardly stop.

When I was in a particularly silly mood, I'd take a small child out of a cart when the parent wasn't looking. Then, I'd hide the kid some-where in the store. Of course, I would pick and choose whom I would play tricks on. I admit that every now and then somebody would get mad at me. But so many of my customers loved it, I didn't worry about the ones who got upset.

One time a woman asked to use a pen at the checkout counter. I had filled one with invisible ink, and I "accidentally" squirted it on her beautiful sweater. She went ballistic.

"Popeye! You ruined my sweater!" she screamed at me.

"Okay, I'll pay for it. I'll pay for it," I said, trying to calm her down.

"I don't want your money, and you'll never see me in here again!" she shouted.

As she was about to leave the store, I pointed at her sweater and said, "Well, I'll be. Look, the ink disappeared."

By this time, everyone in the store was laughing, and her face turned beet red. "Damn you, Popeye!" she said. Then a big smile crossed her face.

The more I joked and entertained my customers, the more my busi-ness seemed to grow. In time, I knew which people appreciated my practical jokes and which ones wouldn't. I developed a sense of timing. After a while, I'd spend only so much time with a customer, always stopping before I overdid it. As they say in show business, you always want to leave your audience wanting more.

■ INTEGRITY AND TRUST

I was a young boy working at the corner grocery store during World War II. I remember how beef was rationed. The government limited how much each family could buy so the overseas troops would have enough. One grocer would butcher a couple of steers in his barnyard and sell it over the counter in his store. Even today this would be illegal because the law requires beef to be inspected, stamped, and sealed.

In those days, sugar and flour used to come in fifty- and one-hundred-pound sacks. Grocers poured it out into five-pound bags. This same guy made a practice out of shorting his customers by several ounces per sale. On top of that, he would grind Wheaties into the hamburger and sell it as 100 percent beef.

Cheating customers is dishonest and stupid. Just think of the message it sends to employees. They have to think, "If the boss cheats his customers, he'll cheat me too." It also truly encourages employees to cheat their boss. We've all seen employees who steal everything from office supplies to inventory and who rationalize it by thinking, "I'm only getting my share."

On the personal side, I came to believe honesty is definitely the best policy. Take the time I decided to go swimming instead of working at the grocery. I slipped out of the store while the owner wasn't looking. I hightailed it down to the pond, swam for a bit, and ran back to the store. When the owner asked where I had been, I said, "Oh, I was in the back with the stock." The owner then directed me to a mirror so I could see how my hair was sticking up in every direction. I learned that it doesn't pay to lie!

I relearned this lesson another time. I was taking an agriculture class in school (I took the class because of the field trips). A prerequisite for the class was to have a farm project. My project was a calf. The only problem was, I didn't really have a calf!

As the year progressed, the dishonesty escalated. For example, I had to report on the calf's status, including what time I fed it, how much it weighed, and even what time it went to bed.

Then one day it happened. The teacher, Mr. Robert "Mac" McMurray, announced, "Class, today we're going to take a trip to see your calves firsthand." My heart almost stopped! I got on the bus and sat in the back, feeling my heart beat faster and faster with every stop we made.

The teacher finally said, "And now let's go see Popeye's calf, Flossie." I sat wide-eyed as the bus neared Flossie's theoretical location. At a fork in the road, the teacher said, "No, I've changed my mind. Let's go see Dave Graves' calf instead. Sorry, Popeye, I don't think we'll have time to see Flossie."

I knew, and he knew, and we knew each other knew. That was a painful lesson, but I told myself if I ever got off that bus alive, I'd never tell another lie.

Well, I've probably told a few more since then, but that lesson always stuck with me. The easiest way out of any situation is to tell the truth.

Integrity is a must in business, and it starts at the top. Management must lead by example. The way a business owner acts (or for that matter, a CEO of a large corporation) affects the whole company. When employees and customers get treated fairly, it sets a standard for everyone. Likewise, when a company engages in one-sided business practices, the workforce takes notice. The same thing happens when a company manufactures a shoddy product. This is the best way I know to destroy an employee's sense of pride. The same holds true when guarantees are made to customers that fall through after the sale. Employees just don't feel good about themselves when their company isn't giving customers a fair shake.

Successful businesses are built on trust, and an employer must prove himself to his people, day in and day out. Never assume that your employees will automatically trust you because you hand them a paycheck. You have to earn their trust. And once you have it, you have to keep on earning it.

One way to win your employees' trust is to show that you trust them. Around two o'clock every day at Popeye's, just after the lunch crowd was out the door, I'd encourage the waitresses to tally up the cash register receipts to see how we did. We made a contest out of it to see if we had taken in more than the previous day. They'd get so excited when we did, and there was always a big celebration when we'd set some kind of a record. The waitresses didn't get anything out of this except the feeling of "ownership." They felt like it was their restaurant, too. This worked so well at Popeye's that we did the same thing at the grocery store.

"You let your employees go through your cash register like that?" people would say. "Popeye, you've got to be nuts. They're going to rob you blind."

I never worried about dishonest employees. I always believed that if I trusted them, they would trust me. Many thought I was taking a foolish risk. But I got bigger returns taking that risk.

■ WE ARE FAMILY

The Pittsburgh Pirates used to play the song "We Are Family" during their 1979 season. It gave them a team spirit that I believe helped them to win the World Series. A family spirit also works wonders for employees.

When I first started in business, there were many things I was unable to do for my employees. I couldn't afford to pay them big salaries. Health care benefits were out of the question. And I couldn't build them a plush workplace. I simply did not have the money. This puts a small start-up business at a severe disadvantage in hiring people. To make it up to them, I worked hard to create a family atmosphere. I grew up in a family where everyone protected and cared about each other. I wanted my employees to have that same warm, comfortable feeling at work.

One way I did this was always to be totally open with my employees. My employees have said, "You always know where you stand with Popeye." I let them know what they could expect from me and what I expected from them. I regularly told them how the company was doing. I let them know when times were tough. Of course, I told them when we were doing well, too, always congratulating them and thanking them for their contributions.

Some employees are associated with your company for so long, how can they be anything but family? One such individual is Anita Rector, who started waiting tables at Popeye's at age fifteen on a part-time basis after school. Anita was a member of a Girl Scouts troop that my wife, Laura, led, and she came highly recommended as a hard worker. She came from a humble background, and since she was a small child had worked at odd jobs like delivering newspapers and housecleaning. I suppose I liked Anita so much because she reminded me of myself at about that age.

Anita worked in the grocery store for me, too, and today she has a management position at Longaberger. With a long-term relationship like we've had for so many years, how can I not think of Anita as family!

Then there's Kenny Birkhimer, who used to drive a bread truck for

Cannon's Bakery. We've known each other all our lives. Because he had the bread route experience, I asked him to work for me in the restaurant. My plan was to teach him the business and let him manage Popeye's. I had just taken over a vacant storefront next door to the grocery. I planned to expand into that space, and then I got the idea that Dresden needed a drugstore. A new business! But I knew I couldn't be in three places at one time. Although Kenny started at Popeye's, he eventually became my first employee when I started making baskets. Kenny played an important role in the early days of the basket company and has remained a loyal employee to this day.

I go way back with Anita and Kenny. We've worked side by side, and we've been close friends. I've seen their children grow up, and they've seen mine grow up. We've shared many good times as well as the bad times. When you develop close relationships like I have with such special people, they are family.

■ MINDING YOUR P'S AND Q'S

Minding our p's and q's means paying attention to details. This expression goes back to when printers set type by hand. They had to pick out letters of the alphabet one at a time, and the letters were backward, so a *p* looked like a *q* and vice versa. Apprentices were told to be careful not to be fooled and confuse the two.

Other people believe this goes back to the time when old English pubs ran tabs for their customers. A *p* stood for a pint and a *q* for a quart. The customers who had a little too much to drink might not be able to tell a *p* from a *q* and would end up paying too much.

Wherever the expression came from, minding your p's and q's in business is always good advice. You have to stay on top of things, which means knowing the nitty-gritty of your business. Once the grocery store got on solid ground, it was carrying a large inventory. But no matter how big we got, I could walk down any aisle and instantly spot when something was wrong. Let's say somebody forgot to order lima beans and didn't want me to know. They might spread out the green bean cans to fill in the empty space. Or they might spread out the lima bean cans, and fill in behind them with the green beans. There are many ways to cover up. It never worked.

I'd say, "OK, who forgot to order the lima beans?" I was so good at this, my employees used to wonder how I did it. I felt it was important to see that I was on top of my business. I think it made them feel secure, knowing that I knew the grocery business backward and forward. Second, it set a high standard, and this, too, is a good message for employees.

It was the same way in the restaurant. I loved to wait tables because it gave me a chance to mix with the customers. I'd chat and tell jokes, and all the while I'd watch what was going on out of the corner of my eye. I always knew when a table needed cleaning, a customer was waiting too long for his check, or a meal was served cold. And when something wasn't right, I'd be on top of it in a flash.

Many people thought I had some kind of amazing ability. I don't think I was doing anything special. I think people who are truly committed to their work are able to detect problems that aren't obvious to someone who isn't interested in doing a really great job. Also, a lot just comes with experience. A guy who's been playing guitar all his life will hear when a note goes flat, even if the audience doesn't hear it.

■ EQUALITY FOR ALL

All too often, business owners and managers draw boundaries between themselves and their employees. They might be subtle so they're hard to see, but they're there. For instance, some bosses insist on being addressed as "Mr." or "Ms." However, starting from day one, every one of my employees has been told either to call me Popeye or Dave—never Mr. Longaberger. I don't like class distinctions, and a lot of pomp and ceremony isn't my style. I like that down-home feeling, the kind that makes people feel comfortable. When an employee can call me by my first name, she feels like she can approach me on level ground.

In some companies, the upper ranks wear business suits. Company dress codes remind me of the military, where the officers stand out from the enlisted people. The military must maintain its strict pecking order so in life-and-death situations there is no debate about the merits of the orders. In the world of business, this approach stifles morale. Good management allows everyone to express their opinions.

When rank-and-file workers sense management is "different" from them, it makes them feel uneasy about making suggestions and expressing legitimate complaints. Such barriers inhibit people from coming right out with what's on their mind. When this happens, a lot of otherwise good ideas never get heard.

■ TAKE A PERSONAL INTEREST

I take a personal interest in my employees, and sometimes I get criticized for this.

"Don't get so close to them," I've been told. "You don't need to take on their personal problems, Popeye."

I can't relate to this advice. If an employee has a problem at home, it will follow her to work. And it will show up in how she does on the job. For instance, if she's worried about a sick child, chances are she'll still be worried when she gets to work. If she can't find someone to care for that child, it would be better if she didn't come in. It's not much of a boss who says, "I own you for these eight hours, and don't you forget it." A boss can't control what goes on in that employee's mind. And that kind of attitude from a boss is guaranteed to make it harder for her to do a good job.

People have also called me a fool for having an open-door policy that permits employees to walk into my office with their problems. I not only permit it; I encourage them to come to me when they need a shoulder to cry on.

"If it's not business, Popeye, stay the hell out of it," people warn me. I'm sorry, but I can't ignore my employees' personal problems. If an employee thinks it's something I should be told, I'll listen. I listen because I truly care about his or her problem. I care about them, and in turn they care about me. This is the relationship I have always sought with my employees. It has to come from the heart; it can't be faked.

■ COMPETING AGAINST MYSELF

I've never measured my success based on how well I competed against others. This may sound strange because from the time we start school, we learn to compete in the classroom for good grades. Later in sports, we're taught to beat our opponent. There's no question that heavy competition is a big part of our American culture. Some people even say it's the backbone of our free enterprise system.

I'm all for free enterprise, and I am not one to back down, but in truth, I have never been motivated to beat the competition. Instead, I have always tried to beat myself. That's right, I compete against myself. I have always set a personal standard for what I want to achieve, and I work toward that goal. When I reach it, I set a higher goal and go after that.

Frankly, I don't care what the competition is doing. It's okay with me if the other guy gets his. More power to him. What really motivates me is doing better than I've done before and improving myself along the way.

I also try to inspire my employees to strive to do their best. I discourage them from competing against each other.

"Just be the best you can be," I say, "and let's work together so we can be the best team." Not a team that competes against other teams but a team that pulls together toward one common goal—to be the best possible company we can be. I believe this can be applied to every business, whether it's a restaurant, grocery store, or large manufacturing company.

■ NEVER FORGET WHO SIGNS YOUR PAYCHECK

As a business owner, never lose sight of who signs your paycheck. If you think it's you, you're not only wrong, you're in big trouble.

Never forget that it's your employees and your customers who sign your paycheck. If you think your employees work for you, you have things backward. You work for them, just as you work for your customers. You're not the VIP, they are. With this in mind, you must keep these VIPs happy.

It's a given that without customers, no business can survive. Everyone understands the importance of catering to customers. But your employees are equally important. Unless you're a one-person operation, your livelihood depends on them.

I've been around companies that do backbends for their customers. They put them on a pedestal and treat them like royalty. That's great, and I'm all for it. But what disgusts me is when these same companies treat their own employees like dirt. Nothing is more hypocritical. When I see someone disrespect his employees, I have no use for him.

In retail, there's a saying, "If the boss screams at a store manager, how many customers feel it?" When an employer screams at an employee, she may as well do the same thing to her customers. What happens? That employee will be down for the rest of the day. And what will he do? He'll take it out on customers. He may not actually yell at them, but he'll feel so bad that he won't be able to be pleasant. Customers will hear it in the tone of his voice on the telephone, and they'll see it on his face and in his posture. The employee might even think he's hiding his feelings, but customers will sense that something is wrong.

It's the old snowball effect. I've seen it in restaurants again and again. The boss chews out a waitress, and she's a bundle of nerves for the rest of the day. She snaps at customers even though she doesn't mean to. She acts impatient when customers are slow giving her their order. Those customers will feel it when the waitress doesn't want them to dawdle at a table after she's brought them their check.

Sales clerks do the same thing. They might as well be saying, "You don't want to buy anything today, do you?" And the customers usually don't!

■ LISTEN TO YOUR PEOPLE

Most people know that it's important to be a good listener. They sometimes seem to leave this skill at home when they go to work. This is especially true when it comes to business owners and managers. It's as if they think because they're high up on the chain of command, they can't learn anything from the people who work under them. They act as if the higher up the ladder you go, the more you tell subordinates what to do and the less you listen.

I once heard about the head of a company who told his employees, "I've been in this business for thirty years and I've been the head of this company for the past ten years. Don't any of you dare come to me with an idea because there is nothing you can tell me that I don't already know." I am happy to report that his company has since gone out of business.

Back in the days when assembly lines were first started, foremen used to say, "You're not paid to think. When you walk through that door and punch that time clock, I want you to check your brain at the door— and don't use it until you punch out. We'll do the thinking for you."

Imagine the morale of people who were told they weren't authorized to think. And what a waste of resources!

Right from the start, I went to my employees and told them how much Popeye's needed their suggestions. I let them know that the restaurant's success depended on the feedback they gave me. Every day, I would ask them various questions:

"How did that man like the ham sandwich? Did he say anything about its size? Did he finish it? How big was the tip he gave you?"

"Did she say anything about our prices? Do you think she didn't order a dessert because she didn't want to spend the money?"

"What do you think we should add to our menu? Is there anything customers have been asking for that we don't have?"

"How can we improve our kitchen service to help you better serve customers? Do you have any complaints about the kitchen?"

"What's your opinion about . . ."

I asked the same kinds of questions in the grocery and the drugstore. I truly believe that the world's best source of information about any business is the people who spend eight hours a day working there. Big companies spend huge fees to bring in consultants, when all the answers (and the right answers at that) are available for free. All they have to do is listen to their employees.

As a bonus, getting your employees' opinions boosts their morale. It's a great compliment when the boss says, "We have a problem, and I'd really appreciate your input."

If you want to see a happy, motivated employee, ask his opinion. If you're sincere and listen carefully, you'll make his day. Remember you have to be sincere about it. If you're not, it will have the opposite effect. He'll know you're just trying to butter him up, and that will make him suspicious.

Back in those early days with my restaurant and grocery store, I'd sometimes wonder why people would stay with me and not take a better-paying job somewhere else. I think that one of the reasons was that I was a good listener. Thinking back on it, I suppose I listened hard because I truly needed their advice. I didn't have the experience for doing what I was trying to do, and letting them take turns at being the coach made them a better team. Later, when I actually used some of their ideas and they worked, I'd give them all the credit.

"How do you like those new menu items?" I'd ask a customer. "Those were her suggestions," I'd say, pointing to a waitress.

Before long, I didn't have to ask for suggestions because my employees couldn't wait to tell me. As soon as one of their ideas worked, they'd say, "Popeye, I'd like to run something else by you."

I didn't always agree with their ideas. And when I didn't, I'd take the time to carefully explain why. Then I'd listen to them again. I was always willing to discuss the pros and cons. Sometimes I'd just play the devil's advocate. I'd say why I didn't think something would work, and then invite them to sell me on why it would. They understood that not every idea could be used, but by turning them down gently, while expressing appreciation, I encouraged them to come back with more.

I even used the same technique with my own ideas. First, I'd always run my ideas by them and then I'd ask, "What do you think? Do you think this will work? Why do you think it won't work? What am I missing?"

I discovered that when employees had ownership like this, they started to see themselves in a whole new way. Some of them began to believe in themselves for the first time in their lives. Suddenly they were part of building a business.

Somebody once said that people support those things they help to create. In business, when you bring your people in during the early stages of a project, they're more apt to buy into it. In a like manner, they'll drag their feet if you make big changes and then tell them, "This is what I've decided we will do." No matter how good an idea may be, if you don't get their support, chances are it's not going to succeed.

Today people talk a lot about the importance of respecting employees. To me that's always been a given. In my opinion, the best way to respect them is just to listen to them. This shows you value them. What bigger compliment can they get?

■ STEPPING-STONES

When I first went into the restaurant business, I was thrilled to be out on my own. I couldn't wait to go to work every day. I loved the fact that I was learning so much about business and, most important, about people.

Today, people ask me if I planned back then to someday operate a company like The Longaberger Company. My answer is, "Definitely no!"

Personally, I don't think any entrepreneur can be so positive about the future when just starting out. First you have to test the water to see if it's hot or cold. And you have to keep testing it, again and again. For the first five years, you're not going to know where your business is heading. That's because all kinds of doors of opportunity will open that you can't possibly expect. As an example, when I was driving my bread route, I didn't plan to own a restaurant. Later, I didn't have a clue I would go into the grocery business until the A&P closed its doors. Even when I first heard about it, I saw it as a chance to expand Popeye's. Then, when the hardware store next door went out of business, my original plan was to use the space to expand the grocery store. Only later did I think about opening a drugstore in Dresden.

It's amazing how things seemed to fall into place for me. Sometimes it was as if my life had been preplanned. As one opportunity presented itself, I'd take a step forward, and then another step with another opportunity. Each opportunity was a stepping-stone, and for a while I didn't know where these steps were leading me.

Although I worked in the restaurant for several years, I always knew I wouldn't spend the rest of my life in that business. Still, I couldn't have told you why, nor did I know where it would lead.

If there is a lesson here, I'd say it is to be sure to keep your antenna up, always ready to act when you spot a window of opportunity. Believe me, there are opportunities all around you. I firmly believe that opportunity knocks, but you have to get up and answer the door.

4

How The Longaberger Company
First Began

I confess that, as a youngster, I wasn't interested in Dad's baskets. I kept busy working after school, so I was never pushed by Dad to help out in the shop. My two older brothers, Jerry and Larry, and my older sister, Genevieve, were the ones who wove the most with Dad. In fact, only on rare occasions was I even allowed in the shop. Dad's big worry was that one of us kids would accidentally start a fire. With all those dry splints on the racks, the shop was a fire waiting to happen. We're lucky that we never had one.

Nevertheless, like the rest of my family, I knew a lot about baskets. There was always talk about basket weaving in the Longaberger house. On hot nights when the windows were open, I'd fall asleep listening to the tapping sounds coming from Dad's shop.

Dad closed his shop in 1955, the same year I graduated from high school. This came as quite a surprise because, all our lives, we had never known Dad to not weave baskets. But that's the way he was. Once he decided this was it, he was through. Dad had retired from the paper mill and had taken a part-time job managing the Dresden swimming pool. Now and then he'd make a few baskets for a little pocket change. He converted one side of his shop into a garage where his pickup truck was stored. The other side became a screened-in porch that had a barbecue pit, used primarily during family get-togethers.

By 1972 the restaurant was taking in $4,000 a week, and the grocery store and drugstore were grossing $20,000 a week. I was making $1,000 a week before taxes, which was a good living in those days, especially in a small town in rural eastern Ohio. Still, I was getting itchy to start something else.

I was watching what was going on in retail in the beginning of the seventies. I sensed people were starting to take an interest in things made by hand, from tie-dyed clothes to wall hangings to crocheted afghans. I thought people might enjoy a handcrafted basket made right here in the good old U.S.A. Americans would like our products because of the nostalgia factor. Longaberger baskets could take them back to the good old days when life moved at a slower, more relaxed pace. I didn't have any marketing research to back this up. It was just a gut feeling.

I'd walk through shopping malls, see wicker baskets, and think that they didn't compare to Dad's. They were imports, so cheaply made that Dad would have been embarrassed to have them in his shop. Every time I'd see shoddy baskets in a mall store, I felt like showing one of Dad's to the merchant so he could see what a quality basket was like. Finally, I asked Dad to come out of retirement and make up ten dozen baskets for me to see if I could sell them. He did.

I took Dad's baskets to the owner of a general store in Coshocton and offered them to him on consignment at $5 apiece. He said he could sell them for $10 each. Sure enough, he did. I went back to Dad and asked him to make up another ten dozen baskets.

"I'll give you six hundred dollars for the ten dozen," I told him. All the years he made baskets, he never got more than a buck fifty apiece for them. "That's five dollars a basket. Will you do it?"

"Sure, Popeye," he said, "but personally, I think you're nuts."

Within a month, I placed them in small gift shops and antique shops. That's when I decided there was money to be made selling baskets.

■ BEWARE OF THE NAYSAYERS

One day in the grocery store, I asked my employees to gather around. I had an announcement to make.

I said, "I think I'm going to start making baskets."

"Like the ones your dad makes?" an employee asked.

"That's right. I think high-quality baskets will sell like hotcakes."

"Your dad is getting up in years," someone said. "You can't expect him to make them for you."

"Well, the Indians make good handmade things," I said, sort of thinking out loud. I was thinking about the fringed leather vests and moccasins and Indian jewelry that were so popular at the time.

"Indians?" someone cried.

"That's right," I answered. "I remember seeing the crafts they sold out West when I was in the army."

Meanwhile, Larry had taught Richie how to make baskets. Every now and then they would make baskets for the family with Dad's remaining basket materials. These were stored in a two-thousand-square-foot building across the street from the restaurant on the corner of Main and Third. Formerly, the building had been a garage. The restaurant was quiet one Saturday night in 1972. I saw the lights on across the street, so I walked over to see my brothers.

"Hey, guys, I've got to tell you what I'm going to do," I said.

Before they could say a word, I was chattering about the huge demand throughout the country for products that were handmade in the United States. Larry and Richie sat there, staring with their mouths half open.

"I'm telling you, people will buy Dad's baskets coast to coast."

Now Dad had sold to a two- or three-county area, and it was strictly a one-man show. I was talking about a big business, far beyond anything they could imagine. Neither one of them had any business experience. Richie was teaching high school, and Larry worked as a mechanic for a construction company. The two of them looked at each other and rolled their eyes.

"Say, Popeye, aren't you just stretching things a bit?" Richie finally asked.

"What needs stretching is your imagination," I said. "You guys want in with me or what?" I asked.

Without the slightest pause, Richie said, "Not me." Larry remained silent. My family had watched me leverage myself up to my eyeteeth with my other ventures. They saw me go into debt to buy the restaurant and grocery store. Larry and Richie knew that being in business with me would be very risky. It was likely they'd have to be willing to mortgage their homes sometime down the road. Plus a business venture with me could cause friction in the family. That's exactly what we didn't want. Nothing was worth doing that could possibly result in a family feud.

"I'm not like you, Popeye," Larry said. "I'm not much of a risk taker.

But if you need it, I'll put up a thousand dollars. There's just one condition." I waited for him to finish. "Will you be willing to buy me out if I say I want out?"

"No problem," I said. Without drawing breath, I started giving details about what I wanted to do.

"Let's call it 'J. W. Longaberger Handwoven Basket Company.' First thing we have to do, Larry, is have you and Dad make up some baskets. My job will be to sell them."

I felt obligated to invite the rest of my family to invest in my new venture. I explained it to each of them. They all reacted pretty much the same way as Larry and Richie. Even Dad didn't think too much of the idea.

If you're thinking of starting your own business, I caution you about heeding advice from those closest to you. They'll tell you what they believe is truly in your best interest. Chances are they'll try to talk you out of it. You'll hear everything from: "It will never fly" to "Don't quit your day job."

It's not that they're trying to discourage you or don't want you to succeed. They genuinely believe such caution stems from good, solid advice. Most people simply reject new ideas, especially risky or revolutionary ideas. People who care about you don't want to see you uncomfortable. They're trying to save you from potential financial disaster.

Now remember: these are the people who care about you. This can make it all the more difficult for you to do what you believe will work. It's also why I never went to the bank to borrow seed money for the company. If I couldn't convince my family and friends, I didn't have a snowball's chance in hell of convincing a bank officer to make me a loan.

Sometimes your friends and family are the least likely people to be financially supportive because they knew you way back when. In Dresden, I was the stuttering kid who clerked at a grocery store, shoveled snow, and mowed grass. I was that kid who took so long to get out of high school. Now here I was with a wild notion of selling baskets all over the country. Well-meaning people would advise me, "You're doing much better in the restaurant and grocery business than anyone could have ever imagined. Now that you have some money in your pocket for the first time in your life, don't blow it on trying to start up a basket business."

One friend said, "There's an old saying that a fool and his money will soon part. Popeye, don't be that fool."

I'm not the first person who ventured into uncharted waters and encountered words of discouragement. When Alexander Graham Bell first tried to obtain financing for his new invention, he was told to remove "that toy" from the banker's office. That "toy" was the first telephone!

In 1968, when Bill McGowan founded MCI, he was warned that it was impossible for a start-up company to lock horns with AT&T, at the time the nation's largest corporation. There are countless stories of daring entrepreneurs who were pressured to scrap their dreams.

Frequently, naysayers don't really understand your business. Assuming that you have done your homework, you're in a much better position than they are to make your own decision. There's much more that they don't know: how much desire and drive you have to make it, or how hard you're willing to work. Many times these simple factors are what determine success or failure.

■ TRIAL AND ERROR

For the next six months, Dad and Larry made baskets. I continued to sell them on consignment to merchants in eastern and central Ohio. Then tragedy struck. At age seventy-two, Dad had a fatal heart attack. He had been in good health, so his passing came as quite a shock. After I recovered from the mourning process, I wanted my basket business to succeed even more. I wanted the family tradition and the memory of J. W. Longaberger to live on. I wanted to build a big company to serve as a tribute to Dad.

I did everything to sell baskets. We put them in our grocery store and any other retail store that would give us shelf space. Most of these weren't actual orders but just a matter of dropping off a handful of baskets on consignment. Every so often, I'd stop by on a Friday or Saturday night to see how our baskets were moving. Our biggest problem was that our baskets were selling for $20 to $30 right beside a similar basket priced at $2 or $3. There was nothing to tell customers about their superior craftsmanship and materials as compared to the cheap ones. If a sales clerk would take the time to explain the differences in quality, an informed customer would understand why ours were special. But seeing the display on a shelf, the customer had to determine for herself why a Longaberger basket justified its price tag.

In some stores, I would hold a small demonstration on how our baskets were made. But this was time-consuming, and I couldn't be everywhere at the same time. I had my other businesses to run.

Our orders were sparse. For the most part, we were placing the baskets in small shops in rural areas. Thinking big, I made an appointment with the buyer for Lazarus, the big Federated Department Store in Columbus. I was so excited, I could hardly sleep the night before the meeting. I had visions of selling the store hundreds of baskets. Then I'd meet with other stores in the Federated chain. I envisioned eventually shipping tens of thousands of baskets to famous department stores across the country. My dream of selling Longaberger baskets from coast to coast was about to come true.

I brought several different baskets to show the buyer. She listened to my presentation and nodded her head. This is it, I thought to myself. That is, until she made an offer that was several dollars lower than our cost to make them. The buyer explained the problems of overhead, including high rent and advertising. So unless we'd sell them at her price, Lazarus had no interest.

"We can't sell them at that price," I explained.

"Can't you lower your production cost?" she asked.

"Every basket is handmade," I explained. "At your price, we'll lose money on every basket we sell you."

Oh well. Our problem wasn't her problem. She thanked me for coming in and wished me good luck.

The seventy-minute ride back to Dresden seemed much longer that afternoon. There has to be a way to sell our baskets, I kept saying to myself. The thought entered my mind that I really knew nothing about baskets and didn't know enough about business to succeed. Maybe all those people were right when they said that my basket business was doomed to failure. I should stop spending so much time and money trying to make it work. I should be focusing on growing my restaurant and grocery businesses. They were my bread and butter, and I had a young family to support. Was I being irresponsible, chasing after a cockamamie dream?

Yes, I sometimes had doubts about whether I should continue or call it quits and keep my losses to a minimum. I wouldn't be human if I never had discouraging moments.

The great thing about being an entrepreneur is that you don't have to bat a thousand to hit a home run. You don't even have to succeed most of the time; in fact, you can fail more times than you succeed and still be a big success. I'm sure that if I had kept score, I would have seen that I had a lot more failures than successes.

■ BEING FOCUSED

I didn't exactly set the world on fire when I started selling baskets. Frankly, a lot of my time and energy was going into my other businesses. After all, the restaurant and grocery took long hours. In fact, my grocery store became the first one in Dresden to be open on Sundays. I figured my customers needed this convenience. People were always running out of something and had no place nearby to shop on Sundays. I liked the idea of being able to sell meat left over from Saturday that would be too old to sell on Monday.

So I was running two businesses that were both open day and night, seven days a week. Talk to anyone who owns a grocery or a restaurant, and you'll hear about the demanding hours in either business. Now I was trying to tackle another venture with the intent to take it national.

Getting a business started requires a lot of sweat and toil. It's unusual for a poorly financed entrepreneur to succeed otherwise. Let's say two people are each starting a new business. The first does it by moonlighting and keeps his full-time job. The second works sixty hours or more per week at his new business. Which of the two do you think is most likely to succeed?

One of the best ways to have a successful new business is to outwork the other guy. If you lack the capital to hire talented people, you'll have to wear several hats during your early years. Working long hours is the price you pay to get your business off the ground. If you can't make this commitment, chances are your new business will die on the vine.

You can see why from 1973 to 1976 we sold relatively few baskets. I sold them only on a part-time basis, and Larry and Richie were weaving baskets when they had time outside their real jobs. No wonder we got off to a slow start.

If you've ever thought about going into business for yourself, take my advice: do what I say, not what I did! I was lucky that I didn't blow my once-in-a-lifetime opportunity. There are any number of reasons why The Longaberger Company could have failed in its early stages. Had it gone under, I would have never known why. Nor, for that matter, would I be writing this book—because there would be no Longa-berger story to tell. With this in mind, if you truly believe in your new venture, immerse your entire self in it. I can assure you this will greatly increase your chances of success.

■ WORKING WOMEN

It was back in 1973 when I formally announced my plans to launch the J. W. Longaberger Handwoven Basket Company. Then we piddled along for the next three years, going through the motions of running a business. Sometimes I'd go days or weeks without selling a single bas-ket. Likewise, Larry and Richie didn't weave for days at a time. Thank goodness nobody else thought there was a future in handmade baskets; had another company been competing against us, they would have cleaned our clock!

It wasn't until September 1976 that I made a truly earnest effort to run this business. That was the year I hired the first weavers who were not family members. Up until then, it had always been a Longaberger family thing.

To get things rolling, Kenny Birkhimer became the first official employee of the basket company. Actually, Kenny was already on my payroll as the manager of Popeye's. However, I had pulled him from that job so he could do some remodeling on an addition to the restau-rant. When I discovered that Kenny had some manual skills, I asked him, "Instead of going back to the restaurant, how would you like to work across the street? I could use you to help me get the basket com-pany going."

I explained that his job would include repairing my father's original basket-making equipment. Once we had the equipment we needed, I planned to have Larry train new weavers. These weavers would train more new weavers, and so on. I also wanted Kenny to build some weaving horses, the frames that hold the wooden form around which a basket is constructed. I knew we'd need some soon. What my father had used wouldn't last much longer.

"Do you think you can make them for us?" I asked.

Kenny shrugged. "No problem." Kenny was game, but he wanted some security, too. "If this thing doesn't fly, I can always go back to the restaurant. Right, Popeye?"

I assured him that he could. Then I continued, "Once we have the horses and forms, I'd like to get started with five weavers. If you know anyone who's looking for a job, send him to me."

I never expected Kenny to approach women about taking jobs with us. Basket weaving in Dresden and eastern Ohio was always considered men's work. Of course, in the old days when my grandfather and father worked at the Dresden Basket Company, married women rarely had full-time jobs. Those who did typically worked as waitresses, cooks, secretaries, nurses, and teachers. So I was surprised that the first person Kenny talked to was his sister, Bonnie Hague.

Bonnie's work experience was three years at the Dairy Twist in Dresden, a job she had quit to raise three children. At first Bonnie had no interest in becoming a basket weaver. Her reaction was much like that of Kenny's wife when he first told her about the new job.

"How in the world can Popeye's company sell enough baskets to support two families?" his wife asked.

Bonnie, too, had her doubts. She later told me, "I didn't want to have anything to do with it. But Kenny kept bugging me. I agreed to come see you just to get him off my back."

Bonnie had to drive around the block three times before she built up enough nerve to knock on the door of my house. When I invited her in, she said, "Kenny said you might be hiring some workers to weave baskets."

I grinned at her. "Are you interested?"

"I might be," she said with a faint smile.

We sat down with a cup of coffee at the kitchen table. I told her what I planned to do. I summed it up by saying, "Bonnie, I don't know if a woman can do it the same as a man. There's a lot of pulling and tugging and moving heavy old forms. It might be too physical for a woman. Why don't you go home and think about it. If I do decide to hire someone, I'll let you know."

That weekend, I told Kenny to tell his sister to come in on Monday to start work. She said, "I'll come in, but not on Monday. That's my birthday."

Birthday or not, Bonnie was there first thing Monday morning. I had also recruited my cousin Sharon Urby. Bonnie became the first weaver outside the Longaberger family to work for me. Larry showed the women around the little shop, then sat down with them and began teaching them how to make baskets.

About an hour later, I walked in to deliver some bad news.

"Ladies, I had been hoping that by this morning I would have been approved for a loan at the bank. No luck on it yet. I'm sorry, but I don't have any money to pay you. You're welcome to stay here and learn the trade. When I do get a loan, I'll pay you for your work."

"When do you suppose we'll get paid?" Bonnie asked.

"I can't answer that," I said. I guess they appreciated my honesty. They had already agreed to work for me for minimum wage—less than $3 an hour at the time. Now they were agreeing to work for only the promise of money.

"Keep track of your time," I told them. "When I have the money, I'll pay whatever is due you."

Bonnie and Sharon agreed, nodding.

I handed a yellow notepad to each of them. "All right," I said, "let's get started."

By the end of the week, I hired three more women, who worked on the same arrangement as Bonnie and Sharon. I really hadn't planned to hire women. But in the beginning, they were the only ones who would work for an IOU. I also told them right off the bat that I couldn't afford employee benefits. Some men had approached me for a job, but upon hearing about the payroll situation, they sought employment elsewhere. Kenny was still on the payroll at the restaurant so he could have a steady paycheck. The weavers were all married to men with steady jobs and family health insurance, so they weren't quite as pressed to bring home money every week.

The women who had small children liked the setup. We didn't call it flextime back then; I just let them work around their kids' schedules. Nobody ever took advantage of this arrangement, but they felt good knowing they could be with their children when it was necessary. I always encouraged my weavers to stay home when children were sick, and I never asked questions when they took a day off for personal reasons.

The women turned out to be excellent weavers, and best of all, they loved making baskets. It showed in their work. Furthermore, this was an opportunity for women to learn a real trade, a privilege not often available to women in the seventies in our neck of the woods.

Back then, my weavers in training didn't get paid at all, but they did get to keep the baskets they made. For many, that's all it took for them to take the job. They would practice weaving for weeks. When I felt they were ready, they were put on the payroll, and I continued to let them make a few baskets on their own time for personal use.

As it turned out, the women handled the physical part of the work just fine. Industrial baskets had always been made of hickory, a very hard wood, and that is what we used when we started the company. We have long since switched to maple, which isn't nearly as splintery. But boy, did a weaver's hands take a beating working with that hickory! Everything was makeshift. For example, tappers are used today to make the weaves tight. Back then, we improvised by using forks with their prongs bent down.

Those women had such a knack for weaving, it was years before we hired men to do the job. It got to the point where our weavers began to think men couldn't be good at weaving because their fingers were too big! Later on, when large numbers of men started weaving for us, it turned out both sexes weave equally well. Still, I have a soft spot in my heart for my female employees because they helped me get the company up and running.

Within a couple of months, all five women were officially weavers. What pleased me the most was that they kept getting better every day. I was so excited with their progress, I talked about hiring still more weavers and started looking for a bigger location to handle a bigger workforce. Larry told his wife about my ambitious plans. I guess it sounded too risky because that's when he asked me to pay back his one thousand dollars. I couldn't afford to pay him in one lump sum, so he agreed to take installments.

In May 1977 those first five women had been working for me nearly ten months. They were weaving and gabbing away when I said, "Ladies, I have something to tell you."

Everybody stopped their work, and the room suddenly became very quiet. "I got the money," I said. "Today is payday." I was finally able to borrow the money to pay them their back wages. I don't know who was more excited, me or them.

I said, "I want everyone to give me their paperwork on how much is due them. I'll have your checks written, and you'll have them this afternoon."

There were many times after that when I handed out checks and had to say, "Please hold off cashing this for three days. After that, it will be good. I'll have the money in the bank."

Bless their hearts, those women had so much loyalty. If they hadn't stuck by me, I would have lost my shirt a long time ago. There is one thing I know now, though, that I wish I had known back then: they really had my number. It was only recently that one of them told me how they'd scheme to get the best of me. When things got hectic in the shop, one of them would pretend to be very upset and start to cry. Believe it or not, they'd take turns doing this. Real tears, too! They knew I couldn't bear to see anyone cry. So to smooth things over, I'd pack everyone into my car and drive to Coshocton for lunch. Sometimes we'd be gone as long as two hours, and I not only was paying for their time, but also buying their lunch!

■ IMPROVISATION

At its peak, the Dresden Basket Company that stood behind my parents' house on Eighth Street used to employ twenty weavers. That seemed like a lot of people for a building that measured forty-two feet by forty-three feet. Well, after it closed I asked my father how so many people could work in such a small shop.

"They must have been packed like sardines," I said.

Dad explained that the demand for basket production was great only when the pottery factories were working at full capacity.

"The twenty weavers were spread out over three shifts, Popeye. So no more than six or seven weavers worked in the shop at any one time. And yes, it was crowded. The working conditions were not the best."

Although I had only five weavers in 1977, I knew we'd soon outgrow our small quarters on Main Street. At twenty-two hundred square feet it was larger than the Dresden Basket Company, but we stored material and supplies in the back. This meant the weaving floor was only a thousand square feet. I couldn't see asking women to work a night shift, and, in fact, nobody would at minimum wage. So I started to look for another location. Because I had no money to make a down payment, this was no easy task. And in a small town like Dresden, there aren't many available properties.

Many years ago, my mother had worked at an old woolen mill in Dresden, over on Chestnut Street. In 1977 the building had been vacant for twenty-two years. From the shape it was in, it didn't appear that anyone would occupy it in the near future. The only positive thing you could say about the place was that it was big. It was a thirty-four-thousand-square-foot brick building. On the negative side, every window was broken or boarded up; part of the roof had caved in; many interior walls had collapsed; and weeds and small trees had sprouted through the decaying floors, some growing all the way through the open rooftop.

I had passed the building hundreds of times. However, when the idea of occupying it struck me, I started to see it in a different light. The more I thought about it, the more determined I became to own it. I drove to Coshocton to meet with its owner, taking several baskets to show him what we did. He said he loved the idea of using the building for making baskets. I'm sure he would have loved any idea that involved buying his property.

We talked for a while, and he mentioned that he owed $7,000 in back taxes on the property. I suggested that figure as a purchase price.

"I'll pay you two hundred a month," I told him, "and when it's paid off, the place is mine. Meanwhile, I'll be fixing it up so we can make it operational. If worse comes to worse, and I don't succeed, you'll get it back in better condition than it is in now."

He agreed, and I owned another property purchased on land contract.

Everyone thought I had really gone off the deep end with this one. All you had to do was take one look at that thirty-four-thousand-square-foot building: it was in such bad shape, it had no value whatsoever. In fact, it had a negative value because it would cost more to tear it down than the land was worth! While I thought I had made the deal of a lifetime, everyone in town thought the old woolen mill was a worthless piece of junk.

Once I had a contract, I loaded up my five weavers and took them to see where they would be working.

They took one look and one said, "We had heard rumors that you were going to buy this place, Popeye. We were hoping it wasn't true."

"Just you wait and see what I do with it," I told them. "It's going to be great."

For a while, most of my weekend time was spent there with a construction crew, getting the place in good enough shape to move in the weavers. I pulled Kenny Birkhimer from his maintenance work at the basket shop to help with the remodeling. Fortunately, I was able to convince a lumber company to supply us and, most important, carry us for a while.

One weekend, I decided it would be easier to burn off part of the collapsed roof than to move it. We notified the fire department, and our building provided entertainment for the day for the good citizens of Dresden. The sirens attracted every kid in town, including my ten-year-old daughter, Rachel, who came riding over on her bike with her friends.

Rachel realized that the fire was at our new building and saw me standing up front giving instructions. She said breathlessly, "Dad, your building is on fire."

"That's right," I said. "We're burning the old roof out."

"You're what?" she exclaimed. She turned white as a sheet.

Telling this story some years later, Rachel said, "I was sure Dad would go broke and I'd be put into an orphanage."

The building was still in bad shape when we moved in. We didn't have central heating, so we used kerosene heaters to stay warm. While my first concern was having enough heat to be comfortable, heat was also needed to keep the wood pliable. Working with wood in cold air causes it to become brittle and break. Kenny made a trough out of PVC pipe, then filled it with heated water. Nevertheless, on a few extremely cold days, we were forced to shut down.

One July we had a heat wave. The temperature hovered around the high nineties for several days. Circulation was bad in the old factory, and at times the temperature must have been over a hundred degrees in there. Boy was it hot! We all became exhausted from the heat. Unfortunately, there wasn't anything I could do. Instead of ignoring the obvious problem, I decided to have some fun with it. At the end of the day, after everyone had gone home, I brought in some Christmas decorations. I made the weaving floor into a Christmas scene, complete with a sleigh and reindeer hanging from the ceiling. I even put fake snow on the walls and ceiling.

The next morning, everyone was greeted with a big sign that read CHRISTMAS IN JULY. It didn't lower the temperature, but it did cool off a lot of hot tempers. We all had a big laugh, and it helped to distract us from our misery.

When we first moved in, I had done only a patch job on the roof. Consequently, on rainy days, it leaked. Buckets were scattered throughout the factory, strategically placed directly beneath a drip. Well, as they say, necessity is the mother of invention. I tacked a plastic sheet over the ceiling. As it filled with water and began to sag, I poked a hole into the sheet where the water collected. The water drained from the hole into a barrel. This way, instead of having a lot of leaks, we had only one! After dealing with all those leaks, one leak seemed minor. The workers got a big laugh out of my solution to our leaky roof. The moral of this story is: in business, you have to make the best of what you have. Then you learn to live with it. When you have a problem that can't be properly fixed, it's not the end of the world!

There were no rest rooms in the building. So at certain times of the day, there were "potty breaks." The five women would pile into my old van, and Kenny would drive them to Popeye's to use the ladies' room.

Within a year, pipes and sewers were installed, and our new factory had its own rest room. There was one slight inconvenience. Everyone had to go through my office to get to it. My desk backed up against the rest room's outside wall, so shortly after a woman went inside, I'd invariably hear the water running full blast. On occasion I worried that the sink would overflow.

Of course, I realized they were embarrassed. The rest room walls were paper-thin. I could have pretended not to notice the sounds coming from the rest room, but I thought that might have made an awkward situation even more embarrassing. So, in my typical fashion, I made a joke out of it.

"I don't know why you ladies turn that water on like that," I'd yell. "It's not like I don't know what you're doing in there."

For a while, they'd come out with red faces, but in time everyone got over her embarrassment. When more women were hired, I had a portable privy set up outside the factory. During extreme weather people spent as little time out there as possible. When I was able to afford adequate rest room facilities, they were installed—much to everyone's relief, may I add, and no pun intended.

■ THE FUTURE IS WHERE WE WILL SPEND THE REST OF OUR LIVES

Looking back at those early years of low pay, nonexistent benefits, and poor working conditions, I see the only thing I had to offer was my personality. Trust me on this one, I never considered myself the life of the party!

About six months after Dad died, I was standing in my little shop, explaining to some of the weavers about how every basket was different and had a unique personality.

"Every one has its own little secret," I said. Then it dawned on me that I had never made a basket in my life. Yet there I was, rattling on like I had made hundreds of them. Perhaps it happened in a split second, but off to the right I saw a faint image of Dad. It was as if he were directing me, putting the words in my mouth to tell the weavers. And he was saying to me, "You're doing fine, Dave."

I've never seen an image of Dad since, but I'll never forget the one I saw that day.

As our company prospered, people sometimes commented, "Wouldn't it be wonderful if your dad could see what happened to his baskets?"

"He has," I always answered.

I started a list of everything my fledgling company could offer new employees. I found myself staring at a blank page. There was absolutely nothing I could do that an employee would write home about. What I could do was paint a bright future. I could tell them about all the wonderful things that would happen someday.

Of course, everything I would tell them about the future had to be believable. What mostly mattered was how much I believed it! I had visions about where the company would be someday, and I wanted to share these dreams with them. I wanted them to imagine what was possible for our company and to see these accomplishments as their own. I knew that if they bought into it, they'd work hard to make it come true.

I felt it was important to share my goals with them so they'd have direction. In this respect, goals are like a road map. Imagine if you were taking a long car trip across the country and started off without a map. Without a map, I doubt that you'd reach your destination. If you had a passenger, he'd feel lost, too. Even if you were sure of your destination but your passenger wasn't, he'd still feel lost. I wanted everyone to know where I planned to take the company, and I wanted them to feel comfortable coming along for the ride. I took it a step further because I invited them to share the driving.

When there were only five weavers, we'd have regular meetings around a small table. As we grew, I'd have everyone gather around in a circle, and I'd stand up on a five-gallon staining can to talk to them. Again and again, I'd tell them what we were going to be. In the beginning, sometimes they'd laugh. I'm sure, to some of them, my ideas seemed too grandiose.

For instance, not long after we moved into our broken-down factory, I talked about how someday we'd have central heating and air-conditioning. It happened to be a chilly day, and the weavers were wearing sweaters and sweatshirts. All anyone had to do was look at the shape the building was in. My visions of the future must have seemed far-fetched. I talked about how someday we'd have color television sets stationed in places so weavers could fight boredom during their work-day. I said that wages would go up and everyone would have full bene-fits, including a way to share in the profits.

I had so much respect for these women, I was constantly praising them. "I don't know how you ladies do it," I'd say. "You go home and take care of your families. You've got cooking and laundry to do. And still you come here every day, eager and ready to work. I really appre-ciate what you do for me, and someday I hope to be able to make things better for you in our factory."

Then I pointed to one side of the factory and said, "Look over there. That's where I think we should set up bleachers."

"Bleachers?" somebody asked.

"Yeah, we'll need bleachers for people who will come from all over the country to see how we make baskets."

That really cracked them up. Later that day, on a bathroom break to Popeye's, Kenny drove the van slowly down Eighth Street. He pointed out the window as if he were conducting a tour.

"Ladies, I want you to look to the right. Now that's where the twelve Longaberger children went to school. Now farther up ahead on the left is the original house where the Longaberger family lived."

When I first started talking about the future, they'd sometimes look at me like I had gone off the deep end. I understood why, but it didn't discourage me from repeating my visions over and over. I wasn't trying to brainwash anyone, but to some degree I suppose I did. Eventually they quit laughing at me. Later, when some of the visions became real, they began to think that I wasn't so crazy after all. It took a while, but in time most of the nonbelievers became believers.

I had gained credibility because I never kept them in the dark. I shared my dreams of a bright future, but I also told them when the company was having a problem. I let them know when I was going to the bank to borrow money, and I didn't keep it a secret when I was turned down. I probably couldn't have even if I'd wanted to. Those women knew me too well. When I was down in the dumps, they could see it in the way I walked and hear it in my voice. I gave them a lot of credit for being so perceptive; they could read me like a book.

When times are tough, I think it's important for a business owner to level with his employees. They deserve that much. Chances are, they know it anyway when your company's having problems. In fact, sometimes they might know before you do! It's not fair to keep this information from them. It's their future, too, that's at stake.

■ A CARING COMPANY

"How can I get my people to take an interest in my company?" I'm sometimes asked.

"When you care about them," I answer, "they will respond by caring about the company."

This, I believe, is the essence of good management. It's also basic human behavior. But you can't fake it. Caring must come from the heart. When it's sincere, employees know it.

You can hand them the world's best fringe benefits on a gold platter. You can provide a work environment with everything from piped-in music to plush decor. You can pay them exorbitant wages. If they suspect your intentions are simply to enhance your bottom line, it's unlikely you'll capture their hearts. You may think business is business, but humans have emotions. They aren't machinery and don't want to be treated as such. When corporate executives and bureaucrats work overtime to remove the emotional aspect of business, they work against themselves. People want management to care about them as individuals. They don't want employers to look at them with dollar signs in their eyes.

A while back, I remember when a group of accounting people came up with the idea of listing experienced employees as assets on the balance sheet. They figured that they had invested millions of dollars in the training and development of these people. So employees had a tangible value and should appear in the corporate financial statement. I guess to them it seemed like a valid viewpoint, but the thought of listing people as property sends a chill up my spine.

The package we give Longaberger employees today is truly impressive. We're proud to give them the best. But this alone isn't what wins their respect and dedication. If this were true, only big companies could afford to finance a motivated workforce. In the real world it's more likely that the owners of small companies are the most admired and loved by employees. Of course, with fewer employees, it's easier for the owner to personally know his workers and have personal relationships with them.

Generally, whether planned or unplanned, the culture of a company is formed during its early years. You still have daily personal contact with everyone, and you're able to build relationships. While large companies enjoy many advantages over small start-up companies, this is not one of them. Take advantage of these opportunities. While your company is still small, it's a lot easier to create a caring environment; if you work hard at it, it will remain intact as your company grows larger.

Nobody gave me this advice when I was starting out. I did it naturally because it came from my heart. I was so grateful to have people who were willing to help me build my business. Your heart may be in the right place, too, but you may be so busy that you fail to tell your people how much you care for them. They must know you appreciate what they do. You can never praise someone too much. Then you can prove that you care by backing up your words with actions. You have to walk the talk.

When I could afford it, one of the first big improvements I made in our Chestnut Street factory was to build a comfortable area where employees could take breaks. I put in chairs and tables and several vending machines.

Other businesspeople told me, "Popeye, you bring vendors and VIPs into that little hole-in-the-wall you call an office. You should have spent that money on yourself instead of that break room. You deserve it."

This thought never entered my mind. My employees put up with a lot of misery in those early days, and I wanted to show them I was grateful. After all, it was because of them that I even had that money to spend.

I'm the first to understand that many small business owners aren't able to afford much for their people. But there are hundreds of small, everyday gestures you can make, and the overall effect of these small things demonstrates that you care for your people. It might be sending somebody home with pay because she has a bad cold, or making sure your employee is given enough time to grieve when a family member dies. I couldn't afford certain job benefits, but I could treat employees to lunch on a regular basis. We'd also celebrate New Year's Eve together and hold a picnic on the Fourth of July. I knew the names of their spouses and their kids not because I memorized them but because I was interested in them.

When I spent time with employees, I did it because I enjoyed being with them. I didn't plan social activities to discuss business outside work. In fact, I used to play a game with them.

"Okay, every time somebody says the word *basket,* he or she gets fined five dollars and it goes to pay for dinner." Believe me, in the beginning I got a lot of free meals this way because I made sure the employees paid up. Eventually, they stopped talking about business because they realized I was serious. I really didn't want to talk shop!

You must develop rapport with your employees while you can. It's a wonderful feeling that builds. You can't wait until you think you'll have more time. Some business owners think they can accomplish it in one fell swoop, when they're ready. That's not how it happens. You do it now.

Certain managers right out of business school preach maintaining a distance from employees. They say, "They have to know you're the boss. You must act with authority at all times. If not, your image will be impaired."

Please! Give your employees more credit. Treat them as mature adults, not children. You're not their boss twenty-four hours a day, so it's okay to let your hair down and have fun with them.

A very silly thing happened at one of our early Christmas parties and has since become a Longaberger Company tradition. We were having a celebration at Popeye's. Some of the employees brought their families, and we occupied three long tables. To get an employee's attention, I threw a roll at her. Suddenly, everyone started tossing rolls at each other. Unfortunately, a roll landed in a cup of coffee across the restaurant and splashed a customer who wasn't part of our group.

I saw an angry man and woman look over at our rambunctious party. I turned to my innocent eleven-year-old daughter and said for all to hear, "Rachel, how many times do I have to tell you not to throw rolls in the restaurant! Don't let me see you do that again."

Poor Rachel, I embarrassed her to death.

From that day on, roll throwing has become somewhat of a ritual at company gatherings. So if you ever attend a Longaberger Company dinner, I advise you, be prepared to duck! A dinner roll could come flying your way!

5

Tell the Story

Without selling, the free enterprise system wouldn't work. No matter what product or service a company offers, remember: nothing happens until something is sold. A company can manufacture the world's greatest product, but it will go belly-up if there aren't enough sales.

Taking over the old woolen mill on Chestnut Street was a gutsy move. Overnight we went from a measly two-thousand square feet of space to thirty-four thousand. The vast difference in size was a constant reminder that we had to sell enough baskets to pay the additional overhead.

In the beginning, the women made baskets on the weaving floor even though the building was constantly under renovation. The pounding hammers and buzzing drills never let me forget that the meter was running. I was well aware that my overhead was surging, and unless the company substantially increased its sales, my fragile, budding enterprise could come crashing down.

Our selling was too hit-or-miss. Our marketing consisted of little more than dropping off baskets at retail outlets on consignment, hoping they would eventually catch on. It was wishful thinking that Longaberger products would simply fly off the shelves and miraculously jump-start manufacturing. I had been around the block too many times. I understood that it was up to me to make things happen. If I chose to wait until there was a huge demand for Longaberger baskets, my chances of success were two—slim and none.

I simply had to find a better way to sell our products. The big question was, How?

■ THE STORY *BEHIND* THE STORY

There's an interesting story *behind* the story that began during the summer of 1977. It's about how I first met Charleen Cuckovich, who at the time was a full-time mother with two young sons in Warren, Ohio. Her husband, George, was a fireman and a part-time building contractor. As a fireman, he worked twenty-four-hour shifts and was required to sleep at the fire station.

Charleen told me that the long hours of being alone were a source of anxiety for her, and once her boys started school, she needed something to fill the void. Perhaps she needed a career. Her high school dreams of being an architect had long since vanished. She thought about a sales job, but the idea of selling was a turnoff when she recalled her part-time experience in a department store during Christmas.

So Charleen spent her free time reading about early American history. In particular, she enjoyed reading about the arts and crafts of yesteryear. She frequently went on day trips with her friends to Middlefield, Ohio, a small rural town with a large Amish community.

"I respected the Amish lifestyle," she explained to me. "I admired their frugality, and in particular, how they didn't believe in waste. I liked their lifestyle because it took me back to a more simple way of life, a time when people were more relaxed."

She bought a couple of baskets from the Amish and liked them so much, she decided to start a collection of baskets.

From that day on, she looked for baskets in antique shops. Charleen's entire collection consisted of only three baskets. She told me that interesting baskets were simply too difficult to find. That August, she and her family went on a camping trip. One rainy day, rather than stay cooped up in the camper, they headed to nearby Walnut Creek, another Amish community. At their first stop, a craft shop, Charleen was ecstatic when she came across a table of baskets, with several dusty ones underneath. These were the most attractive baskets she had ever seen, and, unlike the antique ones, they were in much better condition. In fact, they looked brand-new. Each had a tag reading: "This is a J. W. Longaberger basket. Dresden, Ohio."

John Wendell Longaberger
and Bonnie Jean Gist married
in 1927. This loving, hardworking couple raised twelve
children in Dresden, Ohio.
(The Longaberger Company)

Dave Longaberger was the fifth of John Wendell and Bonnie's twelve children. "The
most important lesson I learned from my parents was to be strong; be firm but be fair,"
Dave recalled. (The Longaberger Company)

Dave was enterprising even as a young boy. His family often called him "the twenty-five-cent millionaire" because of all of his odd jobs like shoveling snow, delivering papers, and stocking shelves at the corner grocery. (The Longaberger Company)

In 1919, Dave's father, John Wendell, began making baskets at the Dresden Basket Company. Over time, John Wendell became well known for his quality craftsmanship. He opened his own basketmaking business, the Ohio Ware Basket Company, in 1936. (The Longaberger Company)

Dave's first venture into the business world came about when he bought the Dairy Bar restaurant in 1963. (The Longaberger Company)

Dave expanded his business opportunities in 1968 by purchasing the A&P grocery store on Main Street. He later renamed it the Dresden IGA. (The Longaberger Company)

From the time he was small, Dave had the uncanny ability to make others believe in what only he could see. When his plans materialized time and time again, those people who had laughed stopped laughing and started to see all the wonderful, exciting possibilities. Then they willingly followed the dreamer from Dresden, Ohio.
(The Longaberger Company)

What an introduction to the Longaberger product line! The World's Largest Basket attracted new customers and potential independent sales associates when it made its debut in 1980. Since then, the basket has been rewoven and permanently displayed on the corner of Fifth and Main streets in Dresden, Ohio. (The Longaberger Company)

The first Longaberger sales convention, known as the Basket Bee, took place in Dresden's Jefferson Elementary School gym in 1981. Dave's mother, known to the sales field as Grandma Bonnie, along with his daughters, Tami, left, and Rachel, greeted and checked in attendees at the registration table. (The Longaberger Company)

Dave's oldest daughter, Tami, graduated from Ohio State University and joined the company's marketing department in 1984. She would go on to lead the marketing division in 1987. She was named company president in 1994. (The Longaberger Company)

Dave's youngest daughter, Rachel, started working with the company in 1987 in the construction division. She would go on to lead the company's human resources and manufacturing divisions. (The Longaberger Company)

In the early 1980s, Dave had to sell his restaurant and the Dresden IGA to keep his basket business going. (The Longaberger Company)

When she asked the sales clerk about the baskets, the only information she got was, "That's the right price on the tag. A real bargain, aren't they?"

Charleen said that she immediately went to the camper and pulled out a state map. "Dresden is about an hour from here," she told her husband. "This weather isn't going to clear up. How about if we drive down and see if we can visit the Longaberger place?"

Charleen said that she always loved the peaceful wholesomeness of small towns. "Had the company been in a bigger town, I probably wouldn't have dragged my family down there," she confided to me, "but there is something about small towns that I can't resist."

When the Cuckovichs finally got to Dresden, Charleen fell in love with the village. She loved the houses with white picket fences and red geraniums in front. When she drove down Chestnut Street and came to our big, run-down building with an old basket hanging next to the front door, she was disappointed. After all, some of the windows were covered with plastic and old boards, and the yard was overgrown with weeds. However, she had driven all this way, so she sent George to see if they could come inside.

Charleen said that George told her, "It's fine to come in. Wait until you see what they have in there, honey."

The first person to greet the family was Bonnie Hague, who stood at the front door and waved at them to come in. Charleen recalled how she noticed three sets of handprints in some new cement outside the door.

Bonnie told her that the big hands were mine, and the small hands were Tami's and Rachel's.

"I know my eyes were as big as saucers walking around the plant," Charleen told me, recalling how she walked through our small factory for her first time. She took in everything—the weaving horses, the splints laid out to dry, and even the pans and buckets catching water from the leaky roof.

Bonnie volunteered to show Charleen how to make a basket.

"Dave, I was in heaven," Charleen told me. "I had never seen a basket made. I couldn't get over how caring and loving Bonnie was with it. She handled it so gently, and she took so much pride in her workmanship."

Mary Ann, a second woman in the shop, asked Charleen how they happened to come to Dresden. Charleen explained to her about finding the baskets in Walnut Creek.

Mary Ann explained that one of her jobs was to go around to different shops and drop off baskets. She remembered the shop in Walnut Creek even though it rarely sold our baskets.

"It's not like me to ask questions of strangers," Charleen told me later, "but I couldn't help myself. I wanted to know everything about your baskets. I started off asking personal questions about if you lived in Dresden and how long have you been doing this. And then I asked all about your family."

She asked questions such as "When did J.W. start making baskets? Where did he first make them? They had *how* many children? Is Dave the only one in the business today? Do his brothers and sisters live here, too? All but one? Which one is that?"

Charleen said she continued to ask questions for the rest of the afternoon. Before she left, she had bought $200 worth of baskets. She said she would have bought more, but that was all the cash they had with them. In fact, she told me that they wouldn't have been carrying that much money, except that they were on vacation. Still, she bought enough baskets to fill up the entire back end of her family's van.

On the two-hour trip back to Warren, the kids and the puppy sat up front with George, and Charleen got in the back of the van with her baskets.

"Dave, I just wanted to touch them," she told me, "and think about all the wonderful stories I had heard that day."

On the way home, Charleen asked George if he thought I would let her sell my baskets.

"He might," George told her.

The following day Charleen ran across the backyard to visit her neighbor and invited her to see what she had brought home.

When Shirley saw Charleen's living room filled with baskets, she became excited, too. Two hours later, Shirley showed up at Charleen's house with her sister, Joyce. Charleen told them about her trip to Dresden and everything she could remember about our family and our baskets. Then Shirley and Joyce started picking out baskets they wanted to buy, and asked Charleen many questions.

That evening, Charleen told George, "You know, honey, I think I could sell those Longaberger baskets."

◼ A LOVE STORY

During the next few weeks, Charleen invited several more friends to see her baskets. Each time, she told them what she had learned in Dresden about the baskets, and they too asked how they might buy some. Meanwhile, every few days, Charleen called me at the basket company but kept missing me. Between the restaurant and the grocery store, I was a difficult person to pin down.

One day George came home and noticed that Charleen was down in the dumps. When he asked her what was wrong, she said, "I keep calling that Longaberger guy in Dresden, but I can't get through to him."

George said he would try.

He just happened to call the factory at a time when I was there, and I got right on the phone. He seemed surprised when I said I recognized his name. George explained how upset Charleen was because she had people who wanted to buy Longaberger baskets, but she needed more of them.

"Can you people come down here to see me?" I asked.

"When do you want us?"

"Could you come on Saturday? Do you know where Popeye's is in Dresden? Meet me there at noon."

When George got off the phone, he explained to Charleen that I had a stuttering problem. "Maybe that's why he never answered the phone," George told her.

Charleen told me how she had worried the whole way to Dresden. "What if he doesn't like me? What if he doesn't let me do it?" she kept asking her husband. George tried to reassure her, but she asked, "What if he doesn't think I'm good enough? I'm just a housewife."

When the Cuckovichs arrived, Charleen said she was both surprised and relieved.

"At what?" I asked her.

She told me, "You came across as very friendly and very shy. Just a hometown kind of guy. And listening to you talk, I just wanted to help you finish your sentence!"

Over lunch Charleen told me about her neighbors seeing the baskets and hearing about her trip to Dresden. "I don't think your baskets have much of a chance just sitting there on a shelf," she said. "But if I could tell people about how you make them, I think they'll sell like hotcakes."

That's all she had to say, and a lightbulb went on over my head. For quite some time I had been thinking about how the baskets might sell if they were sold directly to the customer. I knew if a knowledgeable, enthusiastic person like Charleen sold them, they would sell like hot-cakes!

"I think you're right," I said.

She asked if they could visit the factory with me. I explained that it was closed on Saturday, but I'd be happy to show her around.

"Give me a half hour to run some errands," I said. "Finish your lunch, and I'll meet you there."

With that, I rushed off, leaving Charleen with the check. To this day, she kids me about it.

Since no one was at the factory, we were able to chat without inter-ruption. Charleen was barely inside the door when she began to rattle off question after question. As I talked, she took notes on a clipboard. She asked about Mom and Dad. How did the family first come to Dresden? What did J.W.'s little shop look like? What was it like grow-ing up in a family of fourteen? Why haven't your brothers and sisters bought into your business? How can you run this business along with the restaurant and grocery store?

At one point, I asked, "Why do you want to know so much about my family?"

"Because when I tell things about your family to my friends," she said, "their eyes light up."

"It's hard for me to believe anyone wants to hear stuff like that."

"But they do," she assured me. "When I tell them what I know about the Longabergers, they just fall in love with your baskets."

I suggested to Charleen that she should invite several friends to her house, but this time with the intent to sell baskets to them. "You might even ask some of them to invite their friends to their house; if they like the baskets, some of them could invite *their* friends. This way, you'll always have people to sell."

Charleen's face lit up when we talked. "I love your baskets, and I know other people will love them, too."

"I'm sure that if you show them to enough people, you'll sell a lot of baskets," I said.

"You make them, and I'll show them," she replied.

"That's it!" I said, thinking out loud. "We'll call them basket shows."

At the end of our conversation, I told her, "I know you don't know me, but I am a man of my word. You tell me what baskets you need, and I will make sure you get them."

■ BUILDING THE TEAM

Over the next couple of weeks, Charleen and I talked almost every day. I promised her that the first thing I'd make up would be a price list and a commission schedule. Next I designed an order form. At Charleen's request, I also printed up invitation cards. It wasn't much in the way of sales literature, but it was enough for her to start booking shows.

It wasn't long before she was having a dozen shows a week, with ten to fifteen customers attending each one. Early on, we discovered that offering the hostess one basket at half price was a big boost in booking future shows. For a while, I even paid hostesses $5 for each show. Then I came up with our hostess plan: the hostess received 10 percent of the first $300 sold, or the first fifteen orders. On sales over $300, she got 15 percent. And with over fifteen orders taken, a hostess was eligible to buy a second half-price basket. Later, as added incentive, we made certain baskets available only to hostesses.

The hostess program worked wonderfully. Each show generated even more shows. As with all companies, new prospects are the lifeblood of a growing business. Without the hostess program, Charleen would have run out of friends to sell to within a couple of weeks. This way, she met new people at each show, who in turn agreed to host shows for their friends. Eventually, she was selling to groups of women she had never met—and who had invited her to sell to them!

Every order was paid in advance at the show. Charleen explained that each basket was handwoven to order, so it would take several weeks for delivery. Wisely, she never gave an exact delivery date; she knew better than to guarantee something so uncertain.

It came as a pleasant surprise that everyone was willing to pay in advance. They had total trust in their hostess; after all, she was their friend. They weren't getting pressure from an unknown salesperson, so nobody worried about getting stiffed. Of course, it helped that Charleen was so laid-back. Because she came across as sincere and trustworthy, it was unusual for someone to question her integrity.

I loved calling Charleen to hear about the shows of the previous day. I had to know all the details.

"What did they like?" I'd ask. Then I always added, "What didn't they like?"

"Is there anything they want different that we're not doing?" I'd wonder. And many times Charleen would tell me about a customer's request for a special type of basket. Sometimes it was a hassle to figure out exactly what this custom-made basket ought to look like. Eventually we discontinued special orders because they were extremely time-consuming as well as confusing. Sometimes several calls were made back and forth between Charleen, the customer, and us to get instructions back to a weaver.

Eventually we had developed a line of eighty-five different baskets. Charleen loaded a sample of every one of them in her van and carried them to each show. Keep in mind, we had no product catalog, so this was the only way people could see what our baskets looked like.

When Charleen's orders were ready, she and George would drive down to Dresden, load up their van, and take everything back to Warren. It was a good five-hour round trip, so they waited until we had filled enough orders to make a vanload. They came to Dresden two or three times a month. During one visit, Charleen watched as Bonnie made a basket, and then asked her to sign it.

"Sign it?" Bonnie said, thinking this was an odd request.

"Yes, I want it signed because I'm going to keep it forever," Charleen said, "and I want to remember who made it."

So Bonnie signed her initials on the bottom. What a nice touch, I thought. And why not? Artists sign paintings, and our baskets are works of art. So I told the weavers, "From now on, let's sign every basket." And another Longaberger tradition was born.

Within a couple of months, Charleen was selling so many baskets, I had to hire more weavers to keep up with the orders. Every day I became more convinced that direct selling was the best way to market our baskets. Now I wanted to see firsthand what actually happened during a show. Charleen agreed that I could come to Warren and spend a day with her in the field. On a cold, wintry day, I made the drive to Charleen's, just in time to make it to the hostess's house. By this point, Charleen and I had become good friends, and she knew I used a lot of salty language.

"Please, Dave," she begged, "no cussing."

I promised to behave and told her not to pay any attention to me. I had no intention of saying anything. I just wanted to sit in the back of the room and observe. After helping carry Charleen's baskets into the house, I was introduced to everyone. As the show was about to begin, rather than sit with the group, I picked up my chair and purposely placed it behind where Charleen would stand. Here I would be out of the way, and I could see how the women looked and acted while she was talking.

Charleen was an excellent storyteller. She began by telling how my father, J. W. Longaberger, loved to make baskets, and how his weaving helped him support his family of fourteen. She vividly described our house on Eighth Street, and she talked about the friendly atmosphere in the tiny village of Dresden, Ohio. I studied how the women reacted to what Charleen said. Charleen not only held their attention; they were having a good time!

Finally, she held up one basket.

"This basket is like the one J.W. made for his wife, Bonnie, and attached to her bicycle. When Bonnie went grocery shopping on Main Street, a few blocks from home, she carried the groceries home in her bicycle basket."

Charleen had a different story for every basket, and her audience was captivated by each one. She showed them J.W.'s Easter baskets and small laundry baskets.

"This one," she'd say, "is a centerpiece basket because it's so pretty on a dining room table. See this umbrella basket? Bonnie used it to keep her flower bulbs over the winter. And this one is the banker's basket. The banker in Dresden uses it as a wastepaper basket."

Her favorite story was the one about the pie basket. "Bonnie and the other women in Dresden used this basket to carry pies to church socials. I'm told they put their names on the inside or on the handle so they'd know which was theirs when it was time to go home.

"And this little basket," she continued, "is the one the Longaberger children used to gather eggs from the henhouse. It holds exactly twelve eggs."

When she was finished, the hostess walked off with the egg basket. Soon she brought it back, full of eggs.

"I didn't believe they'd all fit," the hostess said, "but here you are, a dozen eggs!"

Charleen's sales totaled about $800 that night, and she picked up bookings for six future shows. We drove back to her house, neither of us saying a word. Finally Charleen broke the ice.

"Well, Dave, what did you think?"

"We never had chickens," I said.

We both started laughing. "It was wonderful," I said. "But just stick to the facts next time." I was smiling, but I was serious.

"I also like the fact that you don't pressure anyone to buy, Charleen," I told her. "When you're invited into somebody's home as their guest, it's important to make sure they feel comfortable."

"I know some of the older women can't afford to buy anything," Charleen explained, "and I'm happy to see them just being with the group, having a good time. Sometimes they have their own stories to tell me about having baskets when they were little, and I learn so much from them. I would never want to embarrass them or anyone else who doesn't place an order with me. In fact, if there are women who can't afford to buy that night, I encourage them to have their own show. This way, they can make a purchase at half price."

I attended two more of Charleen's shows and then told her it was time for me to conduct a few of my own. After I got the hang of it, I looked for other people to become distributors, and I trained them to sell just like Charleen.

I actually held about ten shows, mainly around Dresden and Zanesville, where I knew a lot of people. I concentrated mainly on having my sisters, relatives, and friends host my shows. I was concerned that some women would feel uncomfortable with a male stranger in their house, especially because most of the shows were held at night.

My plan was to line up distributors in Ohio, and as they were assigned territories, I would no longer sell baskets in retail outlets in those areas. In time, no one could purchase a Longaberger basket except from a distributor or one of her sales associates, who we decided to call "independent sales consultants."

I explained to Charleen that it was essential for me to sign up other distributors, and she, too, should create her own sales organization.

"If I don't recruit other people," I told her, "every salesperson in the entire company will end up being under you."

She understood, and soon we were both recruiting. One criterion was that the person owned a van or a truck for transporting baskets to a show. This was an unofficial but practical rule.

It was a slow process, recruiting one person at a time. After a while, Charleen had her own group of consultants in northeastern Ohio. Every now and then I'd drive up to attend one of her sales meetings. Sometimes, to save her a trip to Dresden, I'd drive a truck and personally deliver her orders. Within six months, she had five consultants— her sister-in-law, her two sisters, and her two best friends.

Meanwhile, I talked baskets to everyone I met, always inviting them to sell for us. I had a display of baskets at Popeye's; that always served as a way to start up a conversation. One customer from Zanesville fell in love with the baskets and asked me to have someone call her to do a show. Actually, she asked me several times. Finally I said, "You invite twenty women to your house, and I'll come do it myself."

On the night of the show, I took Rachel with me. She was excited, but about an hour into the show she became drowsy. Sherry Colling, a cousin of the hostess, took Rachel upstairs and put her in a spare bed.

I sold a lot of baskets that night. Sherry, who was a single mother of two daughters, approached me.

"I'm a dental assistant, and I need some extra income," she said. "I've never sold anything before, but I'd like to give this a try."

"I've got nine shows booked," I told her. "The next one is on May 18. You meet me there."

As the show began that night, I introduced Sherry as our newest consultant.

"I have an announcement to make, folks," I said. "This is Sherry's first show, and she's taking over. I'm sorry I can't stay, but you're in good hands with Sherry."

Just before I left, I handed Sherry a list of dates and addresses for my eight remaining shows. I told her, "You're on your own now. Good luck, kid."

By 1981, Sherry had been selling for over two years and had also become a distributor. With two young daughters, she wasn't happy about selling at night, and she felt insecure working on straight commission. I stopped in at her home in Zanesville one evening.

When she answered the door, I said, "Can I talk to you for a while?"

"Sure, Dave. What's up?"

"Would you like to work for me full-time instead of selling?"

"I don't know. What do you want me to do? And how much will you pay me?"

"I'm not sure what I want you to do, but I can figure that out later. All I know is I need somebody to work in the office who understands the selling end of our business."

"I don't type," she said.

"I'm not looking for a secretary. How much do you want, Sherry?"

Sherry told me what she made as a dental assistant, plus her show earnings, and said, "I need a little more than that."

I tossed out a figure, and she accepted it. "I'll give notice tomorrow," she said with a smile.

"That's fine," I said. On my way out the door, I told her that she could start anytime she wanted.

In 1978 Marge Shipley, who also lived in Zanesville, was invited to a show by a neighbor. When Marge found out the consultant was from Columbus, about fifty miles west, she asked if she could sell baskets in the Zanesville area. Like most of the first consultants, Marge had no prior sales experience. Years before she had worked as a secretary for a manufacturing company and also as a bookkeeper at a bank.

Marge's daughters had grown up and left home. Her husband worked days and spent his nights coon hunting. "It would give me something to do," she said.

By the time I finally met Marge, we had twenty employees in the factory and eighteen sales associates. I already knew who she was, however, because she held two impressive company records. In fact, she sold over $2,000 worth of baskets in a single week, becoming the first consultant to do so. She also had sold more wall plaques than anyone else. That was no easy feat, considering they retailed from $8.95 to $24.95. Besides, those plaques were not really popular. In fact, they sold so poorly we eventually discontinued them. But Marge consistently sold $200 to $400 every week. I had to meet her.

We were both attending a Longaberger miniconvention in Newark, Ohio, at the Sheraton Hotel. "Marge," I greeted her, "I've been dying to meet you and find out how you sell those wall plaques."

After we talked for a while, she agreed to let me come to one of her shows. We set up a time to meet at her house and drive to the show together. Unfortunately, the hostess had an emergency and canceled the show at the last minute. By the time I left for Marge's house, it was too late for her to call me.

When I arrived, she apologized profusely. "It's okay. I just want to know what you do," I said. "Let's have a cup of coffee and talk."

We spent the next four hours talking about selling, and I went home quite impressed with Marge. She has potential for big things with this company, I thought to myself. Two years later, in January 1980, we had about 100 sales associates when I named her national sales manager. I wanted somebody inside who had worked outside. Not only was Marge smart; she also understood the sales field. She spoke the sales associates' language, and they respected her. Marge held this position for six years. With her at the helm, the sales force grew to 3,399. I'd say she did quite a job!

Anita Rector was a high school girl who started at Popeye's and then moved on to the grocery store. In May 1980 I moved her to the sales office. Initially, Anita's job focused on processing orders and customer service. It wasn't long before she had developed a company newsletter.

Meanwhile, Charleen and I spent many evenings talking business and sharing dreams. Sometimes we talked until four in the morning. I told her that someday there would be Longaberger distributors all across the country. I talked about the many products we would sell.

"We'll have a big office building and maybe even a hotel," I said. "We might even build them in the shape of a basket. Someday we'll even sell products for the home."

I don't know how much Charleen believed would come true, but she never seemed to doubt me.

A little over a year after Charleen started, I sat down with her to have a serious talk. I told her I wanted her to quit giving shows.

"You have five women selling for you," I explained. "Now it's time for you to get out of personal production and start building your sales organization."

"But Dave, I like doing shows," she insisted. "And I sell more baskets than anyone else. It doesn't make sense for me to quit."

True, she was our top salesperson. She sold more than $60,000 her first year.

"If I hadn't gotten out of the kitchen," I answered, "I would still be flipping hamburgers. You have to recruit and train people, and then develop them so *they* can recruit and train.

"To make life easier, we'll send a truck to your place on a regular basis so you won't have to come to Dresden. You can keep everything in your garage. Your consultants can come to your place to pick up their baskets. Do you see where this is going?" I asked her.

Answering for her, I said, "We have to figure out how you can make better use of your time. I have big plans for you."

Charleen went with the program. Shortly thereafter, she and George bought a lot out in the country. Before their home was even completed, George put up a forty-by-eighty-foot building for her basket inventory.

■ UNIFORMITY

By the end of 1981, with five distributors and several hundred consultants, we stopped making custom baskets for customers. We were selling a lot of baskets, but each distributor had a different way to sell them. I wanted every show to follow the same format; otherwise, as we grew even bigger, things were bound to get out of control. For instance, somebody in California might tell an altogether different story than what was told in New York.

At the same time, I wanted everyone to be truthful in what they told customers. Without some sort of outline, there was no telling what they might say. Some would eventually stray from the truth, and in time the company would lose its credibility. If that were to happen, we'd have a catastrophe on our hands.

It became obvious that we needed more control over sales before it became unruly. This would be to everyone's benefit. If we didn't make certain changes in 1982, we'd have serious problems down the road. I had studied other successful direct sales organizations and decided we should restructure our sales force as a multilevel organization. This meant we would no longer have distributorships.

One major problem with our current system was that distributors began to quarrel because consultants from one distributorship would sell and recruit in another's territory. This happened a lot because the territories were divided by county. Oftentimes, the consultants weren't aware they had crossed a county line. Women invited their friends to these shows, friends who didn't necessarily live in the same county. You can see how this could lead to all sorts of recurring problems.

With a multilevel sales organization and no territories, everyone could sell and recruit anywhere in the United States. Nobody was limited by a particular boundary. Looking toward the future, this would be a big plus. However, three of our five distributors opposed it. They had become so territorial that, in their minds, the company was taking something away from them. They could not see that we were expanding their horizons. Of course, I understand that some people simply resist change because they have become comfortable. To these people, any change is threatening. For this reason, I met with these women again and again, trying to convince them of the benefits of the new system.

"The new sales structure will have five levels," I explained. "You will be at the top. But instead of being a distributor, you will be a sales director. Every sales director will have the entire United States in which to expand her sales organization. Below the sales director is the zone advisor, followed by the regional advisor and then the branch manager. At the first level is the sales consultant."

I also outlined the sales production and number of consultants required in each position. I included commissions and overrides that would be paid at all levels. It was a fair plan and offered wide-ranging opportunities. But the three distributors wouldn't budge. They wanted to keep their territories and weren't about to give them up. No matter how I tried to convince them that they'd do better under the new system, they resisted.

"We have to have uniformity," I insisted.

They didn't see it that way, and they drew a line in the sand.

"Our attorney says you can't do this," one of them warned me.

"I don't care what your attorney said," I replied. "You just watch me because this is what we're going to do."

I went ahead with the restructuring in spite of their threats. Six months later, I called each of them and said, "It looks like we're going to have to part ways. I'm willing to buy you out."

I made an offer of $150,000 to the top distributor.

"You'll pay me a hundred fifty thousand?" she said in disbelief.

"Yes. I just need you to sign some papers," I told her. "I'll pay you out over the next twelve months."

The other two also accepted my offer. We had to quickly do something with the more than 230 consultants they supervised. Without supervision, they would soon be gone.

A company-owned directorship was set up, headed by Sherry Colling. Many current consultants, branch managers, regional advisors, and sales directors have been developed out of this great group.

■ SOFT SELLING

Because our consultants are guests in someone's home, we frown on high-pressure sales tactics. Some wonder how we can generate so many sales without pressing a customer now and then.

Maybe if we were a little pushy, we could make a few extra sales. But in the long run, customers would stay away from our shows. When we ask women if they'd like to book a show at their home, they know they won't risk putting their friends in an awkward position. Because our sales presentation is kept low-key, a show becomes a fun, sociable night out.

An objective at every Longaberger show is to provide an evening that's not only entertaining but also informative. By talking about our family history, the small town of Dresden, and how baskets were a part of everyday life, we are selling nostalgia along with our products. We go back to when life wasn't so rushed, when people actually knew all their neighbors and merchants took the time to ask about your family. We call up the good old days—before the hustle and bustle associated with computers and pagers and fax machines. During a show, customers feel how it must have been when people seemed to have better values. Having created this atmosphere, we think it would be a shame to kick in with high-pressure tactics. That certainly wouldn't be anyone's idea of a fun evening!

We already have an advantage because our hostess serves as an ambassador to our customer base. There is an established trust because the show is at the home of a friend or relative, which is something we always respect.

"This must be a reputable company, or Paula wouldn't have hosted this event," a prospective customer thinks. This built-in trust is something we cherish and never want to violate. A hostess also serves as a valuable third-party endorsement.

Women and older people often don't like going to shopping malls alone after dark. Not too long ago I heard about a survey on this topic. More and more, shoppers are going out in pairs or small groups. The survey said they actually buy more partly because they have someone to help them make decisions. It's a lot easier to buy an expensive dress when a friend says, "You look so good in that dress. It's definitely you."

I'm sure some of this happens at a Longaberger show. One thing that hasn't changed over the years is that people still have to keep an eye on their bank accounts. This makes spending money really hard for some people, especially wives and mothers. Many times these women feel guilty buying a little present for themselves. But done in a group of friends, buying that present is much easier and more fun.

■ THE BEE

One day in 1980 we had about fifteen consultants come to Dresden to see how the baskets were made and spend some time with me. They each made a basket with the help of a weaver. We had fun talking about the business and the future.

By 1981 more and more consultants wanted to come to the factory so they could learn about how baskets were woven. So we invited them to spend a day in Dresden at what was to become our first annual convention. Someone said, "Back in the good old days, they used to have spelling bees and quilting bees. Let's have a basket bee!" From then on we called it the "Basket Bee," or simply the "Bee."

Tami, Rachel, and Grandma Bonnie worked at the registration desk. The Bee was held in the Jefferson Grade School gymnasium where Tami and Rachel had gone to school. About one hundred consultants attended, spending part of the day watching weavers make baskets. They asked them every imaginable question. They reminded me of newspaper reporters, the way they jotted down answers on note pads. Some of our sales directors and other field people spoke, and I gave some recognition to our leading sales consultants. We also announced new incentives that included prizes such as lawn chairs and thermoses. For many, it was the first time they had met anyone from another distributorship. The best part was watching them get together in small groups and exchange ideas.

Rachel and Tami served cookies and punch, and for entertainment I hired a young local boy who played the organ. It was a hot, humid day, and before long we ran out of punch. Anita, Marge, and Sherry filled 7-Up bottles with water and poured it into the punch bowl. Nobody said a word. They were so thirsty and sticky, it didn't matter—just as long as it was cold and wet.

The next year we didn't have a convention, but so many people told us how much they missed it that we held our second one in 1983. In 1983 and 1984 the Bee was held in tents in Dresden, but the following year we needed more space and moved to the high school gym. To accommodate a larger crowd, in 1986 we moved to the Coshocton High School gym, but as more and more consultants came we had to find a new location. In 1987 the Basket Bee was moved to the Convention Center in Columbus. Now it's a three-day midsummer affair with thousands of consultants coming in from across the country. So many consultants come that we presently have three back-to-back Bees. It's a celebration that everyone in The Longaberger Company looks forward to all year.

While the basic format is the same as at our earlier Bees, the conventions have come a long way since 1981 when we served cookies and punch. Top consultants are recognized and rewarded for their achievements in sales, recruiting, and management. Awards and prizes include special baskets, diamond pins, and savings bonds. Tami, Rachel, and I, along with other company executives and sales directors, present the awards.

One highlight of the convention is the introduction of new products. Here we have a formal presentation that appears on the convention site's main stage and is simultaneously shown on large video screens located throughout the arena. This way, all of the more than three thousand attendees at each Bee can see close-up details of the new products as they are introduced. This is the first time anyone in the field sees the new line that will be available during the holiday selling season. Each new product is individually introduced much like a new dress in a fashion show. And each product makes a statement! The excitement and frenzy that are generated cause the entire convention hall to vibrate.

During the Bee, tours of the home office, manufacturing facilities, and Dresden are also conducted. Finally, the Bee is a chance for our consultants who have come to know each other long-distance to meet face-to-face, as well as renew friendships.

In line with the Longaberger philosophy that fun should be a part of every workday, throughout the three-day event the Bee is filled with festivities. Renowned entertainers perform; past Bees have included such superstars as Kenny Rogers, Paul Anka, and Aretha Franklin. But some of the best entertainment is the skits we perform.

We once did a "Tonight with Dave," borrowing the theme music from "The Tonight Show." I played Johnny Carson. As Johnny, I interviewed three special guests: Marge Shipley, Anita Rector, and Sherry

Colling. As it turned out, most of the skit was ad-libbed, and we had everyone laughing so hard they were holding their sides.

At this point I have to tell you this little story. For years, whenever a waitress would ask, "Is there anything else I can get you?" I would always reply, "Yeah, how about Raquel Welch?" Needless to say, the repetition of this line over the years irritated my daughters.

At the 1991 Bee, I had just given my state of the company speech and was walking off the stage. When Tami walked to the podium, she asked me to come back.

"Dad, we have a little game we'd like to play."

"I'm game," I said.

With that, she asked me to sit down in a chair in the center of the stage. Then she blindfolded me.

"Okay, Dad, we want you to guess who the next speaker will be."

Then, the husbands of three consultants came on stage dressed as women. The audience howled. When I removed the blindfold, I told Tami, "That's it for me."

"Just a minute, Dad, I think you'll be interested in guest number four," Tami said, pointing to the side of the stage.

Out walked Raquel Welch. The crowd went wild. My first reaction was that this was one of those look-alike actresses. "Are you the real one?" I asked.

She gave me what I thought was a sexy smile and a big hug. When I put my arms around her, I knew she had to be the real Raquel Welch. I looked at the audience and said, "I think I'm going to have a heart attack!"

As the Bee's guest speaker, Raquel gave an inspirational speech on exercise and the importance of physical fitness. She also talked about the value of having balance in your life—an important message for all of us. She enjoyed the Bee so much, she spent the rest of the day with us.

Later that day, I said to Tami, "Raquel Welch must have cost us an arm and a leg. How did you ever get the purchase order approved without me?"

"We didn't, Dad," Tami said. "You were busy one day, and I handed you a bunch of purchase orders to sign, telling you they were for the Bee. You just signed them. Had you looked them over, you would have seen one that said, 'For Raquel Welch's services at the Bee.'"

One of my favorite Bees was in 1989, when my daughter Rachel spoke. She was only twenty-two at the time. She was introducing a new cookbook she had written while staying at home with her two small children. Rachel was wonderful, and the consultants loved her.

But perhaps everyone's all-time favorite was in 1985, when Tami conducted an interview with Mom. Tami came up with the idea because newcomers to the sales force always wanted to know more about our family and what it was like raising twelve children in Dresden during the fifties. Tami decided that there was no one who could tell them better than Mom. She called her Grandma Bonnie throughout the interview, and the audience loved it. Ever since, Mom is always referred to as "Grandma Bonnie" throughout the company. Mom's dry humor and witty remarks made her a real showstopper.

Over the years, Grandma Bonnie has attended many Bees, and I can assure you, nobody ever gets a bigger standing ovation!

■ BUILD IT AND THEY WILL COME

It's been said that seeing is believing. With this in mind, there's no better way to tell our story than by having people visit us. This is why, as far back as 1977, I started talking about the day when thousands and thousands of tourists would come to Dresden.

For the record, I never had a desire to be in the entertainment or tourist business. I simply wanted a better stage on which to present our story. I believed that the more people saw, the more they'd like us, and the more baskets they would buy. It's as simple as that. What better way to tell our story than in living color?

As a result, we've worked hard to figure out ways to attract visitors. Take the time we built the world's largest picnic basket, which measures nine feet wide, twenty-seven feet long, and ten feet high, with handles that measure twenty-three feet off the ground. This giant picnic basket is listed as the world's largest in *The Guinness Book of World Records*.

Just how this basket came to be is a story in itself. It started at lunch on a summer day in 1980 when our employees were talking about the company's participation in Dresden's homecoming parade. Once we decided we should build a float, I said, "Let's build the world's largest basket and put it on wheels."

With this seed planted, building a normal-size float simply wasn't good enough for our group. We had to have the biggest. When the question came up about how to haul it, one employee, Judy McGee, said, "We live in a mobile home down by the river. We'll be moving soon, so if you can figure out a way to get the box off the trailer bed, Popeye, you can have it."

I left the building without saying anything and headed straight down to the McGees' house. Judy's husband, Bill, was there. He's one of the nicest, most easygoing guys I've ever known. When I told him about the float, he said, "You can have it right now."

We struggled for about four hours until we finally figured out a way to tow the mobile home. I wanted to get it to our factory, where we could separate the house portion from the bed. As we approached the factory, every employee came outside.

Somebody said to Judy, "Don't look now, but your house is moving down Chestnut Street."

The following day, we started to cut the house off the trailer, but it was a slow-moving, seemingly impossible task. To speed things up, I tried burning the house off, but the fire got so hot the axles melted. For a while, it looked like a hopeless case, but we refused to give up. Finally, three days later, we had ourselves a trailer that would haul the gigantic basket we planned to build. I wanted it to be a company project where everyone participated. So once we started building the basket, every employee—whether or not he or she was a weaver—did some weaving. Then each person could sign a splint, letting the entire town know who helped build it. Working day and night, we finished the basket in two weeks, just in time to enter it in the parade.

The basket caused such a stir, we decided to take it to public events to introduce people to Longaberger baskets. It was a smash hit for the two weeks it appeared at the 1981 Ohio State Fair. Both Tami and Rachel put in long hours at this booth. Later on, the big basket traveled to other state fairs as far away as Macon, Georgia. The basket had an entrance and an exit door, so people could walk through it. Products were displayed on the interior walls, and we also set up an exterior exhibit.

No longer on wheels, in 1990 the world's largest basket found a permanent home in a small park in the center of Dresden, where it's now a big tourist attraction. It's been refurbished, and its doors have been woven shut so you can't go inside. Just the same, people come from all over to see it. Although there are many other points of interest in Dresden, none is photographed more than the big basket. It's become a place where people propose to their sweethearts, and some have even had their wedding ceremonies there.

The Longaberger Company has invested millions of dollars in Dresden. We've put our money into our hometown not only to preserve its charm for visitors but also to help provide a better quality of life for its residents. Few villages in America the size of Dresden can boast about a community fitness center, swim center, athletic fields, and the likes of the Bonnie Longaberger Senior Center. My old grade school building, which had become run down, was restored and is now Longaberger University, a company training center. We take equal pride in the Longaberger Family Center and the Company Health Center, which provide child care and medical care for employees on the Manufacturing Campus just outside Dresden.

From a dying Appalachian town whose best days were believed to have been when canals and coal mining dominated the economy, Dresden has since been transformed into a picturesque community with the charm and innocence of the past. Gift shops, boutiques, restaurants, and small specialty shops line both sides of Main Street. Several bed-and-breakfast lodging houses have sprung up throughout the area. The Longaberger Company has several specialty shops and restaurants, including Popeye's Soda Shop, which specializes in 1950s-style hamburgers and thick milk shakes. The Longaberger Company paved new sidewalks and curbs and invested in landscaping that includes the Bartlett pear trees planted along Main Street.

On the seventeen-mile drive down State Route 16, we built miles of white rail fence wherever we could along both sides of the road. The manicured landscaping along the fence includes lighted, seasonal decorations. Just off the highway on the east side of Newark stands our seven-story office building shaped like a basket. Believe me, you can't miss it!

Remember how I used to love cutting grass? Well, Longaberger crews cut the grass along Route 16 between Newark and Dresden.

Why make such a large investment? We want visitors to "live" the Longaberger story. We want them to personally experience Small Town U.S.A. And we welcome them at our Manufacturing Campus, which employs more than six thousand workers. Here they can walk along our quarter-mile mezzanine and watch weavers at work, while a tour guide answers their questions. When people see what goes into making a basket, they can appreciate its value and price. For a number of years, we've had a Make-a-Basket Shop where you can make your own Longaberger basket with the help of one of our skilled basket makers. And for many, they can see firsthand what Longaberger consultants say at shows. Still, we have other visitors who have never even seen our products. We hope these people will come to appreciate Longaberger products once they know who we are.

It's common to see consultants and advisors visit with small and large groups. A hostess may invite a few friends to join her on a trip to our Manufacturing Campus. Sometimes consultants plan three- or four-day group trips. It's a great getaway for sightseeing and shopping. Sometimes we see mothers and daughters come together, or sisters who want to spend some time together. It's always a delightful, relaxing trip for couples who want to get away from their normal routine. We also see a lot of parents with their children who come to visit and spend quality time together.

As a bit of history, our first tours started back in the late seventies. Actually, when we were still on Chestnut Street, Tami would show people through the factory during the summer. It might be a couple just passing through Dresden who happened to stop by. Or it might be a consultant who drove in to pick up her own baskets. Many people have advised me, "Don't allow people to come through your factory, or you're going to give your secrets away."

"That doesn't worry me," I tell them. "Besides, I see more advantages to letting the public see just what goes into making our products, and what gives them their quality."

When we first started giving tours, on a busy day we would have two or three busloads a day. Now we average twenty-five to thirty buses a day during our busy season. On our record day we saw seventy buses. In 1998 about four hundred thousand visitors came to Dresden. That's an impressive figure, considering we didn't do any advertising to promote it.

When visitors see that everything we do at The Longaberger Company is first-class, it sends a message that we never compromise on quality. What better way is there to tell our story?

■ THE COLLECTOR'S MARKET

As a tribute to Mom, we introduced the Bread and Milk Basket in 1981. That same year, we came out with the Christmas Collection Candle Basket, and we have had a Christmas collection ever since.

Then, in 1983, as a special tribute to Dad, the company had what we thought would be a onetime offering of the Market Basket. The demand for this $32.95 basket far exceeded our expectations, and consequently we decided to offer a different basket for a limited time each year as part of what became known as the J. W. Longaberger Collection. Our plan was to continue this collection until 1994. Because the production of these baskets was limited to the selling period, basket lovers and collectors went wild. We sold more of them than we thought we would, and collectors bid the prices in the secondary market above their original prices. For instance, that original $32.95 basket is currently selling in a secondary market for more than $1,000.

In addition to the Christmas Collection, in the late 1980s we introduced other series of collector baskets, with special editions for Easter, Mother's Day, and Father's Day. Two others are called the All-American Series and the May Series Baskets.

As an offshoot of these basket collections, in January 1996 we established the Collectors Club for our customers and sales associates. Membership entitles the member to a special basket, as well as a subscription to *Signatures* magazine and the *Collectors Exchange*. *Signatures* is a quarterly periodical that features product ideas, members' personal stories, past collections, and so on. *Collectors Exchange* is a monthly publication with listings of past Longaberger products for sale, as well as requests from individuals who are looking to buy specific products.

We tell everyone to buy baskets they love to look at and use. Although many baskets have increased in price in the secondary market, they are not investments. They are wonderful as family heirlooms to be passed down from one generation to the next. They are also popular wedding and graduation gifts.

In addition to the two publications, there are several other advantages to a Collectors Club membership. First, there is an opportunity to purchase exclusive baskets that are not available to nonmembers.

Second, there are club gatherings each year at regional locations across the country. These events are an educational and entertaining experience. For example, a Longaberger basket maker demonstrates the art of weaving. Associates make presentations on the different uses for our baskets—telling how to use our products for cooking, entertaining, decorating, and gift giving. A Longaberger family member is often present. These gatherings also serve as a wonderful place for sharing ideas with other collectors, booking shows, and recruiting new prospects.

Today, we are now the fourth-largest collector's club in the United States, and we're still growing.

■ LISTEN TO YOUR SALESPEOPLE

When we calculate how many customers attend a Longaberger show, we realize there are millions of people out there telling our consultants what they want our company to do for them. All we have to do is listen to what they are saying.

This is one of the great features of direct selling. We go right into the customers' homes, so we have an opportunity to hear exactly what they say. Retailers spend fortunes on research just to learn about their customers. Our consultants are able to find out firsthand what our customers like and dislike. And after a couple of hours with them in their living room, kitchen, or den, close relationships are formed.

That's why whenever I'm with sales consultants, I do my best to shut up and listen. I feel honored to be among so many talented people who spend so much time in the field. The best ideas for our products originate from the feedback our consultants get. It was a customer who told a consultant, "It would be nice to have plastic liners for picnic baskets to keep out the ants." That's all we had to hear, and ever since we have sold plastic protectors as well as cloth liners with our baskets.

Each basket is personally signed by the weaver who made it. As described earlier, this came from an idea our first sales associate, Charleen Cuckovich, had when she asked basket-weaver Bonnie Hague to sign one for her back in 1977. All the brilliant ideas we've implemented are a result of listening to the people who know our customers.

It's a shame, but all too often executives and business owners remove themselves from the playing field and instead sit in their ivory towers, believing nobody knows their customers better. You hear them say, "I've spent thirty years in this business. Nobody knows our customers better than I do."

The trouble is that they haven't had actual contact with a customer for years and years. These so-called experts don't realize that today's marketplace is constantly changing. Unless they're out there on a daily basis, they better start listening to somebody who is.

A direct sales organization such as ours has tremendous momentum, or what I refer to as a life of its own. In this sense, it grows explosively because as we have more sales consultants, more shows are given, and more new sales consultants join our ranks. We have been fortunate that customers have been pleased with their purchases and thus keep buying. Knowing this, we work hard to provide them with what they want. If the past is anything like the future, the company will continue to grow—that is, as long as we carefully listen to our people. I hope that we never stop listening.

However, if you lead a business, you have to know what to do with this important information. Sometimes it's easy. Your customers are asking for more choices in color, size, and so on. Or they're asking for a new product that solves a problem, like the plastic protectors for our baskets. Sometimes it's not so easy.

In 1990 I became convinced that we should sell pottery in addition to our baskets and basket accessories. To me, pottery was linked to our baskets because Dad's baskets had been used by the Ohio pottery industry. Also, Mom always carried her pie plates in our baskets. While no customers were specifically asking for pottery, we did hear that our regular customers wanted something new, not just more baskets.

At our 1990 Bee I announced that we would soon start to sell pottery items. Wow, did I hear from the consultants! Unfortunately, it was mostly negative. They didn't want to have to learn about a new product line and didn't want to lug pieces of pottery from home show to home show.

We launched the pottery line anyway, and it was a success. We started with a few items like the pie plate my Mom had used and grew the line into a whole set of mugs, bowls, plates, and bakeware. In 1998 it accounted for $82 million in sales, or 12 percent of our business. It has grown each year, bringing us many regular customers who buy some and then keep scheduling home shows to buy the new pieces we add.

Another example of doing what your customers want, even if they don't know what to ask for, was our Collectors Club. Tami spent lots of time with the sales field and our customers. She was convinced that many wanted a closer relationship, more information and more exclusive products. She came up with the idea of a Collectors Club to meet those needs and convinced me it made sense. Unfortunately, there was little enthusiasm from our sales and marketing employees and our sales field. Tami heard everything from "It's too confusing to present in a home show" to "We don't have the computer capabilities or the staff to pull it off." But she was relentless, and we launched the club at the 1996 Bee. Once consultants had success selling memberships and the exclusive products, everyone was enthusiastic. Within two years, the Longaberger Collectors Club was the fourth largest in the United States.

So listen to your customers. Listen to your employees and salespeople. They can tell you about the needs and wants of your customers and potential customers. However, as a business leader, it's your job to find the ways your company can meet those needs and wants, and to make sure it gets done—and done right.

6

Growing Up with My Daughters

Y̶ou're not going to believe it, but before 1996 I had never made a complete basket. I had helped my dad from time to time but never made one from start to finish. I figured it was about time to make one. Since I had two daughters, I made two baskets, one for each of them. Afterward, I vowed to never make another one. It took me forever to make those two. Even though the two I made don't get high marks for quality, they are the world's only "Made by Dave" baskets. I hope Tami and Rachel keep them, not because they're collectors' items but to remind them of how much I love them.

When my daughters were born, it was as if I had been reborn, too. From the time I was six years old, people said, "Popeye, you don't have a lazy bone in your body." Sure, I was always a hard worker, but when my daughter Tami was born, I really became motivated. I worked even harder to give my girls some of the things I didn't have as a child. It was as if they gave me a purpose in life. I wanted to build something that would last, although at the time I had no idea what it could possibly be.

Two years after Tami was born, I started my first business. It wasn't that I had a burning desire to own a restaurant. Instead, I saw it as an opportunity to get my feet wet doing something on my own. Once Popeye's was off and running, I went into the grocery business, and a little later, I opened a drugstore that Dresden desperately needed. Even owning three businesses, I had ambition to do more. I wanted to build something big. For years I didn't know what, but I knew someday opportunity would knock, and when it did, I planned to grab it.

Before I became a proud father, I was content to drive a bread truck for Nickles. I did a good job, and I enjoyed the work. Back then, I would have been satisfied to work my way up to supervisor and make a lifetime career of it. For someone who read only at the level of a sixth grader, in the eyes of Dresden, I would have been a success. The fact is, I would have thought so, too.

It wasn't until 1973 that I got serious about selling Dad's baskets. I still had lots of ideas about what I might do, including having a chain of Popeye's restaurants. At that time Tami was twelve and Rachel had turned six. Like most people who have children, I became aware of how fast time flies and how quickly little ones grow up. I was watching it happen right before my eyes. If I didn't try to sell baskets now, I thought, I might never do it.

So although I was making a comfortable living, I was willing to risk it all on a new venture. I was willing to leverage everything I owned to build a business that everyone was sure would ultimately fail. But I wanted something that I thought was meaningful, and I'd risk everything to achieve it. Would I have done the same thing if I didn't have Tami and Rachel? Well, it's hard to say because I can't imagine life without them. They became a part of who I am. So my answer is: probably not. Why? Knowing me, I can't imagine what other reason I might have had.

■ SMALL-TOWN VALUES

Back in the sixties and seventies life in Dresden wasn't a whole lot different than when I was growing up in the forties and fifties. That's the way it is in a small, rural Midwestern town. Sure, things change, but not nearly as much as in the big city.

Everyone in Dresden pretty much knows everyone else's business. While this is not always a plus, being able to go anywhere in town and be called by your first name always made me feel good. It's nice to know that you don't have to lock your doors or that you can leave your keys in the car and it will still be there when you get back.

Things moved slowly in Dresden when the girls were young, and as far as I was concerned, that was fine. I wanted my daughters to enjoy small-town living as I did.

Nothing in Dresden was more than a five- or ten-minute walk away. My restaurant and grocery store were on Main Street in the center of town, so Tami and Rachel always knew where to find me—and I knew where I could find them if I wanted to. They often stopped in at Popeye's for an after-school treat or to pick up something at the grocery store or drugstore. The nice thing was that I got to see them during my workday, which gave me a chance to share a break with them. I looked at it as a "fringe benefit" that I wouldn't have had if I lived in a big city.

Some people feel trapped in a small town because there's not a lot going on. That may be, but I see this as an advantage. Dresden might not have many social and cultural activities, but the church and its youth groups played a major role in my girls' early years. And they were busy with school functions. What better influences on youth than church and school? They also participated in 4-H, which I especially liked because it taught kids about the responsibilities of taking care of animals.

There is also a strong sense of community in small towns. When people know their neighbors, they are more likely to do things together. We always did in Dresden, and I'm told that's the way it is in other rural towns across America. Perhaps what I like most about a small town like Dresden is that there is less discrimination against kids who don't have much. And in Small Town U.S.A., there aren't inner-city kids and suburban kids. Hell, the entire town of Dresden wouldn't fill a decent-sized suburb! Everybody lives pretty much like everybody else. We are all members of the working class.

My daughters grew up treating people equally. They learned to have respect for everyone, regardless of his or her position. As far as they were concerned, everyone who made an honest living was a good person, regardless of the size of his or her paycheck. This attitude would later serve them well, in their business lives. To Tami and Rachel, everyone has an important job that contributes to the ultimate success of the company.

■ FUN TIMES

What I remember most about my youth is all the fun I had growing up in Dresden. I think about the good times with my family and friends. Although we didn't have many material possessions, as I think back, we were always happy. I wanted my daughters to enjoy fun times while they were growing up, too. Every child deserves to have fun.

This is what makes parenthood so special. As a parent, there's so much fun you can have with your children, but you've got to take the time to do it. If you don't, you're depriving yourself of one of life's greatest joys. In my case, I got to grow up again—this time with Tami and Rachel. With them, I was able to relive the same kinds of adventures I had as a young boy. At the same time, I was their father, a role that I took very seriously. I never shirked my responsibility. But this doesn't mean I had to choose between the two. I wanted to have it both ways. I did, and it worked just fine. I was both a parent authority and a good friend. I disciplined them, and I goofed off with them.

To me, their laughter was the sweetest sound in the world. And did we laugh. Once when Rachel was a baby, I was teaching Tami how to change a diaper. She didn't want any part of it. So when she wasn't looking, I put butterscotch pudding on a clean diaper on the bassinet. Then I placed Rachel in the bassinet and called Tami to come in the room.

"Tami, would you help me change Rachel's diaper?"

"It's icky," she said.

"It's not so bad," I said.

Then I stuck my fingers in the pudding and licked them. "Mm, not bad," I said to my six-year-old daughter. "Want to try some?"

Poor Tami couldn't believe her eyes. She looked a little queasy, like she might faint.

I laughed so hard I was in tears. "It's pudding!"

"You're so gross, Dad," she said, trying not to laugh.

But Tami thought it was funny, too, because for days I heard her telling everyone, "Do you know what my dad did?"

I suppose the die was cast, because as the girls got older, we were constantly playing pranks on each other.

There was always a gang of their friends at our house. It reminded me of the house I grew up in, filled with kids. One summer evening, Tami was playing outside with her friends. I ran to them and shouted, "Quick, you kids, go get all the neighbors, and tell everybody to come to our house. Rachel is on TV!"

It didn't take long before we had a full house. A popular variety show was on, and I said, "Rachel will be on in just a minute."

Everyone stared at the set, and just as a commercial ended, I picked up Rachel and set her down on the television set.

"There she is, everyone. Rachel is on TV."

Not all our guests shared our humor, but Tami, Rachel, and I were hysterical.

When Rachel was a cheerleader in junior high, she kept coaxing me to come watch her at a basketball game.

"I know your parents didn't go to games, Dad," she begged, "and I know how busy you are, but won't you please just come see me?"

Tami and I didn't want to disappoint her. So we not only went, but sat in the front row. The two of us kept jumping up and down, and we cheered so loudly throughout the game that Rachel became quite annoyed.

"Okay, you guys, that's it," Rachel told us. "You never have to come to another game."

Another time, Rachel and I teamed up to get Tami. After a high school basketball tournament in Columbus, we stopped at an out-of-town restaurant on our way back to Dresden. We didn't know a single person in the place. After we ordered, Tami excused herself and went to the ladies' room. Rachel and I decided to give her a standing ovation when she returned. We thought it was such a good idea that we got everyone in the restaurant to join in. Well, as soon as poor Tami opened the door, everyone in the place started clapping their hands and cheering. Tami's face turned as red as a beet. She did a complete U-turn and went right back into the rest room. To avoid a repeat performance, she climbed out the bathroom window! She was ready to kill us, but on the way home, we all ended up laughing. Tami swore she'd get even, and, believe me, there have been many times since when she did.

When Rachel was about eleven or twelve years old, she worked as a gofer at the basket factory on weekends.

I nonchalantly said to her, "Hey, honey, I need a wire stretcher. Go get one for me."

"You need a what?"

"You know, a wire stretcher. Now go get me one, will you?" I acted as if I was so busy, I didn't have time to talk to her.

"Geez, okay, Dad," she said, "I'll get you a wire stretcher."

Rachel went to several different people in the plant and said, "My dad needs a wire stretcher. Do you have one?"

"Your dad needs a what?"

"A wire stretcher," she'd say, acting like she knew what it was. "I'm sorry, but I don't have a wire stretcher," everyone kept telling her.

"Maybe you ought to try the hardware store," someone suggested.

At the hardware store, they figured I was up to my old tricks and played right along. "Sorry, Rachel, but we're all out. Why don't you try the paint store?"

Rachel went to the paint store and all over town, looking for a wire stretcher. On her fifth stop someone said, "Your dad is playing a joke on you. There's no such thing as a wire stretcher."

Rachel got so mad, she didn't bother coming back to the plant. When I saw her later that day, I asked, "Did you get the wire stretcher?"

"You're very funny," she said sarcastically.

I explained that when I was a kid, I ran the projector at the Dresden Movie House.

"You won't believe it, Rachel, but the manager once had me running all over town looking for a film stretcher."

"How long did you look?" she asked, grinning from ear to ear.

Hardly a week went by that one of the three of us didn't play a prank on each other. Boy, did we have fun, and we never outgrew it. I believe having a good time at work has a positive influence on people. It helps them look forward to work, and it lets them know they shouldn't take themselves too seriously. These were good lessons for my daughters to learn at a young age. It's something that has carried over into our company as part of our philosophy of fun in the workplace. That's why I hope the day never comes when we stop throwing rolls at each other at company dinners.

■ CONSIDER THE CHILDREN

Laura and I separated when Tami was twelve and Rachel was six. Deciding to split up was difficult, but Laura and I believed it was best. We always got along well. In fact, we've always maintained our friendship, and I value that.

Laura is a wonderful woman, and I would do anything for her or her family. She's such a devoted, loving mother, and she did such a good job raising the girls. We truly like each other, and we have remained good friends—so much so that Laura has worked at our company since 1989 in charge of our employee health clinics.

I realize many couples that break up aren't as cooperative as we were. But when children are involved, and parents love them, I believe every effort should be made to work things out peacefully for everyone's sake. Caring parents should spare their children the unnecessary grief of arguing. You have to place their happiness ahead of your own misery.

The girls always lived with their mother. Although I was never restricted from seeing them, I didn't get to spend as much time with them as I would have liked. Looking back, I realize I could have been a better father, but when I say that to them, they're quick to relieve my fears and say what a good dad I have always been. Of course, that's just like them. Nobody ever says anything derogatory about Laura or me in front of Tami or Rachel because, if they do, they're going to get a piece of their strong-willed minds.

■ GROWING UP IN THE FAMILY BUSINESS

Running several businesses simultaneously didn't leave me a lot of spare time, so I didn't have many outside interests. My life centered around my work. I didn't have time for golf or going out with my buddies. Plus I was consumed with my business ventures. A lot of my conversations with Tami and Rachel focused on business. Of course, that's when they weren't telling me about their interests. Sometimes I could hardly get a word in edgewise.

As much as I tried to leave my work behind at the end of the day, I'm sure my girls heard more shoptalk than most kids do. I didn't plan it that way; in fact, I wanted them to enjoy being kids and grow up having a good time. I just wasn't able to turn off my dreams at the end of the day. In defense of parents who are excited about their work, that's not all bad. Certainly, it's preferable to coming home at the end of the day feeling beat up and wiped out.

Sadly, millions of people go to work each day to a job they can't stand, and their kids know it. It's written all over their faces and in the way they walk in the door each evening. Kids can't help but grow up with negative feelings about work. These children never see work as fulfilling. They learn to view it as drudgery, and they don't expect to enjoy it. What a terrible legacy to pass down to a child.

However, when a parent loves what he does every day, his children eagerly anticipate the time when they can enter the workforce. I believe my passion and enthusiasm for my work rubbed off on my children. As a parent, you should be aware of how strongly you influence your child's attitude toward work.

I wasn't one of those parents who believed in treating my two children alike. This approach never made sense to me because Tami and Rachel are not identical. For one thing, they are of different ages. By the time Rachel reached a certain age, my thinking might have changed from when Tami was that age. Perhaps what I did with Tami was not the best thing to do with Rachel. I learned from my mistakes, and I had no intention of repeating them. So I have always been consistently inconsistent with my daughters. There are just too many variables to give each child the exact same thing. Except love. I love them equally, and they know it.

During Tami's senior year, she enrolled in a program in which she spent half a day at school and worked the rest of the time. At that point I told her she was going to work for me. It was not optional. She started at the restaurant but didn't like being a waitress. Then I put her in the drugstore, but she didn't like that either. Finally I moved her behind the cash register at the grocery store, and she worked there until she graduated from high school.

On the other hand, I never told Rachel she had to work. Rachel was a preschooler when her mother did the restaurant's bookkeeping. Every morning, Laura would stop by to pick up the previous day's receipts, and she'd bring Rachel along. There would always be a steady group of older businessmen coming in for coffee and donuts, and Rachel would be there eavesdropping on their conversations, soaking everything up like a sponge.

One day, I teased her, "As long as you're here, Rachel, I may as well put you to work."

Her face lit up. "Sure, Dad! What can I do?" She was so eager, I started her folding napkins, wiping off tables, and separating coffee filters. She seemed to love it.

Whether they were working, stopping in for a snack, or picking up groceries, Tami and Rachel were constantly exposed to business. As little girls, they listened to my conversations with business associates and employees. They watched me sweat out how we'd meet our payroll, and they worried along with me about that secondhand compressor in the grocery store breaking down. They, too, were concerned about lost perishables when a big snowstorm hit and customers couldn't get to the store.

My business woes were, in part, their problems, too. Likewise, they shared my enthusiasm when things went well. I think this is an edge that entrepreneurs' children enjoy over other kids. Contrary to what some people think, people aren't born with a flair for business or a willingness to take a risk. These are traits that are developed over time, often by watching others. My daughters became businesspeople for the same reason a high percentage of doctors' kids become doctors, and attorneys' kids become attorneys.

For better or worse, children pick up what parents say. Some scientists say they're listening and processing information even before they are born. For instance, after many years Rachel confessed to me how, as a small child, she worried about the second mortgage I carried on the house. Tami told me how it made her feel when people in town would say some of my business ventures were zany and doomed to fail. Of course, some of my business ventures were zany, and, indeed, some did fail. With that many balls in the air, some were bound to hit the ground. I understood the odds as well as the payoff, and I was willing to take the risks. Nonetheless, parents should be aware that their children are also concerned about mom and dad's business ventures. Kids not only worry about seeing their parents get hurt; they don't want to get hurt either! Although they're only children, they do understand how their future rests on the success or failure of the family business.

There's no question that business was the center of our lives. As Rachel recently said, "I was thirty years old before I realized people talked about something other than business at the dinner table." While some families don't think it's appropriate to discuss business at the table, I never had a problem with it, nor did my daughters. In fact, as long as you don't overdo it, the subject can make for interesting dinner conversation. Besides, it beats gossiping about the neighbors.

Unlike some kids, Tami and Rachel never had to worry about finding a summer job. I always had plenty for them to do. Before the basket company, they waited tables, bagged groceries, and worked behind the cash registers. I gave them some major responsibilities at rather young ages, and sometimes this didn't go over well with the locals. For instance, when Rachel was in the fifth or sixth grade, she rang up sales at the cash register in the drugstore. A woman who was upset that I would have my little girl handling money wrote a nasty letter to me. She ranted about how she "considered it an insult" that I would permit such a thing in my store.

I showed the letter to Rachel. After she read it, she ran to her room in tears. I went upstairs and sat down to comfort her. I gave her a little hug and didn't say a word.

"What did I do wrong?" she cried to me.

"You did nothing wrong," I said. "There are people like that woman in this world, and you just can't allow them to get to you. She's just a nasty old lady, and there's nothing you or I can do about it. So just forget it."

"But what should I do if I'm at the store, and somebody tells me that I have no business working there because I'm too young?" she questioned.

"Well, honey," I said, trying to think how I could turn this around, "you have every right to work in our store. And nobody has the right to tell you who you are. That's up to you. You can't let one person discourage you from doing what you're entitled to do."

"But what could I say, Dad?"

"Well, honey, if this ever happens again, you have my permission to tell that person to go straight to hell."

Rachel gave me a long look. She had been taught always to be polite to grown-ups. Plus, she had never said a swear word in her life. The idea of saying such a thing to an adult went against everything she had ever been told.

"Let me think about this," she finally said. "Okay, Dad?"

About an hour later, Rachel came downstairs.

"I thought about what you told me, Dad, and I know what I'll say the next time it happens."

"That's good, Rachel," I said. "What are you going to say?"

"I'll tell that person she can go straight to heaven, and when she gets there, she can make a complete U-turn."

I just about lost it when I heard that.

■ THE BOSS'S DAUGHTERS

By the late seventies the basket company was getting big enough for the girls to get involved. When we started putting product tags on all baskets, Rachel helped with that job. She also worked in the staining and shipping departments. By then, Tami was old enough to pinch-hit for a secretary or a bookkeeper on vacation. One week, Tami would sub for someone in personnel, and the next week she might be in the accounting department. When people traveling through Dresden would drop in at the factory, if Tami or Rachel was around, she'd get to conduct a tour. These were probably some of the earliest tours conducted in a Longaberger facility. About the only job neither ever had was weaving, and that's because it took eight weeks' training to become a weaver. It didn't make much sense to have them in training for two months and work only one month.

Nobody knew better than Tami and Rachel that the boss's daughter has no entitlements or privileges. They were never treated differently from anyone else. In fact, sometimes I was tougher on them than I would be with another employee. Many times I would call them into my office, shut the door, and read them the riot act for a good solid hour. Later I found out it had become a standing joke. On their way to my office, they'd say to my secretary, "Looks like another one of Dad's lectures, doesn't it?"

When the girls and I took car trips to Zanesville, Hartville, and Columbus, they'd refer to them as "lectures on wheels."

From time to time when Tami or Rachel disagreed with an employee, I'd always side with the employee. The girls may have been in the right, but I wouldn't give them the benefit of the doubt. Later, in private, I'd explain why I did what I did.

"But I'm your daughter," Rachel would say. "You should have stuck up for me."

"Because you are my daughter," I explained, "is exactly why I didn't."

Once I made my position clear, both girls understood. When these rare incidents occurred, they learned to cope with them. And because I discussed it with them privately, they never complained.

On the plus side, being the boss's daughter meant my secretary always put their calls through to me, no matter what I was doing or whom I was with. It didn't matter if they called me in the middle of a meeting with a bank president. This doesn't mean I had extended conversations with them while visitors sat twiddling their thumbs. Naturally, I'd tell the girls that I was tied up and promised to call them as soon as I was finished. Tami and Rachel always knew they were my number one priority and I was available whenever they wanted me. Even later in their careers here at the company, they always knew they could walk into a meeting to speak to me. I wanted them to know what was really important to me—they were. Nothing has ever been more important to me, and nothing ever will be.

The same is true at home. I rarely make or take a business call at home after work. The only two people who call me about work are Tami and Rachel. I'm always available to them.

In the early stages of my career, I struggled to keep my head above water. There were many times when there wasn't enough money to meet the payroll and have anything left over for the family. Both Tami and Rachel were old enough at the time to understand the financial problems I faced. During their early childhood, and particularly Tami's, we lived very modestly; there were a lot of things my daughters were denied because we couldn't afford them.

Later, as the business started to prosper, our lifestyle didn't change a lot. The money I made was always poured back into the business. For instance, the girls lived in the same house from the time they were born until Rachel graduated from high school in 1985. At this time, we were the biggest employer in the county, but their standard of living hadn't changed from when the company was just a hole in the wall.

By that time, I had taken the girls on a few nice vacations to places like Acapulco, Cancun, and the Bahamas, but those were only one-week trips. Afterward, life would go on as usual in Dresden.

I remember Rachel once saying how she envied her friends whose parents had regular jobs. "They had a paycheck every two weeks and a pension at retirement," she said. "But what was going to happen to us if these baskets didn't sell?"

As far as I was concerned, I liked it this way. I didn't want my daughters to feel like the little rich girls in town, even though that's how many people in Dresden perceived them. My daughters could very well have felt like that, but fortunately they never did.

When Tami turned sixteen, like every teenager with a driver's license, she wanted a car. I liked the idea of her having the freedom to go where she wanted, because I didn't want her to have to depend on any Tom, Dick, or Harry—some irresponsible kid—to drive her. With her own car, she would be more in control; she wouldn't have to accept a ride with someone I wouldn't trust in the driver's seat. I knew that with Tami behind the wheel, there would be no drinking or speeding. Just the same, owning a car is a big responsibility for a sixteen-year-old kid, and I wanted to make sure she knew that.

After a long discussion, I agreed to make the down payment on a late-model used car, but she would have to make the monthly payments.

"Before we discuss this any further," I told her, "I want to know how you'll be able to take care of maintenance and repairs."

The next day, she sat me down and presented a detailed account of how she would handle every possible expense. I was impressed with her figures. She outlined how many hours she planned to work at the restaurant and grocery, and based on her hourly wages, she had it all figured out.

She anxiously watched me as I studied it over. "This looks great, Tami. You did a thorough job, except you forgot one thing."

"I did?"

"Yes, gasoline and oil," I said. "Based on these numbers, you'll only be able to drive thirty miles a week."

With that, she revised her plan and came up with a new one that required her to work a few more hours. Although I intended to help her—and we both knew I would—Tami realized she had better get serious about work if she wanted to drive a car.

We bought it the next day, and she did put in the extra time. She even worked during high school football games when she was dating the team's star. Tami didn't like it, but she lived up to her part of our deal.

I made lots of deals with my girls when they were growing up. Sometimes, I negotiated deals with them where I ended up with the shorter end of the stick. I know people who negotiate with their kids and think that because they're the parents, they should always come out on top. I disagree, first, because I wanted to teach my girls to negotiate win-win situations versus thinking the object is to outsmart the other person. Second, if a parent doesn't let his child win sometimes, the kid will grow up with a dislike for negotiating. Third, and perhaps the most important lesson to teach, is that a deal is a deal. Once you make a deal with someone, you never renege on it. Children learn by the examples set by their parents.

By the way, seven years later when Rachel turned sixteen, she, too, wanted a car. I didn't put her through the same exercise as Tami's. One reason was because now I was able to afford it. When Tami was sixteen, I didn't have the money. So with Rachel, I simply went out and bought a car for her. Like I said, I wasn't consistent in how I treated them. But

Rachel was always eager to work at just about any job I would give her. Of course I always had to pay her. In fact, she made me pay her top dollar, particularly after she got her new car.

Once when I was discussing a summer job with her, she said, "How much will you pay me?"

When I told her, she replied, "That's not enough. I could get more in Zanesville, and I need the money. Either pay me what I want or hire somebody else."

"Why, that's highway robbery!" I blurted out.

"Look at it this way, Dad," she interrupted, "you should be happy you didn't raise any stupid daughters."

Rachel got what she asked for. And she made me proud. Like I said, it's good for the kid to negotiate with a parent and win sometimes. Winning lets them enjoy the benefits of making a good deal, and it's good for their confidence.

■ DON'T BE A HYPOCRITE

We've all heard a young person swear that the last thing he'll ever do is go into his father's business. So many kids who work in a family business grow up despising it, and their parents can't figure out what went wrong. What I think often happens is that the child becomes disillusioned because he discovers that his dad's business ethics fall short of what's been preached at home. Imagine the poor example I would have been for my daughters if I adjusted the scales in my grocery store so customers would receive a fraction of an ounce less on each order of meat. Or if I shouted at employees, wanting them to work harder. And what would they think if because I was the boss, I acted as a know-it-all and never listened to anyone else's ideas!

You can't tell your kids that they should never cheat on a test in the classroom if at the same time you cheat in your business. You can't tell them it's wrong to tell a lie, and then misrepresent what you sell to a customer. When children see their parents act hypocritically in business, it's a big turnoff. Think about it. For years they put Mom and Dad on a pedestal; they've lectured to them that being honest and working hard is the right thing to do. Then they witness how Dad takes advantage of people at his business. "Everything Dad's taught me is a sham," they think. No wonder teenagers revolt!

At The Longaberger Company, we tell our managers that they must walk the talk. As a parent, you must also walk the talk at home.

■ THE EMOTIONAL SIDE OF A FAMILY BUSINESS

One thing most people don't consider prior to starting a family business is its emotional side. They don't think about the fact that no matter what happens at the office, they all go home at the end of the day and turn into parents, siblings, spouses, and so on. Needless to say, what happens on the job can strain a personal relationship. Nothing is worth risking that.

Of course, there are some strong advantages to being in business with your family. I want to emphasize the trust factor. I have explicit trust in my two daughters. Not all business associates are able to make this claim. From a father's viewpoint, I take comfort in building something that will continue in the family when I'm no longer around and that can be passed on to future generations. With Tami at the helm of The Longaberger Company and Rachel leading our newly established foundation, I am confident both entities will be in good hands. I also know my daughters. They not only are women of high character and integrity but also have good values. That's the way their mother and I raised them.

Then, from a selfish point of view, working with my daughters means I get to spend a lot of time with them. Today many grown children live far away from their parents, and family get-togethers may happen only once or twice a year. I see Tami and Rachel every day. To me, this is a luxury. And because we work together, we share a common interest. Unlike some father-daughter relationships, we're never at a loss for words; we always have something to talk about!

Of course, the downside is that when business is bad, it carries into everyone's lives. Rachel was too young to endure the stress of the company's severe financial difficulties throughout the early and mid-eighties. As Rachel says today, being in a family business is the best of the best and the worst of the worst.

"The most rewarding thing," she says, "is that your emotions are involved." Then she adds, "The really bad thing is that your emotions are involved." Rachel emphasizes that it's a two-edged sword, because when you're down, there is no one to go to. But when you're up, you celebrate together with your family. "It's a package deal," she explains.

Tami concurs that there is a strong emotional side to running a family business. "It has put me in some difficult situations where I had to have conversations with my father and sister that were strictly business. If we take personally what each other says, it can be very painful. It gets awkward at times, because we're constantly flipping back and forth from a personal mode to a professional mode."

Nevertheless, I have enjoyed my front-row seat watching my two daughters grow and thrive in their professional lives. I can pat myself on the back because I was able to play a significant role in their growth. As top dog, I had to walk a delicate line just bringing Tami and Rachel into the business. The line got narrower when I promoted them into management. I had to avoid favoritism so other deserving employees wouldn't be hurt. At the same time, I didn't want to hold back because they were my daughters. I couldn't promote them too soon, or they'd be in far over their heads. I would be putting them in a position to fail when, if they were left where they were, they would have succeeded. This is food for thought for other family-run businesses. When a family member fails, that's another story—and usually a tragic one. In our case, we were fortunate because everything worked out fine. My daughters have become superstars. Both found roles they enjoy and perform well.

Believe me, it wasn't a piece of cake. After Tami graduated from The Ohio State University as a marketing major, her plans were to land a job with a company such as Procter & Gamble. When she joined our company in January 1984, in her mind it was only until she could find what she considered "a real job." Tami was so proud of her degree that she brought her diploma to the office to show me.

"Here, Dad, look what I've got," she said.

"Tami, you can take that and stick it where the sun doesn't shine," I blasted her. "Until you learn that the only way to make it in this company is to get out there on the floor and travel in the sales field, that diploma isn't going to cut it around here. First, you have to treat everyone as an equal—and show them that you care about them. Second, you have to find out what they want. It's not what you or I want, but what they want, and you have to get them on your side. That's the only way they'll ever accept you. You have to earn their respect; I can't give that to you. Now, what I suggest you do is watch me when I go out talking to them. You learn from me, and you'll learn a lot more about people than they can teach you in any college."

Tami's first position was as a marketing manager, although at the time we didn't have a marketing department. In fact, she was the first college graduate to work for us. She had to be careful not to step on people's toes. Certain employees had their own turf that carried over to Tami's projects. For example, one of the first things Tami did to become familiar with the sales organization was to establish what would become a customer relations department. Here she responded to complaint letters and customer suggestions. Within a year, she was in charge of new product development. This evolved from her following up on products that customers wanted. Most impressive was Tami's willingness to spend a lot of time in the field with sales consultants. She not only attended shows but even held them at her own house, something she does to this day.

Tami made a big hit with the sales organization. She loved working with these women, and to this day she's very involved with our growing national sales organization. I think she won the hearts of the consultants at the 1985 Bee when she interviewed Grandma Bonnie. Her genuine love and respect for her grandmother made everyone feel warm all over.

As things turned out, Tami, bless her heart, put in a good five years walking the floor at the plant and working with our sales consultants. She spent a lot of that time asking people, "What do you think?" and "Dad's thinking about doing this or that, but I wanted to hear what you think about it." And now she's running the whole company.

Like Tami and me, when Rachel headed manufacturing, she walked the floor every day, always spending lots of her time with plant workers. Even though she was very young, nobody resented it when she was given high-profile positions.

One of the times I was proudest of Rachel was a time most people wouldn't have even noticed. It was on a hot summer day when the temperature hit the hundred-degree mark. Rachel, who had only been with the company a short while, had just returned from a meeting in Columbus and was wearing a black suit. As she got out of her car in the parking lot, a tour bus full of guests was unloading. One woman recognized Rachel and asked her to sign her basket. Rachel ended up standing in that blistering parking lot, signing baskets for a good solid hour. I happened to witness this, and it made my day. Rachel put aside her busy schedule and her own personal comfort for the customers. She understands that people always come first.

■ SHOOT FOR THE STARS

As young girls, my daughters had a front-row seat watching our family business grow. They were there to witness all the early struggles and obstacles I had to overcome. I also made sure they understood where I came from—being one of twelve children, having difficulties in school, spending years driving a bread truck, and getting some hard knocks starting my own businesses. I've constantly reminded them that if somebody like me could succeed in this world, they could achieve anything they wanted. Thank God, they believed me.

Their mother and I always encouraged Tami and Rachel to shoot for the stars. As girls, they never faced barriers or restrictions, and so they became women who believed no glass ceiling would ever limit their growth.

When it was time for college, I asked each one, "What do you want to be?"

"I don't know, Dad. What do you want me to be?"

"I don't know."

"What do you think I should do?"

"Do whatever you want," I'd answer. "You could run this grocery store. Shoot, there's nothing to it. If I can do it, you can do it. You could run The Longaberger Company. It's up to you to do whatever you want."

I suppose they heard Laura and me tell them this so much that they never had any doubts about how far in this world they could go. Their destiny was in their hands. They controlled it.

Unfortunately, many parents handicap their daughters. They may not do it intentionally, but they do it all the same because they limit their ambitions. Many of these same parents encourage their sons to set lofty goals, but by not doing the same for their daughters, they lower the bar by subconsciously setting lower standards.

Many fathers do this unwittingly by talking business only with their sons. Entrepreneurs do it when they invite their young sons to work in their business but exclude their daughters. Perhaps these parents want to protect their little girls, or they think girls shouldn't sweat or get their hands dirty. Consequently, when these girls are older, they don't understand the nitty-gritty of the business because they weren't allowed to experience it. No wonder many daughters are unable to relate to coworkers; they never had to roll up their sleeves and work side by side. Unknowingly, many parents make it difficult for their daughters to achieve success in managerial positions.

As you can see, it's not just what parents tell their daughters; it's what they show them as well. It's one thing to tell little girls they can be anything they want, but it's another to back up your words with actions. You have to walk the talk.

Entrepreneurs who fail to realize that their daughters have equal potential in joining the family business miss out on a golden opportunity. My objective was never to groom Tami and Rachel to work with me in my business. I only wanted them to grow up to be strong, confident women. I was never concerned about whether they would someday choose to work for The Longaberger Company. That was strictly their option. Their coming aboard turned out to be a blessing for me far beyond my expectations. They have made tremendous contributions to the company, and without them I can't imagine how we could have succeeded as we have today. Both have been members of the board of directors for many years, and each has held a variety of management positions. In 1998, at age thirty-seven, Tami became CEO in addition to president of The Longaberger Company. That same year, I established The Longaberger Foundation and appointed Rachel, age thirty, to be president.

As an added bonus, as a small company, we operated as a family business. We worked hard at making our employees feel like family. And today, even with seven thousand employees, we work hard to preserve that family feeling.

When I take a look at Tami and Rachel today, it's hard to believe that these two lovely, charming women could be my daughters. They are such a source of pride and joy to me.

I am a very lucky man.

7

Hard Times

In Dresden, when we say, "He's been to the fair," we're talking about someone who has had his share of ups and downs and survived them. Having been to the fair, I can tell you nobody is so charmed that he or she can whiz through life without adversity.

I had my share at an early age. In addition to epilepsy and a terrible stutter, I had a learning disability. But back then that's not what they called it. In those days, if you did poorly in school, they called you a dummy. A kid held back three times was destined to become the village idiot.

"Poor Popeye, life dealt him a bad hand," some people said.

I never looked at it that way—not even as a kid. I consider myself blessed because my early adversities toughened me up. They enabled me to handle much larger problems later in life. The person I feel sorry for is the guy who has life so easy, he never has to push himself to do well. He never studies to make the honor role, he is the school's top athlete, and he's so good-looking, every girl in school has a crush on him. Life has been good to him. So good, it could eventually come to haunt him. In time, it could make him soft. Adversity might catch him off guard, and he'll be devastated.

When I look back at the trials I had, I can see that I was being prepared for much higher hurdles to come. Had I never met adversity head-on, the difficulties I faced in business would have likely overwhelmed me.

I once read a story about Winston Churchill, who had been asked to give a commencement speech and say something that his young audience would never forget. He walked up to the podium with a written copy of the speech in his hand. He looked at his audience and said exactly five words: "Never, never, never give up."

Then, without another word, Churchill walked away from the podium. I believe that for the rest of their lives, everyone in that room remembered his message. Had he spoken for two hours, he couldn't have made his point more clearly. To me, the key is the ability to get through tragedy, get over it, and thrive afterward. Believe me, we've been through sixteen kinds of hell to get our company off its feet, but we never gave up.

When I started The Longaberger Company, I knew it was a risky venture, that I was highly leveraged, and that I had very little margin for error. Being thinly capitalized, if I didn't fix problems as they occurred, I wouldn't be around to handle new ones.

An entrepreneur is by definition a risk taker. But in my case, risk was greater than normal because I was headed into uncharted waters. In the seventies it seemed nobody made baskets domestically. Decades had passed since an American basket company had prospered. Then, along came Dave Longaberger with a vision that the American consumer would crave a product that had gone the way of the buggy whip. To most people, I might as well have started a buggy whip company!

I always had faith in our product because our baskets were superior to anything in the marketplace. I knew that some people wanted only the best and wouldn't settle for anything less, but in retail outlets the baskets sat and collected dust. Virtually all attempts to sell them retail failed miserably. It was only after I met with Charleen Cuckovich that I realized we needed to take a different approach, and so we got into direct selling. But setting up a successful direct sales organization is no easy task. It takes a great deal of time and patience to build a strong sales force and an adequate infrastructure.

When outsiders look at our company today, they see a prosperous business with large manufacturing facilities, a beautiful headquarters, professional full-color sales materials, and a dynamic sales organization. It doesn't appear as though we've ever struggled. They say, "Dave Longaberger is a lucky man who was in the right place at the right time."

But building that dynamic sales organization was one of my first obstacles. Many associates I asked to sell our products were constantly being warned by their families that it was "just a matter of time before

Dave Longaberger would be out of business." Admittedly, my style of doing business has always been a tad peculiar. In the eyes of many, I didn't appear to know what I was doing. And those husbands dragged to Dresden by their wives only had to take one look at our dilapidated building to see that we were a rinky-dink operation, doomed to fail. It didn't get any better when they met me. My cussing offended many of the women, as well as their husbands. (Of course, I was not the sophisticated, well-mannered man I am today!) I was just trying to be me, but those people didn't understand. Plus the first handful of women who worked for me in the plant had to wait six months before I could finally pay them. Sometimes they were even told not to cash their paychecks for several days after I had signed them. It's not surprising that a job with The Longaberger Company didn't look like a choice career.

Now remember that back in the seventies, fewer women had careers outside the home than they do today, especially in Dresden. Women mostly relied on their husbands' judgment; business was a male domain. Men simply didn't think much about baskets, and they saw zero potential in our company. In addition, back then many people viewed direct selling as a dead-end job, something you did because you couldn't get or hold down a "real" job. Finally, selling on straight commission is nerve-racking for many folks. It was bad enough that our consultants had to overcome their own fears and insecurities. They also had to contend with their families' fears and insecurities.

Today the casual observer, familiar with the phenomenal growth we've enjoyed in recent years, sees this as an easy business. People say, "Why didn't I think of that?"

But those who had front-row seats in the early days have a different perspective. They remember the dilapidated factory with the leaky roof. They went to the one-day sales convention in a grade school gym and drank warm, watery punch. And they squirmed while listening to some guy called "Popeye" stuttering through his dreams that stretched the imagination.

We've come a long way, baby! To our good fortune, we've been able to recruit top-level outside management. Tom Reidy, our general counsel, was formerly with Porter, Wright, Morris and Arthur, a large Columbus-based law firm. Stephanie Imhoff, who had worked with our auditing firm, Ernst & Young, joined us in 1992 as a senior executive. Today Stephanie is our chief financial officer. Tom and Stephanie are just two of an impressive group of young, vibrant managers. Many of our sales directors have six-figure annual incomes. This, too, is a mark of our success.

With a string of record-breaking years behind us, people tend to forget the hard times we faced. I hope we never do.

■ WHEN I LOST POPEYE'S

Our failures and near disasters are as much a part of our history as our successes. Fortunately, we have learned from these past mistakes, and while we will surely make others in the future, we don't intend to make the same ones again.

I bought the old woolen mill in 1977 when we had five weavers. Although I bought it for a song, I spent a lot of money making it functional. Just roofing a thirty-four-thousand-square-foot building is a big expense. But in addition to a roof we needed everything from plumbing and heating to adequate wiring, and these were just the basics. We also needed equipment, inventory, and everything else it takes to run a manufacturing plant. Within two years, we had 94 consultants and 35 employees, and by 1980 we were up to 236 consultants and 130 employees. This meant a lot of spending to support this growing business.

In 1978 I expanded Popeye's to seat 164 customers. By 1980 I was $400,000 in debt to the bank. Three times I had used the deeds to my house, the restaurant, and the grocery as collateral. As long as interest rates were reasonable, being highly leveraged was a good business strategy. Since I had no money, I really had no other choice. I had bought the restaurant, the grocery, and the old woolen mill on land contracts. Interest rates were well under 10 percent during the sixties and early seventies. I generated enough to pay off my debt and still have a decent after-tax profit. Even in the seventies I could still borrow with no money down, although by 1972 interest rates had started to creep up. In fact, in early 1972, the prime rate was around 5 percent, but by September 1973 it had jumped to 10 percent. This was the first time in decades it had reached double digits. It finally peaked at a record high of around 21 percent in December 1980. You know that the prime rate is what banks charge their best customers. That left me out. I didn't qualify. So I was borrowing money above prime rate.

Can you imagine paying interest of 23 percent? This had jacked up my loan payments to $10,000 a month. Tami was in college, so I was also paying her tuition. I was having a serious cash flow problem.

The restaurant and grocery were making good money. I could have covered my debt with those two businesses. My financial problems were caused by the basket company. Month after month it lost money, and I kept pouring more into it, taking away from my two healthy businesses. Even though the basket company revenues were growing, costs kept skyrocketing. I couldn't cut back on overhead; that would have meant no growth. Without growth, the company would never operate in the black. I truly believed that it would eventually turn the corner and be self-sustaining.

Most people looked at me and figured I didn't have a worry in the world. But I kept thinking about all those bills and wondering where I would get the money to pay them.

The most obvious solution would have been to shut down the basket company. Along with my accountant, my brothers advised, "Get out while you can, Popeye. It's a losing battle. If you stay in it, you'll not only lose the company; you'll lose everything."

"No," I said. "I'll sell Popeye's."

"Why would you sell your cash cow? Get out of the basket business while you still can!" But I was set on keeping it.

I approached the bank and asked to refinance my loan on the restaurant. I figured that if I could have more time to pay off my debt, the payments would be low enough to allow me a little breathing room. The bank refused and instead financed the purchase of Popeye's by a family with no business experience, let alone a restaurant background. The bank also extended the loan to them over a longer period at a lower interest rate. Why in the world would they pick them over me, I kept asking myself. I really know this restaurant business, and I know how to make it work. It made no sense to me that the bank would force me to give up Popeye's.

I cried for two days after I lost Popeye's. I was heartbroken.

■ INTERNAL REVENUE WOES

Selling Popeye's reduced my bank debt, but it didn't solve my cash flow problems. The restaurant provided me with a steady stream of revenue to support my basket venture. It also gave me money to live on. Now the grocery would have to carry everything until the basket company could turn a profit. This put added pressure on me. The year was 1981, and I had yet to make a dime selling baskets. There was no guarantee I ever would.

The biggest thing that made me toss and turn in my sleep was the $50,000 I owed the Internal Revenue Service. It was as if I had a one hundred-pound monkey on my back and I couldn't shake it off. I had never been in trouble with the IRS, but I had heard horror stories about people who had fallen behind in their taxes. I had always believed that the only thing worse than owing money to the IRS would be owing money to the Mafia.

My IRS troubles began when the basket company failed to pay its withholding taxes. I couldn't meet the payroll and pay the taxes, too, so I decided I'd give what money I did have to my people. They had to buy groceries and make mortgage payments. Paying them was always my first priority. I decided the government could wait for its money. Now, I had every intention of paying these taxes, but I would do it when I had the money to spare. After all, you can't get blood from a turnip. I wasn't living high off the hog. At the time, our revenues were around $5 million, and I was living in an efficiency apartment.

When the agent from the IRS arrived at the plant early one morning in 1982, I wasn't surprised to see him. I knew that sooner or later, the government asks for its money. Besides, I had already received calls and letters warning me to pay up or they'd padlock the place. At the time, both the plant and the office were on Chestnut Street. So it looked like he only needed to make one trip.

I was shaking like a leaf when this short, mean-looking man said, "Is there a place where we could talk privately, Mr. Longaberger?"

"Yes, sir. Just follow me," I answered, leading the way to my office.

Boy, I thought, he looks tough as nails. Of all the IRS agents in the country, I had to get this one.

When we sat down, I thought, I've got nothing to lose, so I'll make one last pitch. What the hell, what's the worst thing that could happen? He won't shoot me.

"I know I owe the money, and I intend to pay it," I said.

He gave me a cold stare and said flatly if we couldn't pay the taxes, he'd come prepared to padlock the building.

"You leave us no choice," he said. "I intend to close you down today."

"If you put us out of business," I said, "I'll never be able to pay a cent. And all these people who work here will be out of jobs. You know if they're unemployed, the government will have to pay them until they find other jobs. And they won't pay any income taxes, either. Isn't that right?"

The agent didn't respond, so I continued, "If there's a way we can work things to stay open, I'll eventually pay every penny due the IRS. The government won't have to lose anything. Don't you think that's a better solution for everybody? The government gets its money, I stay in business, and all those employees and their families stay off welfare. Isn't everyone better off this way?"

Still he remained silent, with a blank expression on his face. Never play poker with this guy, I thought.

"Would you please take a look at our records? I'd like you to know a few things about our company."

He nodded, so I took out our books and spent the next hour showing him our financial statements, explaining why we were having such serious problems. Then I offered to show him around the plant so he could see how our baskets were made. He said that he would like that.

I talked a lot about what I wanted to do with the business in the future. He took it all in, hardly saying a word. He spent the next three hours going over the books a second time.

"You can see that our sales keep going up," I explained. "You can also see how we're starting to reduce labor and material costs. Unless I'm missing something, anyone can see that it's only a matter of time until we're in for a big payday."

Looking at me over his glasses, he said, "Dave, there is no reason why the bank shouldn't give you $50,000 to pay us."

When he said that, I said silently, thank you. "Would you call my banker and tell him that?" I asked.

The agent consented to call the bank the following morning. Just before noon the next day, my banker called.

"Dave, you don't ask the Internal Revenue Service to call me to lend you money to pay your taxes."

"Well, I did," I said. "Are you going to lend it to me?"

"No."

I called the IRS agent and gave him the news.

"I thought it over," he said. "We're going to set you up on payments."

"You're going to lend me the money?" I blurted out.

"Now, you can't miss a single payment," he warned me.

We didn't. We paid back $50,000 over the next twelve months. The bank was willing to let me go down the tubes, and the IRS became my knight in shining armor. I took back all those bad things I had said about the agent. He might have been a mean-looking guy, but he had a heart as big as his whole body.

If someone tells me today about how he cheated the IRS, I always ask, "What do you have against the government?"

"Nothing," they answer. "Everyone does it."

I tell them what my dad always said: "This is a great country." Then I add, "If we don't pay the government what we owe, we can't keep it going. Then what will we do?"

■ THE HANDSHAKE

In the mid-1970s, I first met with Charles Kimberly and his wife, Wilma, who owned the Asplin Basket Company in Hartville, Ohio. I worked out a deal with "Kim" so his veneer company would be our source for splints. We were still in our first little building on Main Street. Every Saturday, Kenny Birkhimer, one other weaver, and I would make the two-hour trip to Hartville in my old truck. Asplin would cut the wood we selected into splints, which we loaded onto the truck and took back to Dresden. Back at the shop we'd spread the splints out on the ground to dry just like my dad did it. On Sunday, we'd go back to the shop to flip them over. Later that same afternoon we'd rebundle them so they'd be ready for the weavers on Monday morning. As you can see, this process basically took up the whole weekend. I never really had a day off.

By the early eighties we had become the Asplin Basket Company's biggest customer. Meanwhile, Kim was getting up in years and decided he wanted to get out of the business. Since his company was my only source for raw materials, I had no choice but to figure out a way to buy him out. Like every other time I bought real estate, I didn't have any money. The property itself had little value, and the machinery was obsolete. These were the company's only tangible assets, and obviously not the kind of collateral a bank wanted to justify a loan. So once again, the bank refused to finance me.

Nonetheless, I made an appointment to meet with Kimberly. My attorney, Bob Beam, accompanied me to the meeting. On the way to

Hartville, Bob said, "Dave, tell me how you're going to buy this company."

"Well, I don't have any money, Bob," I answered, "so it will have to be on a land contract."

"Do you have some money for a down payment?" Bob asked.

"Not even that."

"You know, Dave, people usually want something down. How do you expect to make this deal?"

"With your knowledge, Bob, and my personality," I said with a smile.

Bob was rightfully skeptical, but I had known Kim for several years and I felt confident we could work something out. I knew that Kim wanted to retire and there was nobody to take over the business. If he didn't sell to me, he'd have to close up, and that would mean getting nothing. Hartville was a small town just like Dresden. Hartville's bank wasn't going to finance that building for Kimberly any more than Dresden's bank would finance it for me. I thought I was Kim's ray of hope.

Kimberly had also told me in previous conversations that if he could come up with $3,000 a month to live on, he'd retire in a heartbeat. So I set my offer high at $540,000, at payments of $3,000 a month for the next fifteen years, but with no money down. He agreed to the terms.

"It's a deal," I said, shaking his hand. "Bob will draw up the papers."

"My wife and I are going on vacation," Kimberly said. "We'll be back in a couple of weeks."

"I'll have the paperwork done when you get back," Bob promised.

About two weeks later, on a Saturday night, a fire broke out, and the Asplin Basket Company was burned to the ground. Kimberly carried only $50,000 on the place, less than 10 percent of its value. Both of the lathes were destroyed. The only thing salvageable in the entire thirty-thousand-square-foot building was the boiler. Kim's plans for retirement had gone up in smoke, and he was devastated. Already in his sixties, he was broke and saw no way even to find a job, much less retire.

I set up a meeting to see him.

"It doesn't look like we'll be doing any business," Kim said, with tears in his eyes.

"Kim, this was my fire," I told him. "It wasn't yours."

"We never signed any contract, Dave," he said.

"As far as I'm concerned, the deal was made. I gave you my word."

I paid $3,000 to Kimberly every month for the next fifteen years.

The Asplin Basket Company was two hours away from Dresden. It would have made sense to build a veneer facility at or near our existing plant, but then all the Asplin workers would be unemployed. Kim had a good crew, and I didn't want to see them lose their jobs.

I formed my own construction crew to rebuild the plant. In spite of our money problems, we managed to get it up and running in a year.

■ A LETTER TO OUR ASSOCIATES

The Hartville fire burned up more than the veneer plant; the fence we'd been walking financially went up in smoke, too. At the end of 1983, I mailed the following letter to our employees and consultants; I think it reflected the severity of our problems as well as our mood.

December 1983

DEAR ASSOCIATES:

I must now sell my only income to keep the basket business alive. There were no second thoughts about it. Every year our labor and material costs are going down and our sales are going up. To meet our bills and make sure everyone got a paycheck, I've sold my IGA store and put the money into our company.

I have heard that there are some folks who think I was foolish for selling two profitable businesses that I worked so hard to build in order to pay the bills for our company which has continued to lose money. Let those folks say what they will. I have faith in our company, in its products, and in the people who work here.

I have shown my faith by putting everything that I own into our company, and I am confident that I will not be disappointed. Each year in the life of a growing company like ours has a special meaning, and the years 1983 and 1984 will be no exception.

This year 1983 has been the most challenging year in our company's history. We have faced many challenges and many hardships together, and through hard work and patience we have overcome them. We have moved ahead and improved Longaberger Baskets in many ways in the face of challenges and hardships in a depressed economy that would have made other people quit.

As you know, our Hartville veneering plant was completely destroyed by fire in February 1983. Some companies would have closed the Hartville plant, giving up making their own high-quality weaving material.

Instead, we rebuilt that plant, installed more modern equipment, and further improved the quality of our weaving material. This decision will mean a great deal to the future of our company. Unfortunately, for 1983, it meant putting our company further into debt by one million dollars. As most of you know, Longaberger Baskets faced layoffs in the past more often than any of us wanted. When there were not enough basket orders, we just could not operate, and employees went without a paycheck.

To keep everyone working this year, we offered a hamper special in February and a magazine basket special in May. Instead of selling the 8,000 hampers that we expected, we sold 20,000 hampers. Instead of selling the 24,000 magazine baskets we expected, we sold 44,000. These sales figures are a credit to all of us and our high-quality product.

However, the sales figures, through the specials and tremendous increase in our other sales, meant that we faced the hardships of working on weekends and were forced to expand our operations even more quickly than we had planned. We had to move departments around, open a new plant in Millersburg, and hire hundreds of new people.

In 1983, we also faced additional challenges in the financial area. The Hartville fire meant that we had to buy veneer at double our cost to produce it ourselves. Specials meant extra overtime pay and additional shipping expense. The tremendous expense of training so many new people was a substantial investment of time and money.

This has been a challenging year for all of us. Of course, 1983 has not been all hardship. We have had a lot of laughs together, and we have continued to see improvements in our plant facilities that make our workdays more enjoyable and safer. We have also seen improvements in the size of our paychecks. I am proud of our accomplishments and our determination to overcome the hardships and frustrations that we have endured.

While there may be many different challenges in the years ahead, the future looks much brighter because of our efforts and determination. By training so many talented new people, we are more prepared than ever to meet the increase in demand from new customers.

We have faced challenges this year that other people might have run away from, and we won. Let's look forward to 1984 with excitement based on the knowledge of what we have achieved in the difficult days of 1983.

Sincerely,

Dave Longaberger

A VOTE OF CONFIDENCE

The same people who criticized me for selling my restaurant thought I was insane when I sold the grocery in 1983. I now owned one company—and it had never operated in the black. There were some who didn't believe we'd ever make money selling baskets.

Meanwhile, in the same year I incurred more debt to rebuild the Hartville plant, I purchased the local paper mill in Dresden because we needed additional work space for our employees. I thought surely nothing else could go wrong when a special assistant to the president of the United Food Commercial Workers came to our area. This union organizer had come to organize a nearby food processing plant. When he caught wind of us, his mouth started to water. There we were, a company with hundreds of employees, getting paid piece rate and receiving no benefits. Being on the edge of a coal mining region also worked against us, since coal workers belong to unions. Plus our working conditions left a lot to be desired. To the union, taking on our company looked like shooting fish in a barrel. If ever there looked like a sure thing to organize, we were it.

For six months, the union tried to induce our employees to unionize. It was a very difficult time for everyone. One day, the union rented the high school auditorium and invited all our employees to a formal presentation. To guarantee full attendance, the union had invited Crystal Lee Sutton as a guest speaker (Sally Field's character in the movie *Norma Rae* was based on Crystal Lee). Although she was a big attraction, only a handful of people showed up. I'm sure the reason for such a small turnout was that our people understood the company was having financial difficulties and we were doing all we could for them. With so few people in the audience, the union representative announced that the projector had broken and the meeting was canceled. Not long after that, the union organizer stopped coming around, and the employees who had been involved with him lost interest.

I was deeply touched by how our employees stood by us. Their loyalty made me all the more determined to someday give them good wages and benefits. But I was beginning to wonder if that day would ever come.

■ THE 1986 CRISIS

Although the company was growing, it continued to operate in the red. With debts of $7 million, I was facing the most difficult decision of my life.

On April 22, 1986, Tami and Rachel returned from hosting a sales incentive trip with a group of eighty sales consultants. That night, I called Tami at her home in Zanesville.

"I'd like to see you and your sister immediately," I told her. "Could you come to my house right away so we can talk?"

"I'll call Rachel," Tami said. "Give us a half hour, and we'll be there." At the time, Tami was twenty-five, and Rachel was only nineteen. They were so young that I hesitated to tell them what they soon would know. Just the same, I had never kept anything from them and I wasn't about to start now.

After graduating from The Ohio State University two years before with a degree in marketing, Tami had joined the company. She quickly found a niche in customer service and was doing a terrific job working with the sales organization. Rachel was a freshman at Ohio State. Both daughters had grown up in the business. I felt they were mature and strong enough to handle the bad news I was about to deliver.

I paced back and forth waiting for their arrival, running through my mind how I'd tell them I was getting ready to shut down the business.

Rachel arrived first. We sat down at the breakfast table and chatted while waiting for Tami. After Tami arrived, I put on a pot of coffee, and they told me about their trip with the sales field.

But there was no ignoring my anxiety. "What's up, Dad?" Tami asked.

"It's over," I said.

Neither said a word.

"It's done," I told them. "There is no way we can make it." They looked at me in disbelief. They had never heard me be so pessimistic about the future.

"It can't be," Tami said. "There's no way we can do that."

"I don't know what else we can do," I replied.

"We have to make it work, Dad," Tami said in a determined voice. "Let's focus on what we can do to stay in business."

For the next two hours, the three of us brainstormed on how to turn things around. When we concluded, we decided to have an executive meeting in the morning and present the facts to our vice presidents and directors. At the meeting, I explained that we were carrying a total of $7 million in debt.

"We have two choices," I said. "We could declare bankruptcy, or we could try to erase our debt."

Once bankruptcy was ruled out, we collectively came up with a plan. We would raise prices by 18 percent. We would eliminate specials, which at the time represented 40 percent of our sales. We would cut our product line from 170 to 70 items, and sales commissions would also have to be reduced. The hardest part of the plan included massive layoffs of our employees.

I personally knew almost every person in the group. This made it all the more important that I be the one to tell them, and it made it more painful to do so. I thought about the early days when the company was tiny, and I'd have state-of-the-company meetings with all of us sitting around a lunch table. As we grew, I'd talk to them standing on a milk crate or stain can. This time, we would all gather outside the building, and I would stand on a picnic table so I could be seen and heard by all.

"I am so sorry I let this happen," I began, accepting all the blame. I explained our predicament, giving all the details.

"It's nobody's fault but my own," I said. They could tell I was speaking from my heart, and they listened quietly. I explained how the company was paying off debt at rates as high as 23 percent. I went on to tell them how our sales organization had generated more sales than our infrastructure could handle, and as we threw money at the problem, our debt just kept growing.

"I believe we can beat this," I continued. "But to do it, nine hundred or more of you will have to be laid off, and the remaining will have to take at least a 15 percent pay cut. Hopefully, in six to seven months, I'll be able to bring you all back."

I finished speaking, and I was surprised at their reaction. Everyone seemed positive and supportive. People called out, "We're behind you, Popeye," and "Do whatever you think it takes, Popeye." They were solidly behind me—except for one guy who stood up and sounded off.

Everyone else started booing him. They even threatened to throw his butt in Wakatomika Creek, which runs behind the plant. He got the hint and left the premises.

Our next step was to communicate with our sales organization. By 1986 we had over three thousand sales consultants around the country; they, too, had to be informed about our crisis. It was imperative that we get to them quickly to avoid their hearing it through the grapevine. In all organizations like ours, bad news can spread very fast. I wished I could have spoken to all of them at the same time, but that was physically impossible. So Tami and I flew all over the country, going in different directions to meet with groups of our people. Again, we said exactly what happened, taking all the blame and always speaking straight from the heart.

Our message was that we believed the company could be saved, "if we all pull together, do our part, and make some sacrifices." We were cutting out specials, liners, and covers; raising our prices and cutting back our product line; and changing the commission plan. Finally, there would be a reduction in sales commissions. Delivery time would be tripled, and consultants were advised to notify their customers immediately. Refunds would be made to anyone who didn't want to wait.

Since orders for Longaberger baskets are paid in advance, some top-level salespeople had already sent in personal checks as big as $10,000 to $20,000. We weren't sure how they would react. We were expecting many to be angry and thought some might even resign. But we were wrong.

Incredibly, as a testament to these wonderful people, they were behind us all the way, sharing our commitment to turn the business around. Because we had always been truthful with them, they showed great faith by sticking with us. Some of the sales directors even volunteered to postpone receiving their commission checks. Tami and I were deeply touched by their loyalty.

And twenty-five-year-old Tami came through like a true champion. She worked tirelessly, crisscrossing the country, winning the respect of the entire sales organization. At first I hesitated to burden her with such an awesome responsibility. Then I quickly realized I couldn't have picked a better person. I couldn't have done it all by myself anyway. There were simply too many people to see in too short a time.

I guess the thing that touched me most through the entire ordeal was that Tami took a pay cut even though she was working harder than ever. As a result, she couldn't afford the payments on the new car she'd had for only four months. She had to sell it and buy a used car. I knew how proud she had been of her new car, and watching her trade down struck me to the heart. Although she never once said a word about it to me, it served as a strong, tangible reminder to me every day when I came to work and saw that used car in the parking lot.

Three months after our cross-country visits, we had our annual sales convention. Knowing that our top sales people would be getting together in private groups, we weren't sure what to expect. Obviously, there was a chance they could mutiny against the company—perhaps ganging up on us and demanding certain concessions.

Our worries proved foolish. In fact, our sales consultants went out there and worked harder than ever. They gave us their full support. We actually had a 10 percent increase in sales during this period. With their faith in us, our confidence was restored. It was truly a tribute to the people of The Longaberger Company—and it's something I'll never forget. We were convinced that we had the greatest sales organization in the world, and with these fine associates leading us, we were sure to succeed.

■ A BLESSING IN DISGUISE

While we never embraced adversity with open arms, I can honestly say that it has made us a better company today. It's rare to find any person or company that has scored one success after another without encountering failure along the way. Study the long-term financial charts of great companies such as IBM, General Electric, and Ford Motor Company, and you'll see valleys as well as peaks.

Speaking for The Longaberger Company, our 1986 crisis made us stronger because it forced us to work together as a team. Everyone had to pull together in a concentrated effort. It helped that everyone wanted to do his or her part. I don't recall seeing or hearing about a single slacker. The company also benefited because of the understanding that came from seeing how interdependent we all were. Even though certain people worked in one area, more or less in their own little world, they learned how and why their department needed the support of other departments for the entire company to succeed.

Throughout this ordeal, we kept everyone posted on our progress. Yes, we made some mistakes along the way. When we did, we never tried to cover it up. The message repeated again and again was: "We think we can keep going, but we need everyone's help."

There were days and weeks of burning the midnight oil. But after six months, we began to feel hopeful. We knew we were going to survive.

This crisis was also an excellent learning process for management. As Tami has said, she felt fortunate that she had been with the company since 1984 so that by 1986 she could participate in and contribute to its turnaround. From my perspective, Tami was put through a fast-forward executive training program, and she evolved into a top-notch executive. Her management skills were sharpened to an extent that otherwise would have taken several years. In short, she earned her stripes and took on a larger role in the company, leading sales and marketing at age twenty-five.

The company grew rapidly throughout the late eighties and the nineties. I believe the 1986 crisis enabled our management to meet challenges we later faced due to certain stresses on our infrastructure. While we turned the corner and actually made some money in 1988, we operated in the red in 1989. But this was the last time this happened. Again our losses were due mainly to growth, such as having to pay overtime for speeding up production so orders would stay current. We managed to hobble through 1989, and ever since 1990, with the work of a solid financial accounting department, we've made a profit.

8

Every Business Is a People Business

You hear the expression "People are a company's most valuable asset" so much that it sounds trite. But I don't think you can say it enough. Alfred Sloan, CEO of General Motors in the 1920s, once said, "Take my assets—but leave me my organization, and in five years, I'll have it all back."

In the early stages of my business career, there were times when my liabilities exceeded my assets. On paper, I had a negative net worth. When you study a financial statement, physical things like inventories, real estate, and accounts receivable are listed as a company's assets. But what financial statements don't show is the quality and loyalty of the people on a company's payroll. Nor do they put a value on the sum total of these people's experience and skills, which represent the most valuable asset of our company.

When I went to borrow money, loan officers turned me down, never considering the talent of our people. For instance, the sixteen weeks of training we give a newly hired weaver means nothing to the bank. But each skilled weaver represents a value, and now that the company has thousands of weavers, their combined total value is indeed greater than any of the company's tangible assets. The same goes for our asset-filled sales organization.

Think of it this way: if you took away all our people and left only the real estate, equipment, and other assets, how much would our company be worth today? Or, for that matter, any company? When bankers fail to place a value on people, they are way off base because people truly are a company's most valuable asset.

Of course, the value of workers is also determined by how well they are managed. If a company has poor management, the workforce won't be productive. People are not nearly as valuable when they are not properly led. Managing people is considerably different from managing any other asset. Unlike real estate, inventories, machinery, and other assets, people have emotions. So, for good reason, at The Longaberger Company, having people skills is the number one quality we evaluate when hiring, promoting, or, for that matter, demoting employees. As far as we're concerned, this is what management is all about.

■ THE PEOPLE PERSON MANAGER

A small business owner should seek out employees with people skills in the company's beginning stages. By making this a priority early on, it becomes deeply ingrained into the company culture. This concept is difficult to instill in a large company if it's been absent in the past. Making such a change is akin to a mature person trying to change his or her personality. It can happen, but it's not likely.

The phrase "people person" has a lot of different meanings, so let me tell you how I relate it to management. Simply put, to be a good people person, you have to genuinely care about other people. This means you have a sincere desire to help and serve others.

The best thing I had going for me at the start of my basket business was that I was a people person. In fact, that might have been the only thing! I couldn't afford to pay decent wages or provide benefits, and working conditions were deplorable.

A people person manager respects the individual. No matter what position an employee holds in the company, he or she deserves your respect, if for no other reason than they work for you. That's right, if someone is good enough to be employed by your company, this is enough to make him or her special. When you respect a person, it demonstrates that you care. Caring and respect go hand in hand. This attitude should also be extended to vendors and customers for the same reason. It's an attitude I believe must start at the top of a company and trickle down, because managers take their cues from the CEO and owner of a company. The lead dog sets the pace.

This doesn't mean if you give people everything they want, they will be happy, loyal employees. This is no way to run a business, and employees realize your company has to make a profit. So they don't expect to get everything they want. But everyone deserves to be treated fairly, honestly—and always with respect. And employees have every right to expect that.

Top salespeople, for example, are motivated by doing what's best for their customers. I realized this long ago during my days as a Fuller Brush salesman and later as a bread route salesman. I always did what was in the best interests of my customers. Nobody had to tell me to do it. I did it instinctively because I truly care about people. Of course, I won their loyalty, and as a result my sales grew. I wasn't doing it to make extra commissions, but that was the end result.

Later, when managing Popeye's, I observed how the best waitresses truly cared about pleasing customers. They didn't provide great service to get big tips; they did it because they wanted people to enjoy themselves. And again, while they didn't do it for the money, they were rewarded for their efforts.

In fields where you constantly deal with human beings, people skills are vital to your success. People persons make the best doctors, nurses, lawyers—and managers. It all starts with wanting to do what's best for the other guy.

"But how do I know what's best for the other guy?" you may ask. Frankly, if you're a people person, you probably won't ever have to ask this question. You just naturally treat the other guy as you would want to be treated. Believe me, this isn't complicated stuff. Just pretend you've traded places. It's that simple.

How did I keep good people? By letting them know how much I cared about them. They, in turn, cared about me. This mutual affection didn't grow out of lip service. I earned their loyalty by action. I walked the talk.

For starters, I always ran ideas by our employees, looking for feedback. This showed that I valued their opinions and judgment. I shared my visions for the future with them. By being so open, I stood on level ground with them. And I always listened to what they had to say—not just once in a blue moon but continually. It showed I thought they were important as individuals. Over a period of time, a good relationship with my people grew. To me, this is what good management is all about: building relationships. I'm constantly reminding our managers that listening builds trust and trust builds relationships.

I have always admired Sam Walton, the founder of Wal-Mart, who is known as "Mr. Sam" to his employees. There was a time, in fact, when his store managers wore buttons that said, "We Care About Our People." A driving force behind the company's success is the way Walton treated his people. One night he was unable to fall asleep, so at 2:30 A.M. he got up, headed to an all-night bakery, bought four dozen doughnuts, and headed to a Wal-Mart distribution center. He sat down at the shipping dock with some workers and had a long chat, during which he discovered that there weren't enough shower facilities. That very day Walton set about making sure two more shower stalls were installed for those workers. There are many such stories about Sam Walton, who is revered to this day, years after his death.

A word of caution: if you're going to invite your people to share their opinions, listen closely to what they tell you. Notice how Walton not only listened; he also followed through. Too often, managers go through the motions of listening but don't really hear anything. They do it because management books tell them to listen. But if you do it only for show, it's worse than not listening at all because you'll end up insulting your people. If you don't like what they tell you, let them know why. Otherwise, they won't think you're serious about wanting their feedback, and they'll stop giving it. And no matter what they tell you, thank them for being honest. Then invite them to participate in implementing their ideas.

Believe me, this kind of caring can be as effective as bonuses, stock options, and fringe benefits. Otherwise, The Longaberger Company would have never been able to hire and keep good people in the early days. Nor, do I suppose, would any start-up company.

On occasion I've done things that seemed like poor business. I did them anyway because they were good for our people. For instance, after the Asplin plant burned to the ground in 1983, it would have made more sense to rebuild near Dresden. Instead, we constructed the new plant right there in Hartville, over two hours north of us. I didn't want all those workers to lose their jobs. Well, they're intelligent people who realized that I cared about them, and they responded in kind by being loyal, caring employees. So even with the additional costs associated with having the plant two hours away, the high productivity of our Hartville employees more than makes up for it. Did I anticipate this? Frankly, I'm not that smart. But somehow, when you do the right thing for your people, it seems to come back to you in the long run.

■ RESPECT FOR THE INDIVIDUAL

Every individual who works for your company is entitled to your respect. (If I have to give you a reason, you won't get it anyhow, so I'll save the ink.)

Respect for the individual applies across the board, regardless of position or title. Every person on your payroll should be treated with equal respect and made to feel important—without exception. In Japan, companies go to extremes to demonstrate respect for the individual, emphasizing equality for all. Japanese manufacturing companies have managers and workers dress alike in jumpsuit-style uniforms. There are no private offices or executive rest rooms or dining rooms. Automotive companies like Honda, Toyota, and Mazda that have opened plants in the United States have applied their management principles in this country. Now, because of cultural differences, what works in Japan doesn't always work here, and vice versa. Nonetheless, certain aspects of human nature are the same everywhere. In my opinion, you can never go overboard in showing respect to your people. End of story.

When I bought the Hartville plant in 1983, we inherited all its employees. One of those was Stanley Patchin. If you add all the years he worked at Asplin prior to 1983, he's got over thirty years of employment with us (even though our company isn't thirty years old—go figure). Stanley, who has a profound learning disability, has a particularly hard job. He collects rubbish and scraps from the floor in the veneering area and carts them to the boiler room, where he dumps them into the furnace. The heat in the boiler room can be intense, so Stanley's job is physically demanding. It's enough to exhaust a vigorous, robust person within a few hours. Yet Stanley does this work eight hours a day, year-round.

Stanley's my buddy, and whenever I visit the Hartville plant, weather permitting, I sit with him on the dock, where we have been known to have long chats. Our people are required to wear hard hats at this plant. Stanley takes such pride in his work, he is the only employee whose hard hat is always shiny. That's because he takes it home each night to polish it. He's a delightful man, with a lovely wife and family.

Years ago, a new manager was hired who evidently didn't know about my personal relationship with Stanley. Once, while I was visiting

Hartville, I was walking through the plant with the manager. For some odd reason, I guess to impress me, he started to give Stanley hell. Stanley is a quiet person who would never cause trouble for anyone, and here this manager is jumping all over him, screaming and shouting.

"Have you ever collected rubbish all day?" I asked the manager.

"No, I can't say I have," he answered.

"Stanley," I said, "come over here. I've got a new job for you for three days."

Then I turned to the manager. "I want you to learn about Stanley's job," I continued. "I want you to do Stanley's job for the next three days. Stanley, your job is to stand and watch him."

Guess how long that manager lasted on that job? All of thirty minutes! He stormed out of the plant, and we never saw him again. Never came back, and good riddance! We don't need people like him at our company!

When our former corporate offices were at the old woolen mill in Dresden, I mowed the grass. Even when annual revenues passed $100 million, it was not unusual to see me on our fifteen-acre property, riding back and forth on my mower.

"Popeye," people would ask, "why do you still cut the grass?"

"Because I like cutting grass," I'd reply. "And it gives me a lot of time for thinking without interruption."

Having just finished mowing one hot summer afternoon, my greenies covered with perspiration and grass, I walked into the lobby. Whew, did I smell! A single waiting salesman sat reading a magazine. I stopped and said hello. He turned his head the other way.

"Hi," I repeated in a friendly voice. "Hot as hell out there today."

The salesman grunted and never looked up.

"Where you from?" I asked.

With that, he gave me a look that said, "I'm too important to talk to a mere custodian. Don't waste my time. Can't you see I've got better things to do than talk to you!"

It was clear that I was too insignificant for even the courtesy of a hello.

I went to my office immediately and asked the receptionist which purchasing agent was expecting this salesman. A half hour later, I placed a phone call.

"Mike, I know you're in a meeting with a vendor. When you're finished, would you bring him to my office?"

"Sure, Popeye," he said. "Our president wants to meet you," I heard him tell the salesman.

The salesman excitedly replied, "That's great."

Fifteen minutes later, the two of them walked into my office. I sat at my desk, still wearing my greenies. The salesman's face turned white.

"Mike, whatever business you placed with this person today, forget it. I want you to rip up the order."

Then I turned to the salesman and said, "When you learn to treat everybody as an equal, you're welcome to come back here. I don't care who the person is, whether it's an old guy mowing the grass or the man who sweeps the floor. As long as he works for this company, I expect you to treat that person with the same respect you'd show to Mike or me. But anyone who treats somebody poorly isn't welcome here. In fact, I'd rather give the business to somebody else at a higher price. So I hope you think about what I told you before you call on this company again."

I make no bones about it. That Hartville manager who mistreated Stanley and that nasty salesman really got my goat. I won't tolerate anybody treating any of our people with disrespect. In my opinion, there's simply no place in business for such behavior.

■ THINK SMALL

When we were a small company, nobody fussed about how I spent my time or with whom I chose to talk. But now I'm expected to play the role of a VIP. Frankly that's just not me! Today, some critics aren't the least bit amused when I toss a dinner roll across the room or use a cuss word at the podium. Well, the hell with them! Personally, I'm not good at putting on airs.

They say, "A man in your position shouldn't be cutting the grass, Popeye. It's not a good use of your time."

Others thought it was inappropriate for me to spend so much time with Stanley at the Hartville plant. "It doesn't look good for a CEO to be seen sitting on a loading dock with a boiler room worker," they'd say. Of course, nobody ever actually told me to my face that I shouldn't be talking to Stanley. That's because they knew I'd be all over them for putting him down.

There were things we did as a small company that got us where we are today; these are things I believe we should work hard to keep. Sure, I understand that things change as a company expands. There was a time when I personally knew every employee, as well as their spouses' and children's names. I still know a lot of employees by name, but I can't possibly keep up with all seven thousand of them, particularly the new hires. And it goes without saying, I couldn't go to lunch with all fifty thousand sales consultants—even in small groups. There aren't enough days in the year!

But believe me, we want to remember how it was when we were small because we don't want to lose what made us what we are. So while everyone else is thinking big, we're thinking small.

Yes, I know all the positive-thinking gurus preach "think big." Much of the time, no one thinks bigger than me. I think in my life I've shown that I don't have a problem thinking big. I have been criticized for thinking too big! But there is also value in thinking small. We never want to lose our personal touch. To this day, I'm either Dave or Popeye; nobody ever calls me Mr. Longaberger. Likewise, Tami and Rachel are addressed by their first names, as are all other executives. Any employee can find Tami's, Rachel's, or my phone number or e-mail address in the company directory.

As you know, factory people in small towns like Dresden, and everywhere else, don't wear suits and ties to work. I never liked getting dressed up and would have felt uncomfortable walking around the plant in a coat and tie. I dressed like everyone else on the factory floor. Frankly, I thought it would be inappropriate to do otherwise. Had I "dressed up," it would have separated me from everyone else, and I would have stood out like a sore thumb. On the floor, I wanted to blend in and be one of the guys. I didn't want to look like I didn't belong there. I've always believed that when the "suits" of a large manufacturer visit their plant, they automatically set themselves apart from the workers. It's as if they're saying they are the ruling class. What a terrible message to communicate. I want our people to feel comfortable around me so that they'll speak their minds rather than saying what they think I want to hear.

To this day, the only time I wear a tie is when we have a meeting with one of our bankers. It's not that I have anything against wearing a suit and tie. If I worked at a bank, a law office, or an investment firm, I'd wear one, too. As they say, "When in Rome, do as the Romans do." But in our business, dressing up would serve as a detriment because it could make the people in our plant feel uncomfortable. In the early days, everyone knew whenever Tami or I had an important meeting outside the company because we each had a special outfit for such occasions. When Tami first joined the company, I gave her $400 to buy clothes, and she spent the whole amount on one wool suit. She got teased a lot for blowing the money on one suit, but she knew what she was doing. Tami wanted to look her best when we met with bankers and other important people, and she sure did.

There's an old expression that says you can take the boy from the farm but you can't take the farm from the boy. I suppose the same is true with a small-town boy: I'm that boy. I've always felt most comfortable in and around Dresden, and I have no intention of ever living anywhere else. My roots are here, and this is where I belong. People around here say I haven't changed over the years. I hope I never do. I still drive a jeep, visit all my favorite stomping grounds, and have the same friends as when I didn't have two dimes to rub together.

My employees razz me about the many occasions when they had to pick up the tab because I never used to carry any money. The truth is, I still don't, and I still leave them with the check. Rusty Deaton, our vice president of development, has never let me forget the time he and I were on our way to a real estate closing in Newark. We stopped at a little diner for breakfast, and when the waitress handed me a check for $6.70, I pulled out my wallet. It was empty.

"Do you mind taking care of this?" I said, handing it to Rusty.

Rusty didn't have any money either, so he asked the waitress if she'd take a personal check. She said the diner didn't accept checks. Rusty turned to me and asked, "What are we going to do?"

"Do you have any money in your car?" I asked him.

Rusty said there would be some change for parking meters and so on. He left the diner and a few minutes later returned with two paper cups full of change. He poured out the change, and we counted $5.20. "That's not enough," I said to him. "I might have some nickels and pennies in my car. Give me those cups."

Five minutes later, I came in and poured my change on the table. We had just over $7. We placed all the money on the counter, and I said to Rusty, "We're out of here."

Now, in my briefcase there was a certified check for over $1 million. And I didn't have enough cash on me to leave the waitress a decent tip!

■ A BIG ADVANTAGE TO THINKING SMALL

Billion-dollar companies are prone to lose their competitive edge; they often shy away from new ventures that seem too small because they offer only marginal short-term potential. For example, a national grocery chain wouldn't have much interest in acquiring a mom-and-pop food market. A large department store chain would pass on testing a young men's specialty store in a shopping mall.

Entrepreneurs who operate on a shoestring benefit from being forced to learn the ropes from scratch. Basically, they serve an apprenticeship, and in the process they gain invaluable firsthand knowledge of what makes the business work, many times through trial and error. Expansion comes gradually, one step at a time. This is how McDonald's Ray Kroc and IBM's Thomas Watson, Sr., actually began.

Although it may not be apparent, start-up companies enjoy a benefit that money can't buy—and could ruin. Big companies tend to throw money at problems that can't be solved with money. Doing this is a waste of both money and time because the problems don't go away. Small companies with empty pockets must rely on innovation to find solutions. When companies reach the point where they try to buy their way out of problems, something precious is lost. And those who scrimp and scrape to survive eventually become formidable competitors.

The bigger The Longaberger Company grows, the harder we work at thinking small.

■ BREEZE TIME

Nearly twenty years ago business management gurus Tom Peters and Robert Waterman Jr. wrote a best-selling book called *In Search of Excellence*. It introduced America to their philosophy of MBWA: "management by wandering around"—and set America's business community on its ear. MBWA says that managers should listen to workers and customers. To do this, they must get out into plants and retail outlets and meet people. Then, they must listen. This way, they will learn solutions to their problems.

Long before *In Search of Excellence* was published, I was wandering around, talking and listening to our people. Some managers, however, only wander; they go through the motions of being on the factory floor, but they don't "connect" with anyone. That's because they come across as insincere. Their employees are unlikely to level with them. Those managers only go through the motions, but their hearts aren't in it.

For instance, the boss will start out asking, "How's it going today?"

The worker says, "Everything is just fine, boss."

Then he'll ask, "Any problems? Are you being treated okay?"

That worker just nods. "Things couldn't be better."

It reminds me of those old war movies where the general would visit the troops. What else can an enlisted man say when asked, "You doing okay, soldier?"

The soldier says, "Yes, sir." No way is he going to tell it like it really is.

"How's your sergeant treating you?"

"Fine, sir."

"The chow all right?"

"Fine, sir."

I walk the plant floor so often that I can call many of the employees by name. And I don't wear a suit. In fact, I sometimes wear my greenies, so some of the workers are actually better dressed than I am. I ask important questions like "Did your wife have that baby yet?" or "How's your golf game?" I don't just do it to make small talk. I genuinely want to know how they are. Sometimes I'll tell them a joke, and they know I like it when they tell one back to me. At our company, we call this "breeze time," as in "shooting the breeze."

If somebody calls me Mr. Longaberger, I'll say, "You must be new here. You can call me Popeye or Dave, but please don't call me Mr. Longaberger."

When a manager walks the floor and her people don't look up, that company has a major problem. I've seen executives walk through their plants, and as they go by, everyone's head goes down. You can tell they're thinking, "Boy, I better look like I'm doing my job." The message is that the people don't feel comfortable around their managers.

In every organization, there's a grapevine. Some CEOs do their best to ignore it, but I consider it very important. Even as a kid when I heard customers talk in a grocery store, I would pick up on what they liked and disliked. At The Longaberger Company, whenever I wanted to hear what people were thinking, I'd go sit in the break area. While I was talking to somebody, I'd have an ear open to what people nearby were talking about. I can go out on that floor today and pick up information about what's going to happen a month from now. More often than not, it comes true. I'm talking about things that I'd never learn about so soon at the corporate office. You can talk all you want about today's sophisticated communication systems, but no computer in the world can keep up with the grapevine.

On any given day, although I can't remember all the names, I can still say hello to people instead of just walking by. I love it when I'm on the floor and they come up to me saying, "Popeye, how are you doing?" The fact is, they swarm around me—and there's nothing that makes me feel better.

A lot of old-timers are still around, and because they feel comfortable walking right up to me, the newer people do, too. This comfort level was established over time because it's built on relationships. And relationships don't just happen; you have to work at them.

In June 1997 I was diagnosed with renal cell cancer, and recently I have been receiving treatment at the M. D. Anderson Cancer Clinic in Houston. We shared my news with our employees, and they're kept current on my condition. A couple of weeks ago, they were told that the cancer had spread; there were some small tumors on my brain. When I returned from Houston, I visited the plant. This is my therapy. I needed a shot of those warm feelings I get when I'm out on the floor. Mary Farmer, executive director of basket making, who has been with us for more than twenty years, drove me around in a battery-powered cart because I was feeling weak. At one work station, a dozen or so old-timers gathered around to wish me well.

Although I knew each of them like my own family, I pretended I didn't know them. I said to Mary, "Who's that?" I pointed to a few and said, "Those people look familiar. Do I know them?"

Evidently I must have pulled off my little joke too well! Suddenly everyone became very quiet, and some even had tears in their eyes. Those employees who have been with us for years had no idea that I was acting.

"What's wrong with you people?" I asked. "Do you think I have lost my mind? I know who you are!"

When everyone realized I was kidding around, they burst out laughing. I had a terrific time. Although I was tired, touring the plant was the right dose of medicine for me.

While my wandering had started on the plant floor, it's now routine at the home office. Supervisors are encouraged to take time to listen when someone has a personal problem. Some companies think this is a waste of valuable time; letting an employee vent her troubles is considered taboo. Not us! If they lose half an hour, so what? We believe it pays off in the long run because it shows people we care about them. For this reason, Stephanie Imhoff resisted moving to an office on the seventh floor next to Tami's. Tami wanted Stephanie, our chief financial officer, close by so they could brainstorm. Stephanie was flattered, but she wanted to stay closer to her department, which was on another floor. Stephanie had the right idea. She was overruled because her expert financial advice is in such demand on the executive floor. But Stephanie is such a great people person, she goes out of her way to spend as much time as she can downstairs with the people she supervises.

I believe it's vital for managers to stay in touch with their people. In fact, I think a good CEO or chairman should spend 75 percent of his time out in the field or on the floor. Only then will your people feel at ease in your presence—and comfortable enough to tell you the way everything really is. Why are people like this? It's human nature to avoid confrontation, especially with senior management.

Customers behave the same way. They don't want to set themselves up for an unpleasant experience.

"What do you think about our new line of sportswear?" a department store CEO who's walking the floor asks a middle-aged couple.

"We like it very much," they reply.

Once out the door, the husband says, "What garbage! That's the last time you'll ever see me in that store."

What did the couple have to gain by telling the truth? By giving an honest opinion, they might risk offending the CEO or getting stuck in an uncomfortable conversation. So what do they do? They take the safe road. Who needs the aggravation?

I once introduced myself to a customer in a local Dresden furniture store and asked her opinion on a dresser. I myself didn't like it.

"It's very nice," she said sheepishly.

Several other customers reacted the same way. I thought, it must be my taste. Maybe it really is a nice piece of furniture. But their body language said they weren't being straight with me. That evening, at a friend's house, the host asked me if I liked their new sofa. It was gaudy, but I couldn't tell him that so I nodded, saying, "Looks fine to me."

So there I was, being polite to avoid confrontation. I was just like those customers at the store who keep their opinions to themselves because I didn't believe he really wanted to hear the truth. He simply wanted reassurance that he had done the right thing.

When business is down, big corporations spend lots of money hiring consultants. That's a joke because consultants don't know beans about these companies. The saying goes, "A consultant is someone you hire to tell you the time with your watch. Then he keeps the watch."

My advice to anyone who has brought in consultants: kick them out. Then get in there with your people, tell them your problems, and ask for their help. When you do, speak from the heart. I guarantee you they'll open up, and it won't cost you a dime.

■ THE BEST SOURCE FOR SOLUTIONS

At The Longaberger Company, we have seven thousand employees, with experience totaling tens of thousands of years. Who better to give me the answers? Among them are the solutions to all problems we may have. And when we consider the knowledge of our fifty-thousand sales consultants, we have hundreds of thousands of years' worth of experience. That's quite a large source of information. It would be nonsense for a company to have this available resource and not tap into it.

I'm smart enough to realize that all those people working for us know a hell of a lot more than I'll ever know. Only a fool would refuse to ask for their opinions. I believe the secret of good management is to go out there and get all those ideas, put them in a blender, turn it on, and see what comes up. You just have to get out and do it. Don't send a memo or let them know when to expect you. Just show up. Later on, in your managers' meeting, you'll be informed. You won't be second-guessing anybody or wondering what's going on. This approach works in big business just like in small companies.

During our 1986 crisis, Tami and I went in separate directions to meet with our salespeople throughout the country. We told them about our mistakes and asked them how they thought we could fix things. Today, as our CEO, Tami is constantly asking our people for feedback.

While Tami may be the head of the company, she never claims to know all the answers.

"We're just average people," says Tami. "I've never run a $700 million company. Every year I have to do things that I've never done before. I'd like you to tell me what you think. I enjoy the challenge of new adventures. But I would never go on an adventure alone. It takes all of us, so tell me what you think."

When Tami says this to our staff, she speaks from the heart. And because she's so sincere, they tell her what they think—from the heart.

■ HAVING A SENSE OF HUMOR

Believe me, a good sense of humor is a strong asset in business. Sometimes it can be just the right thing to soothe an otherwise stressful situation. Like the time we were roasting that summer at the old woolen mill. I didn't have the money to install a cooling system, so I put up Christmas decorations in the middle of July. Instead of everyone complaining, they laughed and sweated out the heat wave while maintaining a good attitude.

Then there was the time when the Dresden Swim Center was being completed. The new swimming pool had just been filled with water, and I was talking to a construction crew when Rusty Deaton came by. He had just come from an outside meeting and was wearing a suit and tie. There were two diving boards. I was standing on one, and Rusty walked to the edge of the other.

"Hey, Dave," he challenged me, "let's be the first ones in the pool. If you jump in with your clothes on, so will I."

"Okay, Rusty, the last one in is a rotten egg."

"Hey, Dave, I was just kidding," Rusty said.

"Oh, no, a dare is a dare," I insisted.

"Let me take off my suit jacket and shoes," Rusty pleaded.

"Nope, we both jump in just like we're dressed," I answered.

On the count of three we both jumped in. The poor guy. But we had a good time, and the construction workers got a great laugh!

Years ago, I walked into the office of Terri Baldwin, a member of our accounting and finance group. Her office was so small it was like a closet. Although Terri never complained, I knew she wanted more space.

"Do you know what this office needs?" I said to her. "It needs a window."

"Yes, would you please give me one?" she said.

"Yes, ma'am," I said, and I drew a window on her wall with my pen. "There. Now shut up," I teased her. "You got your window."

Almost always I'm able to find a place for humor in business. While some people don't consider it appropriate, I think it serves a purpose. If nothing else, humor relaxes people. In awkward situations, it can be an excellent icebreaker. Humor is also a great motivator. A light touch of humor at the right moment puts everyone in a friendly mood so we can work toward the benefit of all sides.

Of course there are many kinds of humor. I've been known to tell some off-color jokes, but I never aim to insult another person. I'm more likely to make myself the butt of the joke. By making fun of yourself, you come across as nonthreatening. People with disabilities sometimes do this to put others at ease. For instance, a blind person might say, "I love what you're wearing," just to let people know that he doesn't have any hangups about what others might perceive as a problem. It's as if he's saying, "I know you know I have a disability, but since it doesn't bother me, you shouldn't let it bother you." This lets people know that he's really not that different from any other person.

■ THE POWER OF BELIEVING

I often wonder what would have happened if one of my schoolteachers had encouraged me. Not one of them ever said, "I have confidence in you, Dave, and I know if you apply yourself, you can be a top student." What a difference that could have made in my life. I would have thrived on it. We all need to have somebody believe in us, especially as kids.

Growing up, I got my strokes outside school, working at the grocery store, mowing grass, and shoveling snow. The more people praised me for being a good, hard worker, the harder I worked so I would not disappoint them. I didn't want to let down anybody who believed in me. I learned this lesson early on, and I have applied it throughout my life. By believing in people, you raise their level of commitment because they don't want to disappoint you.

It's amazing how people who lack self-confidence or formal training will rise to the occasion when they know someone believes in them. That's because when they see you have faith in them, they will begin to have faith in themselves.

In 1979 Mary Farmer started with the company at $2.95 an hour making basket bottoms. A year later, she was weaving baskets. By 1982, Mary was an operations manager, and she was promoted to plant manager in 1986. I had to coax her to take that job. Mary had a young child at home, and the new position was too much for her. Three months later she asked to step down. She started working as a coordinator on the factory floor, where she felt less pressured. Mary explained how she was at a time in her life when she didn't feel comfortable taking on so much responsibility. I respected her decision and said she should do what she felt in her heart. Since then, Mary has worked her way back up, and in 1998 she was named executive director of basket making, with three thousand people under her. Mary is doing a terrific job, spending very little time in her office. Like me, she loves to walk the floor, visiting people on the line.

Back in 1991, I sat down with Rachel and told her we needed to hire a human resources vice president. "We keep hiring people from the outside," I said, "and we should really be hiring someone who understands our culture."

Rachel looked at me and nodded.

"I'd really like you to do it," I told her.

"Yeah, right," she said, thinking I was joking. "If you'd like, Dad, I'll help you find someone. I'll help you interview."

"No, I really think you would do a good job," I said. "You know this business, Rachel. You grew up in it."

Rachel grinned. "What are you going to pay me?"

Rachel took over our Human Resources Department and quickly learned on the job what she had to do. She was so good that two years later, when she was twenty-five, I promoted her to vice president of manufacturing and human resources, a position she held until 1996; at that time she decided to devote herself to her most important responsibility, raising her three small children. Professionally, she focused her attention on a part-time basis on the company's philanthropic efforts.

The power of belief is a two-way street. To be a good leader, you must believe in yourself. This is how you get others to believe in you. In my case, I believed in the future of this company so much that our people started to believe in it, too. Of course, it helped that I was totally honest with them, always letting them in on the bad news along with the good news. Because they were kept informed, they learned to trust me. Their trust accounts for how they stuck with me during those bad years throughout the 1980s.

Employers should give their people credit for being smart because, believe me, they know when the company is in trouble. Oftentimes, they're the first to know. So when management denies or covers up the truth, it hurts morale. Employees conclude that management doesn't have enough faith in them to tell it like it is. It makes employees feel like they are being treated like children.

When one of our people comes to me with a new idea, I'll play devil's advocate and ask a lot of questions. I'll even give them reasons for why I think it won't work. Then I shut up and listen. I'm more interested in the person's conviction than anything else.

Sometimes an employee will say, "I'm sorry, Dave, but I can't explain to you why I think it will work, but my gut instinct says it's the right thing to do."

When I sense this person truly believes in it, I'll give my okay, even though she can't articulate her reasons. I'd rather have a person with conviction and enthusiasm institute a new program than someone who has all the answers but isn't a true believer herself. How do I know when someone believes? I can tell from the tone in her voice, her body language, and her facial expressions. As you probably know by now, I place a lot of value on these nonverbal forms of communication.

Everyone who works here knows that I welcome far-out ideas. In fact, the crazier, the better. While the first thing some managers do is think about why an idea won't work, I skip that step and focus on why it will work. I love it when someone suggests an idea I hadn't thought of, and I invite people to argue with me. They know I'll challenge them, so they come prepared to defend their position. But I do it in an unthreatening way, and I never intimidate anyone. As a result, we have an environment that encourages people to make suggestions. There's no fear of being criticized for suggesting something that doesn't make sense.

Sometimes I'll approach one of our professional people such as Tom Reidy, our in-house legal counsel. Having worked with him for a long time, I have complete confidence in Tom. I'm comfortable with his advice because he doesn't tell me what I want to hear, but instead he presents the parameters to me in which I can operate.

Sometimes Tom will say, "Dave, I hear what you've said. Now tell me what you're trying to accomplish. I'll get back to you with an answer in a day or two."

Tom might add, "What you're talking about will be difficult to implement. But after I've played with some options to get you from point A to point B, I'll review them with you, and we'll figure out how to do it. Now, it may not be how you want to do it, but as long as we get the same end result, that's what counts."

I like working with Tom because he's straightforward, yet he never tells me, "That can't be done" or "That would be illegal." Instead, he focuses on my objective and then comes back to me with some alternatives that are within the law. He'll also challenge me on how I think we can get there.

Sometimes he'll give me advice I don't want to hear and tell me, "That's the law, Dave."

Frustrated, I fire back at him, "Well then, change the law, Tom." Of course, I'm only teasing him. Then we'll review my original plan, and it will evolve into three different ideas; frequently, the alternatives are even better than what I first wanted.

Over a period of time, Tom and I have developed a wonderful rapport—again, it gets back to relationships. Tom is effective because he listens not only to my words but also to the intent behind my words. I believe in his advice and take comfort in knowing that just because I'm the boss, he won't tell me what I want to hear.

■ IF YOU'RE GOING TO HAVE A PURPOSE . . .

Every company should have a mission statement. Here's one bit of advice on the subject: make sure it's short, preferably ten words or less. Otherwise, nobody will ever remember it. Then what good is it?

I've seen mission statements running three to four paragraphs in length, but nobody remembers them. This defeats the purpose of having a mission statement. Its purpose is to give all employees a clear idea of the company's goals. This is our purpose: *to stimulate a better quality of life*. Everything we do at The Longaberger Company should do just that—stimulate a better quality of life. This philosophy is applied across the board: to our employees, independent sales associates, vendors, customers, and respective communities.

■ THE CORPORATE CULTURE

We're a $700 million company. We've grown from three hundred employees in 1981 to seven thousand in 1999. As we grow, we're making a strong effort to maintain our company culture.

There's a sense of family here, and we consciously work at keeping it, or else we'll lose it. And just like in a family, we care for one another. Right from the beginning, I let our employees know how much I cared for them. Being completely open keeps a family functional. We only confide in people we care about and trust. This openness is deeply ingrained in our company culture. And because we place a high value on relationships at our company, we have created an environment that makes people feel comfortable. It's like the relaxed feeling you get at the home of a close relative or dear friend. You feel so much at home, you can slip off your shoes.

Having fun is also part of the Longaberger culture. Generally speaking, people think they aren't supposed to have fun at work. But here, much as families set aside time for fun, say, at the dinner table or on weekends, we do the same at our company. We place such an emphasis on having fun, we even put a number on it. We think work should be 25 percent fun!

I am well aware of the value of high-tech and how it will take us into the twenty-first century. This is why we have more than one hundred people working in our Information Systems Department. These individuals are among our most dedicated and skilled employees. In an age of high-tech, part of our company's culture is what we call "high-touch," which refers to the relationships we form with our people. This is something we never want to lose. For this reason, when a new manager comes aboard, I say, "If you get hired here, I won't be the one who fires you. It will come from your employees. They'll tell us if you're treating them right and if they trust you. If they do, we'll know you have a good relationship with them."

We have quite a mix of managers. Some, like me, have no college education, and others have advanced degrees. I believe in education, and we provide tuition reimbursement for all our employees. However, I do remind everyone what counts is not how many degrees in business you have but the degree of experience you have in managing people. I've told more than one new college graduate that if you can't get along with people, your degree means nothing.

Change is also a significant part of our culture. Rather than resist change, we embrace it. From those early days when I'd stand on a staining can to tell everyone about my dreams, we were gearing ourselves for change. Everyone got used to hearing that expression from me. After we'd make a plan to do something, I'd always conclude by saying, "subject to change."

Admittedly, our company culture is not what you're likely to find as a textbook example. Many view us as a maverick company with an unusual management style. As a result, working here is great for some people, but not for everyone.

In their book *Built to Last*, James C. Collins and Jerry I. Porras explain that visionary companies have their own brand of company culture. Newly hired employees discover rather quickly whether or not they fit in. Those who don't stick around for only a relatively short time. Generally, that's the way it seems to work around here.

9

Having Vision

The word *vision* is so overused in business today that most people aren't sure what it means. Some people say it means being able to tell the future. Others use it to describe having the gift of amazing insight. Before I give my views on it, let me say that I think some people carry this idea a little too far. I know one CEO who said he had a vision while spending a weekend stranded in the wilderness on a mountaintop during a snowstorm. He went back to his company and prescribed a dedicated path to follow. Another CEO was inspired by a near-death experience that forever changed his life and way of management.

Hey, if that's what it takes to rally the troops and choose clearly defined objectives, so be it. I won't knock it. Visions like this can be effective, especially when they zero in on an exact goal. There is a definite need to have vision in business.

I have not, however, been blessed with this form of vision. My vision is the good, old-fashioned kind, not nearly as exciting as a divine revelation. My vision is the result of hard work and burning determination. I've put in long hours, and I've done a lot of thinking about solutions to my problems. I think back to my past experiences. And I think about where I'd like to be in the future and what it will take to get there. I allow my imagination to wander without limits. I think outside the box. This is where some people have said, "There he goes again. Popeye just went off the deep end." Let them say what they want. I refuse to allow them to restrain my thinking or dictate what I do.

When I first started my career, my vision about the future was all I had. Without money, why else would anyone work for me? The present was dismal, so I had to make them think about the good things that would come.

Remember, too, that the future is forever. The present is only now. The future is where people spend the rest of their lives. Our employees understood this and were willing to sacrifice a few dreary todays for many glorious tomorrows.

■ THE ESSENCE OF GOOD LEADERSHIP

My definition of leadership is to lead people into the future. A leader can only go forward. Going backward is the opposite of leading.

Right from the start, I provided leadership by talking about my vision of the future while standing on a staining can. Today Longaberger employees watch their own television network called LTV. Tapes are made in our own production studio, and broadcast over 244 TV sets located throughout our plants company-wide. These days no one has to try to hear someone talking from on top of a picnic table. We just go on TV and simultaneously talk to everyone. The network serves as a medium to broadcast announcements to our workforce. It is also a way to entertain our plant workers. We televise everything from local and national news to sporting events, but we concentrate mostly on music.

Critics said that LTV would distract workers and lower productivity; instead, it has increased their output. That's because bored factory workers don't perform well. So, once again, we demonstrate to our workers that we care about them, and they respond by caring about us.

Good leaders understand the future will be different from the present and they must embrace change. It is said that change is constant, so we must accept it. There is no alternative. Although most people know we live in an ever-changing world, they resist change. They view it as threatening because it always comes with uncertainty. Also, change requires people to do something. Accepting the status quo requires no action. When people are required to take action, there is always the possibility they could do something wrong. So they think it's safer to do nothing!

But as we well know, doing nothing is not a good way to do business. A company that never changes is doomed to fail. A good leader will not permit this to happen. His antenna is always up, constantly looking around, searching for ways to implement change, thinking ahead to the future.

People want to be led, and they will follow a good leader with vision. However, because people resist change, a leader must constantly tell them how change will make their lives better. If people continually hear what the future could hold and how to get there, in time it will seem familiar. I think the businessperson who fails to talk about future plans makes employees feel insecure. This is what starts rumors about owners selling out and laying off chunks of their workforce. You have to let people know where you plan to go and how you intend to get there. As long as your employees are with you, your future is theirs, too.

Remember, too, that visions of the future don't have to be accurate in every detail. The important thing is that you share them. As a leader, your job is to give people direction into the future. You're not a prophet, and there are too many variables along the way. You must anticipate changes that come and have backup plans. My motto, "subject to change," is well known throughout the company, which I believe is positive. Your employees will understand if you make revisions along the way, as long as you keep them informed. And as you move forward, always listen to your people. When your vision is realized, it might not be identical to the original, but it could very well be even better.

Sharing your visions with your people invites them in "on the ground floor" and gives them ownership. They know where you want to go, and with an open-door policy, they feel welcome making suggestions along the way to implement and improve on your vision. It's when employees are kept in the dark that they're most likely to resist change. Good leaders encourage their people to become involved.

Admittedly, in the beginning, some of what I told my people seemed so far-fetched it was hard for them to swallow, such as when I told them we'd sell baskets all over the country. At the time we had accounts with only a handful of tiny retail stores in and around Dresden. I promised them that someday they'd work in a large Longaberger plant that had not only central heat and air but also piped-in television. Many thought this sounded more like pipe dreams! There was no reason for anyone to believe me, except that I repeated the message over and over. I believed what I told them, so I said it with conviction. Plus I "bet the farm" on the business when I sold my restaurant and the grocery. I never shied away from putting myself into debt. A person with lesser faith would have bailed out. When others see that kind of commitment, they can have confidence in the future.

I guess they started to think I might be right because they stopped laughing. As little successes trickled in, and some of what I said came true, they would say, "You just might have something there, Popeye."

The key to being a visionary is how much you believe in your vision. To continually repeat what you yourself don't believe is downright deception. It's nothing more than telling a big lie again and again.

■ SHARE YOUR DREAMS

Many people keep their dreams to themselves. Not me. I've never been shy about telling people about my dreams. In fact, when I set a goal, I usually announce it to everybody.

I talk about it for several reasons. First, by letting my people in on it, it becomes their dream, too. I invite them to participate in making it happen. The more I involve them early on, the more supportive they are. As far as I'm concerned, it's never too soon to have your people get involved.

Second, when they're involved, I get their feedback. This helps a fuzzy idea to be shaped and improved into a spectacular idea. Most of my ideas probably would have died on the vine without input from other people.

Third, and perhaps most important, by voicing a dream or a long-term goal, I commit to it. To tell everyone about it and then not do it is like breaking a promise. A lot of people take a different approach. They keep their dreams to themselves; if they fail, nobody will know. In truth, these people have never convinced themselves that they could succeed. What's more, they don't have the conviction to give it their all.

Fourth, telling about a dream makes it a goal. Goals are essential in business because they provide direction. Without direction, individuals as well as companies drift and never get anywhere.

Have you ever had somebody confide in you that she wanted to write a book, quit her job and start her own business, or go back to school for a degree? "Promise you won't tell anybody," she insists. Over the years, I've noticed how few of these people ever reach their goals or, for that matter, ever get started.

Many times I've blurted out a particular goal to my employees, and afterward I think, what the hell made me say that? But once I'm committed, I have to find a way to make it happen. I believe that even a mediocre idea pursued with enthusiasm is far better than a great idea that just sits on the table. Sometimes, in fact, the enthusiasm and support your people give you are what make your idea succeed.

■ THEY CAN'T PUT LIMITS ON YOUR DREAMS

There's a difference between having big dreams and being a big dreamer. Walt Disney had a big dream, and so did Bill Gates. Most people, however, are just big dreamers.

One day, my accountant, my attorney, and I were getting ready to go to the bank for some money. Since banks lend money based on the customer's ability to pay it back, we were putting together some financial projections. The following day, we would present our numbers to a bank committee to show that our company would be able to meet its debt service with future earnings.

Again, let me point out that nobody has a crystal ball. A business plan that shows future income is at best a "guesstimate." If you're too conservative in your estimate of earnings, your numbers will be too low for the bank to justify the loan. If you overestimate, the bank might conclude that you're unrealistic or—even worse—that you're not very smart and don't understand your own business. In either case, you'll get turned down. The trick is to come up with financial projections that are neither too high nor too low.

My financial projections had a 30 to 50 percent compounded growth rate over the next five years. Based on our sales growth, I felt these numbers were realistic.

My accountant looked at them and laughed. "Come on, Dave," he said, "we can't show these to the bank."

"Why not?" I asked. "I believe we can do this. With some luck, we'll do even better."

"They don't mean anything," the accountant said. "They're too high. Now listen, Dave, we have some serious financial problems. We need this loan to see our way clear to get us out of this thing. Forget about your dreams, and get real."

"It's my dreams that will get us out of this thing," I answered.

Bob Beam, the attorney at the meeting, understood what I was saying. A realistic man, he advised, "I believe in your dreams, Dave, but the banker will think you're stretching things."

"The only thing that needs stretching," I said, "is his imagination."

"You're right, Dave, but we have to put some limitations on these numbers in order to have credibility at tomorrow's meeting. I recommend we put down some lower numbers that will be acceptable to the banker."

I followed Bob's advice, and we got the loan.

I've grown to admire Bob Beam since I met him years ago when we started making baskets in 1973. A friend who owned the lumberyard in Dresden recommended Bob, and I made an appointment to meet with him at his office in Zanesville. I figured the best way to explain what we did was to show him some baskets, so I carried five baskets with me and placed them on his desk.

After shaking hands, I said, "Mr. Beam, my Dad has been making these baskets for years, and I think we can sell them. I realize everybody else in the world is trying to figure out how to do things faster. But I think there will be a big demand for handmade baskets."

Bob asked me a lot of questions about my background, my Dad's basket weaving, and why I thought the handmade basket industry had disappeared. He listened intently when I explained why I believed millions of Americans would be receptive to reviving what had become a dying industry. As we talked, I was impressed with his questions and even more impressed with his sincerity in listening to my answers.

My past experiences with attorneys had been negative. Most of them only seemed interested in impressing me with how smart they were. Instead of listening to what I had to say, they would tell me what I was doing wrong, as if they were trying to make me believe I'd go out of business without their advice. Bob wasn't like that. Bob has always been straightforward with me; most important, right from the beginning, he believed in me. I felt he really cared about me, and he's been my friend and attorney ever since.

■ LITTLE IDEAS GROW INTO BIG IDEAS

You never know what can spring up from a small idea until you give it a try. For instance, our first plant tours began when a sales consultant would stop by and ask to see how we make baskets. One of Rachel's summer jobs in her early teens was showing the occasional visitor around the plant. It wasn't a major part of her work, usually only a few tours each week. Then, as the word got around that a plant tour was available, more consultants came.

"Well, let's do it for a couple of summers," I suggested, "and see how it goes."

When Rachel was in school and not available to give tours, consultants would ask, "Do you mind if I just stand around and watch the weavers?"

How could we refuse? Our receptionist would say, "Okay, but stand back here. Please don't go any closer because they have to concentrate on their work."

But the consultants were so inquisitive that they couldn't resist asking questions—and they did. The weavers complained because it slowed up their production, so we started to assign certain weavers to take turns demonstrating to visitors. After that, we hired a person to be in charge of plant tours, and she developed a video for visitors to watch. As you can see, what started out as a small idea just kept on growing.

In 1991 Sherry Colling was put in charge of guest relations. At that time, about 12,000 tourists were coming to the Manufacturing Campus each year. As more people came, we had to do more to accommodate them. That's when we got into lodging, food, and retailing. Now, with a golf course and Longaberger Homestead, this division will itself become big business. And it all started from those first tours Rachel gave at the old plant on Chestnut Street.

■ THE ART OF DELEGATION

All the vision in the world won't do you any good if you don't delegate. That's because you can't do everything yourself. There's simply not enough time in the day to get it all done. The secret to being a good manager is to surround yourself with good people and let them execute your visions. Any manager worth his salt knows this.

We've all seen executives who are weak at delegating and who spend too much time on trivial matters that could be handled by subordinates. Not only is this poor time management; it also kills team spirit.

When people are shut out, they can't be supportive. Then, too, some executives simply don't think anyone else is capable of getting the job done. It gets back to being surrounded with good people. I pick people who are smarter than I am. This way, I have complete confidence knowing they'll do what I would do.

A word of caution: while you may have bright people, even some who are specialists in their fields, as the CEO, you are the one who makes the business decisions. For example, an accountant might point out a specific way to handle an inventory problem, but he might not be aware of the effects that his approach would have on sales and marketing. He's focused on his area of special interest, but as CEO you must look at the big picture. The job of business leadership is to collect and analyze any advice received and then make a final decision. Remember, too, that specialists often have their own agenda. It's similar to how doctors might treat a cancer patient.

A surgeon says, "Let's cut out the tumor."

An oncologist says, "Let's do chemotherapy to shrink the tumor."

A radiologist says, "Let's use radiation and kill the tumor."

Each has his own approach based on his specialty. Sometimes a combination of all three approaches is the right solution.

Likewise, in business, there is a budget to meet, and each department head has his own special interest. The vice president of sales and marketing, for example, thinks that the best place to spend money is on advertising and sales promotion. The vice president of manufacturing wants to upgrade machinery and equipment. And the vice president of finance wants to reduce everyone's spending. The CEO must consider all points of view before reaching a decision.

Then, too, a business leader must evaluate the source of information he or she receives. For instance, my attorney may give me his expert legal opinion. But good legal advice is not necessarily good business advice. As the CEO, I have to make a good business decision, and how I approach it from a legal viewpoint is only part of the big picture. A lawyer might tell me to submit a one-sided, ironclad contract to a third party. "You have to protect yourself," he insists. But I might think a more relaxed agreement would be better.

"It's the spirit of the contract," I argue. "Do we really have to take such a tough position?"

From past experience, I know that taking a hard line may provoke the other party to bring in his attorney. In an effort to protect his client (and make himself look good), the attorney may insist on certain revisions in the contract. Before we know it, the lawyers are at each other's throats. What started out as a friendly, low-key deal is now in the hands of the attorneys.

Now I don't want to mislead you into thinking that I don't listen to my lawyer. I pay him too much to not listen to his advice.

■ IF THEY COULD PUT A MAN ON THE MOON . . .

When we moved into our new corporate office building in Newark, Ohio, at the end of 1997, it was a dream come true. I must confess, however, not many CEOs have dreams like I do. Like constructing a $30 million freestanding giant replica of the company's trademark: a basket! The *Wall Street Journal* described it as "one of the more inventive architectural designs to hit corporate America in recent years. With a clay-colored stucco exterior and 'handles' that tower overhead, the seven-story structure has the look of the real thing."

The building is a dream I've had for so long, I'm not sure when or how it originated. I also had other visions about things with a basket theme. I once envisioned having our sales consultants drive vans that looked like a basket. When parked, they'd push a button and a handle would pop up from the roof. It would tell people a Longaberger show was in progress. I even suggested building a high-rise hotel in the shape of a Longaberger hamper basket. And I talked about having basketeers who would dance like the Rockettes. That's right, they'd be dancing baskets.

For years I spoke about building an office in the shape of a basket. In the beginning, whenever I talked about it, people looked at me like I was nuts. However, I believed in it so much, they could see I was dead serious. Besides, so many of my zany ideas came true that they started to think that anything I dreamed up could happen. These days, when I talk about one of my visions, our people start doing research on it.

I had the vision of such a building fixed in my mind, but the exact image of it was fuzzy. It made perfectly good sense to me. After all, a basket is our signature. I figured if Walt Disney could build an empire around a mouse, the Longaberger home office building could resemble a basket.

We brought in architects to design the building, and they said it would be impossible. We had several meetings, and they always said the same thing: "It can't be built."

Finally I told them, "Look, they can put a man on the moon and bring his butt back, and you're telling me we can't construct a building that looks like a basket?"

In the middle of one meeting, I walked out of the room. I came back with a medium market basket with two swinging handles, which happens to be my favorite basket. I set it on the conference table and said, "This is what I want. If you can't do it, I'll find someone who can!" I left the meeting and there was no more discussion.

Once they accepted the idea, they found a way to build it. We now have a building that's 160 times larger than the medium market basket. It measures 192 feet in length and 126 feet in width at grade, widening to 208 feet by 142 feet at the roof. The building has 180,000 square feet of office space and houses five hundred employees. Its atrium has a glass roof that allows natural light to pour down the center of the building to the first floor lobby. A grand staircase leads to conference rooms and a set of glass elevators. The building also has a 142-seat auditorium. A majority of its cherry woodwork and trim was harvested from the Longaberger Golf Club in Nashport, Ohio, dried and milled in our Malta facility, sawed and shaped at our construction wood shop, finished in our construction paint booth, and installed by our construction division. Two Longaberger 725-pound gold-leaf tags are attached to the sides of the building, each measuring 25 feet by 7 feet by 3 feet. They resemble the brass tags placed on Longaberger feature baskets, such as the Christmas Collection.

Admittedly, there were some tough issues to resolve. One was that the dimensions varied from floor to floor. The seventh floor extended about eight feet farther out than the first. We were also limited in the number of windows we could install as a result of the basket "weave" carved into the stucco. The architects suggested we etch a wood design on glass windows or put a giant basket "shell" around a traditional building. I was convinced that if I wavered even one iota, they'd jump on it like crazy. So I remained firm. Each time they mentioned a compromise, I'd point to the basket, and say, "This is what I want!"

The most difficult part of construction was the 150-ton handles, which took eighteen months to complete. The handles are two 300-foot pieces of assembled, galvanized steel that rest on 18-inch pins, just like on a real basket. A special heating element was installed to warm up the handles when the temperature drops to avoid having icicles form that could ultimately damage the glass rooftop.

Friedrich K. M. Bohm is the chairman of NBBJ, the Columbus architectural firm that designed our building. He said it "is a monument, it's a piece of pop art, it's a gigantic billboard." He adds that "the trick was to make it elegant but not kitschy—and it could have gotten kitschy very easily."

It wasn't only the architects who warned against building it. Everyone opposed it, including local residents, bankers, and even employees. But once my mind was made up, I was determined to see it through. Come hell or high water, nothing was going to stop me.

After purchasing the site, we approached our bankers. Financing on a $30 million building that looks like a giant basket was not exactly the kind of loan those guys were apt to meet with open arms. We didn't get a warm reception. They thought the rendering of the building looked silly. They were certain that I had gone off the deep end this time.

■ DOES IT SELL PRODUCT?

The cost of the building came in considerably over estimate. Today, however, the consensus of everyone—even the critics—is that the building is a home run. It's not only a magnificent headquarters; it's also a marketer's and publicist's dream come true. People come by the busload every day to see it. Touring the building is a must on every Dresden visitor's list. We've received millions of dollars of publicity in national publications such as the *Wall Street Journal, U.S. News & World Report,* the *New York Times,* and *People* magazine. When you add this into the equation, we think the price was a real bargain.

As a criterion for major expenditures, I always ask, "Does it sell product?" It's a question you hear a lot at our headquarters. For the record, our basket-shaped building sells product. It is the Longaberger crown jewel property along the twenty-six-mile corridor between Dresden and Newark, not far from our Manufacturing Campus, where tourists can stroll along a quarter-mile mezzanine to watch weavers at work and tour the gallery to learn about the company and our products. Longaberger Golf Club, an eighteen-hole championship course designed by renowned architect Arthur Hills, is currently nearing completion. This tournament-caliber course will offer five sets of tees to accommodate golfers at every skill level. It will include a twenty-five-acre practice facility with target greens, a short game area, and two putting greens. The pro shop will carry a complete line of Longaberger golf clothing and accessories.

Also under construction is Longaberger Homestead, a retail, entertainment, and dining complex with a theme of early American craftsmanship. The Homestead will capture the true essence of home and family. The "At Home" area will offer a unique experience. Shoppers will be able to wander from room to room and see how to replicate them in their own homes. Showcased products coordinate with our direct sales merchandise, suggesting inspired decorating, accessorizing, and entertaining. The Homestead will remind tourists that our entire business is centered around the home. Our products are sold in the home, our independent sales associates have their businesses in the home, and our products are used in the home.

The "At Home" area will offer a variety of demonstrations and classes. In the garden area, an expert floral designer may discuss container gardens, herb growing, or flower arranging. Children will enjoy the Play Room and our life-size Tree House. At the Crawford Barn, activities will include arts and crafts, hayrides, square dancing, and a traditional farmers' market. Visitors will see replicas of the Longaberger family home and Dad's original workshop. The Longaberger Heartland Deli and Flossie's, an ice cream shop, will offer quick meals. Or visitors can sample Italian cooking at the Terrace Café or visit the Longaberger Homestead Restaurant for some good ol' home cookin'. Diners can relax in a homey atmosphere, reminiscent of the days when Grandpa used to sit in a rocking chair on the front porch, waiting for the family to gather around the kitchen table.

I believe the millions of visitors who come to Longaberger Homestead over the next decade will go home with a highly positive feeling. They will reconnect with the past. By allowing them to witness our family history and our company heritage, we are taking our story to the next level. We will do something that's never been done before.

A single common denominator exists throughout the entire "Longaberger experience." Everything about it—from the white rail fences and manicured landscaping along Route 16 to the fine architecture—is first-class. We believe this sells product because everyone who comes here will associate our company with quality.

We never cut corners on quality. When we built the mezzanine at the plant so visitors could watch the weavers, people said we were spending too much money. Even our employees told me I was wasting money. It was expensive. We used as much steel in the mezzanine as we did in the rest of the plant walls. Why did we do it? Because it passed the "it-sells-product" test.

Needless to say, the bankers couldn't understand why a basket company would spend so much money so that people could watch its products being made. Nor, for that matter, did it make sense to them for us to invest millions of dollars in Dresden.

"Why would you put curbs on Main Street?" they challenged us. "Why would you pave new sidewalks? And why would you spend your money to plant Bartlett pear trees?"

They discouraged our buying Dresden storefronts and restoring them, especially since much of this spending occurred when the company was still losing money. I understood the bankers' concerns. The problem was that they didn't see the big picture. They could understand financing manufacturing facilities, but not to promote tourism. It wasn't our core business. You can imagine the resistance we would have gotten from shareholders had we been publicly owned!

At a town meeting at the high school auditorium, I presented our plans to the Dresden residents.

"We're telling our story across the country," I told them. "Someday, visitors will arrive by the busload. They'll need places to eat and sleep, and they'll want to shop. There's a wonderful opportunity for you people to accommodate these visitors by putting up hotels, bed-and-breakfast inns, restaurants, and shops. Why don't you get together and call it the Dresden Village Association?"

Their reaction was lukewarm at best. They listened but didn't do anything. Evidently, they didn't share the vision I had for Dresden. To them, it was a ramshackle town, a dying community whose best days were over. They thought no person in his or her right mind would come to Dresden on a pleasure trip.

A year later, I met with the people of Dresden a second time. Nobody had made the least effort to open a tourism-driven business. I never wanted us to get into retail and food businesses, but if nobody else did, then we'd take the lead. This time I told them very nicely to get the hell out of our way because we were going to do it. We started buying property on Main Street. Our first retail business was the Village Etc. Shop, a small gift shop operated by my sister Ginny Lou. As several stores and restaurants began to prosper, some locals and some out-of-towners decided to join the band. More than eighty new businesses have opened since the Village Etc. Shop, including restaurants and specialty shops that are Longaberger owned.

Many businesses have piggybacked on our success, and some of them disappoint me. The town is starting to get too commercial. Some outsiders have converted places into shops that hurt the integrity of the town. I swear, they'd turn outhouses into gift shops. It upsets me to see some of these people come in who don't care about Dresden but only want to make a quick buck.

Dresden won't be able to accommodate the large numbers of tourists we expect within the next five years, and it would break my heart to see the town become a tourist trap. That is why we decided to build Longaberger Homestead, four miles outside of Dresden, adjacent to the Longaberger Manufacturing Campus. Everything is moving forward on the Homestead project, and I anticipate we will grow to one million tourists a year. Once everything is completed, instead of being a six-hour visit for tourists, the area will take two to three days to cover.

Longaberger Homestead will complement Dresden by helping to preserve the best aspects of the town's residential community as well as its heritage and history. It will keep the number of business establishments at a level that will allow the town to remain quaint and charming. We do not expect the Homestead to take business away from the existing shops in Dresden; instead, it will attract additional tourists who will choose to visit both places.

Unfortunately, not everyone sees how Longaberger Homestead and Longaberger Golf Club tie in with the core direct-selling business. That is why some people ask, "Why are you building two golf courses?" They have even suggested I'm building my own private courses. For the record, the last time I played golf was several years ago when I hit a ball into the weeds on the ninth hole. I threw my clubs down and said, "Why am I spending all my time looking for this little ball that I can't even hit straight?" I've never hit a golf ball since.

I can't wait to have the course completed so I can sit in the clubhouse and tell people, "I want you to know that this course has never beat me," and I'll be telling them the truth.

Both golf courses will be open to the public and will be the best in

Committed to revitalizing his hometown of Dresden, Ohio, Dave invested millions of dollars to beautify Main Street. He opened Popeye's Soda Shop on the corner of Fifth and Main streets, across from the World's Largest Basket, in 1990. (The Longaberger Company)

In response to the growing interest in his basketmaking business, Dave opened a variety of retail shops and restaurants in the early 1990s to expand the guest experience for his visitors. (The Longaberger Company)

In 1992, the twelve Longaberger children posed with their mother, Bonnie. Dave is pictured in the top row, third from the left. (The Longaberger Company)

Today, hundreds of Longaberger basketmakers enjoy a state-of-the-art work environment on the company's manufacturing campus, located two miles outside of Dresden on Ohio Route 16. (The Longaberger Company)

A dynamic speaker who could captivate and motivate an audience, Dave often shared his dreams and visions for the future of The Longaberger Company with his employees, sales associates, and the surrounding communities. (The Longaberger Company)

Sales associates and customers loved to have Dave sign their baskets. Often, once he started signing, a line a block long would form. Not one for the spotlight, Dave would offer a warm smile, share a funny joke, and then thank the guest while he signed the cherished basket. (The Longaberger Company)

Charleen Cuckovich became Dave's first consultant in 1973. Today, she serves as one of The Longaberger Company's national sales directors. Dave presents Charleen with the Spirit of Longaberger Award at the national sales convention in 1995.
(The Longaberger Company)

Located just thirty-five miles east of Columbus, Ohio, in Newark, the Longaberger home office building is modeled after the Medium Market Basket. Dave's dream of creating the world's largest basket building became a reality in 1997. Today, it is home to over 500 employees.
(The Longaberger Company)

As he received the Ellis Island Medal of Honor in 1997, Dave said, "Giving back to your people and your country is absolutely the right thing to do."
(The Longaberger Company)

The Longaberger Company celebrated its twenty-fifth anniversary in 1998. Over 6,000 employees helped celebrate this important milestone at the company's home office in Newark, Ohio. (The Longaberger Company)

Three generations of the Longaberger family. From left, Tami, Rachel, and their father, Dave. Seated is Dave's mother, Bonnie. (The Longaberger Company)

In keeping with the company's mission statement, "To Stimulate a Better Quality of Life," The Longaberger Company opened the senior center in 1988. The center offers activities, meals, and transportation for area seniors. The company expanded the center and, to honor Dave's mother, renamed it the Bonnie Longaberger Senior Center in 1998.

(The Longaberger Company)

Adding to her role as president, Dave named his daughter Tami CEO in 1998.
(The Longaberger Company)

Dave named his daughter Rachel president of the Longaberger Foundation in 1998.
(Photograph by Jeffrey A. Rycus, © 2000 Rycus Associates Photography)

Dave was a dedicated father and grandfather to his daughters and grandchildren. Pictured from left to right: Back row: Tami's daughter, Claire; Tami; Dave; Rachel; Rachel's daughter, Kaitlin. Front row: Tami's son, Matthew; Rachel's sons, Dustin and Benjamin. (The Longaberger Company)

As part of Dave's vision of creating guest destinations, the Longaberger Golf Club opened in May 1999. The eighteen-hole championship public course, designed by renowned architect Arthur Hills, was named in the "Top Ten You Can Play" by *Golf Magazine* in its first year. (The Longaberger Company)

Longaberger Homestead, a retail, entertainment, and dining complex, is another attraction Dave envisioned as part of his plans for creating guest destinations. Opened in June 1999, Longaberger Homestead receives hundreds of thousands of visitors each year. (The Longaberger Company)

The Crawford Barn, considered to be one of the largest barns in Ohio, is just one of the many interesting elements at Longaberger Homestead. This barn was given to The Longaberger Company by the Crawford family when Dave agreed to move and preserve the barn for future generations to enjoy.

(The Longaberger Company)

Longaberger products have come a long way since the first baskets were displayed in Dave's grocery store. Today, Longaberger offers baskets, pottery, wrought iron, and home decor products in a variety of styles. Longaberger has become a leader in home lifestyle and decorating across the United States. (The Longaberger Company)

the area. As public courses, they will enhance the entire community. They will also be a good recruiting tool for hiring new people. I'm sure our employees will get a lot of use out of them. I anticipate the golf courses will, at best, break even. But these two beautiful properties will enhance the corridor. Visitors who don't enjoy a day of shopping just might enjoy a day of golf. It will add to the Longaberger experience. All those doubting Thomases will see the golf courses, our world head-quarters, and Longaberger Homestead and will think, "Wow!" That's the feeling we want everyone to have when they visit.

Back to the question, Why two golf courses? The answer? It sells product.

■ JUST A ONETIME COST

I've bought a lot of real estate in the Dresden-Newark area and paid top dollar for it. One reason that I pay the price is because I always buy it in our name. I don't have a dummy company to keep the owners from knowing who wants their property. That's done to keep a seller from thinking the buyer is a fat cat who can afford a high price. My track record on real estate purchases proves that if I want a property, I'll pay for it. I don't mind; there are worse reputations. This way, when people here decide to sell their property, they generally approach me first. When I buy real estate, I think about its value based on what it will be after I develop it. This way, even when I pay more than its pres-ent value, I gloat over what a great bargain I'm getting.

In 1995 Rusty Deaton and I were driving through the country look-ing for a site for future plant expansion. A large tract of land with a FOR SALE sign caught my attention. I told Rusty to pull over so we could take a look. We got out of the car and started walking up and down across the hilly, wooded area.

Ten minutes later, I said, "Look at that hill over there, Rusty. It's got a perfect dogleg to the left."

He nearly fell over because he didn't think I even knew what a dog-leg was. When the architect saw the land, he asked how we were able to find such a perfect spot for a golf course.

As vice president of development, Rusty frequently accompanies me in land acquisitions. I also discuss other major expenditures with him.

He's one of the key people whose input I've sought when we've made large capital improvements or acquisitions. Being a top financial man, Rusty lets me know when he thinks I'm spending too much money.

"It's just a onetime cost," he's heard me say many times. "Let's do it right the first time, and we won't have to do it again."

This is advice every entrepreneur should heed. Too often, people try to cut corners and end up spending more and getting less for their money. In the long run, quality pays—even when the dollars are bigger on the front end. In my opinion, it makes good sense to weigh the long-term value against the few measly dollars you'll save in the short term. This advice applies whether you're buying real estate, cars, or computers. Let's say you buy the smallest computer you can find because you're only going to type letters on it. It may serve your needs for the next year or two, until you discover it's faster and more efficient to do your bookkeeping on it, too. You end up buying the more expensive model you should have bought the first time around. You can't get your money's worth out of your old computer, and your onetime cost would now look like a real steal. See what I mean?

■ I LIVE IN THE FUTURE

Today, the single most important question I ask about every decision concerning this company is: How will it play twenty years from now? The present is already here, so it doesn't concern me. By tomorrow, today will be history. I focus on the future. I want to know how something will play in the year 2020. The decisions we make now chart the course of this company for years to come.

These days, when I think about twenty years down the road, everyone around here understands everything is subject to change. The farther out you go, the bigger the bumps are likely to be along the way. There are simply too many things that can happen. The world is changing so fast, it's impossible to accurately predict the future. Just over ten years ago, who could have predicted the collapse of the USSR, the decade-long bull stock market, or the impact of the Internet? These are only three external events that directly or indirectly affect every business in America.

Then, too, internal changes can't be precisely foreseen. In spite of my vision for this company, I'm the first to admit that it doesn't resemble what we talked about around the lunch table in the late 1970s.

This doesn't mean we shouldn't make long-term plans. Only a fool would ignore the future. It's essential to have vision in order to have direction. And a company moving toward that vision must constantly make changes along the way. An operational plan may realistically go out as far as five years, but it should always include contingencies. As changes occur, the vision provides focus and a target, which ultimately may be altered.

Some years ago, Tami and Rachel talked me into buying a condominium on a golf course in Pinehurst, North Carolina. It was a peculiar place to own for a man who doesn't play golf. But at the time we thought it would be a good retreat for executives and family, so I bought it. I used it only once in the summer of 1991, but did I ever get my money's worth. I went there alone and locked myself up. When I emerged two weeks later, I had written in longhand a twenty-year plan for our company. At the time, our sales were $140 million. I projected annual revenues through the year 1999, as well as a number we'd hit by the year 2010. These projections included sales consultants who would join us. At the time, we had 16,000, and I projected 48,000 by the end of the decade. As we began in 1999, we had over 50,000. So I actually underestimated by about 10 percent. Basically, I forecast sales based on the growth of the organization, increasing the annual sales per consultant according to what I thought the average show per consultant would bring. I included budgets for key departments. My projections were on target for each of the first five years.

My plan stressed the importance of investing back into the business by using the U.S. steel industry as an example. I pointed out how American steel companies failed to reinvest and refused to modernize. Our steel industry lost the ability to compete with foreign steelmakers, in particular the Japanese.

One of my pet sayings is: We have to mow our own grass first. My plan revealed that in 1991, we were selling to only a small percentage of the U.S. market. Since this is the world's most lucrative marketplace, we shouldn't be thinking about overseas expansion because "we have a lot of grass to mow in the good ol' U.S.A." Nevertheless, we should study the cultures of other countries during the next ten years or so.

I also covered the need to develop more skilled workers. I proposed future products and discussed the need to recruit and train additional management. How well we understand that it takes a different set of talents to run a $5 billion company than it does a $500 million company. The opportunities in the future present great challenges; the planning must be in place now so we will be prepared to meet them.

Copies of my handwritten twenty-year plan were distributed to our top managers, and it has served as a road map for the company to follow. It provided direction. And like a long road trip, there will be many detours and speed bumps along the way. A good map will get you around the detours, but the destination remains the same.

As a result of our long-term planning, we expanded our Information Systems Department to more than one hundred people. For a company our size, that's big! I confess I have no expertise in this area, but we have employed people who do. I am aware that our infrastructure depends on the department to support our long-term plans.

Accompanying the twenty-year plan for our company, I also wrote a second document that was a ten-year plan for the community. With projections of a workforce of thirty thousand, we must create an environment in which people will want to live and raise their families. The community plan focused on Muskingum, Coshocton, and Licking Counties. Several meetings with the Dresden Village Association and other chambers of commerce have since taken place. Copies of our community ten-year plan have also been distributed to civic leaders. We've had a lot of outreach, a lot of working together, and it's an ongoing effort. We view it as a partnership with the local communities.

■ THE SUCCESSION PLAN

When Tami was eighteen years old, I made her secretary of the company. She was just a freshman at The Ohio State University, but I needed somebody to sign tax returns and other official documents (many forms require signatures by two corporate officers). She and her sister were my closest kin, and Rachel was too young, so Tami got the job. To get her signature, I'd either mail papers to her or drive up to OSU. Tami enjoyed my visits because she always got a free dinner. I know I might have been jumping the gun, but I was hoping both of my daughters would someday play a major role in the company.

After graduating in 1984, Tami came to work here. During her first years, I must have told her a thousand times: "Tami, this place is not a birthright. You're going to have to earn your place. And that means earning people's respect. I can't give that to you. You earn people's respect through hard work."

I was always proud of Tami, but I confess I used to come down on her pretty hard.

"I'll tell you what I'll do, Tami," I would say. "I will give this place to someone walking down the street. I'll do it if I think he or she cares more about this place than you do. Let me tell you, young lady, it's not something you're handed just because you're my daughter."

She got the message. And did she ever rise to the occasion. She joined the company during a very difficult time, but she got right in there and rolled up her sleeves. From 1986 to 1994, when she was our sales and marketing director, our sales volume increased 2,000 percent. Over that same period, she continued to increase her level of responsibility and proved over and over again she was headed to the top of our company. In 1994 I named her company president, and in 1998 she also became CEO, both titles she truly earned.

Outside the company, both of my daughters have excelled and are making a difference. In 1994 Tami was appointed by the governor of Ohio to serve on the boards of the Ohio Building Authority, the Capitol Square Review, and the Advisory Board. She also serves on the board of the Wexner Center Foundation and the Ohio State University Board of Trustees. I've been active in the Direct Selling Association for years, so it was a happy day for me in 1993 when Tami was elected the DSA chairperson. She became the organization's youngest leader ever and was only the third woman to serve as chairperson in the eighty-six-year history of this national group.

Like her sister, Rachel has become an important member of the community. She, too, serves on many boards in a leadership role. In 1995 Rachel was appointed by the governor of Ohio to serve a five-year term on the Ohio Bureau of Workers' Compensation Oversight Commission. She is also a board member of the Ohio Manufacturers' Association, Children's Hospital in Columbus, Good Samaritan Medical Center in Zanesville, and Muskingum College. My prediction is that both women are destined to be pillars of the community—on a local, state, and national level. This makes me burst with pride.

I often wonder where my daughters find the time and energy for their busy schedules, especially as working mothers. Tami has two children, and Rachel has three. But as somebody once said, "If you want something done, give it to a busy woman."

As I've been saying for a quarter of a century, America's greatest untapped resource is its women. Today, women represent 65 percent of our company's management, and they're starting to make headway in corporate America. I predict that by 2025, a majority of the CEOs and presidents of all U.S. companies will be women. Men shake their heads when I say this, but just look at what many women are doing. I don't know many men who could manage a home with a family of four. I certainly couldn't. When I look at how my mother ran a house full of twelve children, I think about all the wonderful organizational skills she obviously had. While Tami, Rachel, and I are called overachievers, Mom was a star in her own right! In the area of time management, women have it all over men. And you can add intuition on top of that. Women are a lot more comfortable going with their gut than men are.

As you can see, I am a proud father, one who believes 100 percent in his two daughters. They are remarkable women, and while I won't take the credit, I will admit that I must have done something right. Maybe it was nothing more than believing in them, giving them some coaching and encouragement, and then being smart enough to get out of their way. Whatever it was, the three of us have a wonderful relationship, and for this I consider myself a very blessed man.

I know one thing for certain. Tami and Rachel have learned this business well over the years. Today they share my philosophy, as well as my vision for the future. I also know they have their own interests and visions, and I wouldn't want it any other way. The next generation isn't supposed to be a duplication of their parents. Tami and Rachel have high goals, and I am confident they will raise the bar.

Several years ago, prior to my bout with cancer, I began transferring my company stock to my daughters. I did this because it would soon be time to turn over the reins. When that time came, I wanted it to be a seamless transition. I've witnessed other family companies that haven't planned a smooth succession, and consequently, all hell broke loose with a sudden illness or unexpected death. I put my heart and soul into this company. Plus I love my daughters and our people too much to be a burden to them when it's time for me to check out.

A top priority of every CEO should be to put a succession plan in place. Anybody at the top who doesn't do this is irresponsible. When a plan doesn't exist, you'll generally find somebody with a big ego. It's probably a CEO who either doesn't believe anyone is good enough to replace him or foolishly believes he has plenty of time. Whatever the reason, it makes the company highly vulnerable. Without a smooth changing of the guard, a healthy company can crumble. We've worked too hard at The Longaberger Company to let that happen.

My daughters share my vision. They understand where I'm coming from and where I want this company to be. We spend a lot of our time together talking about the future. When we do, it's just a matter of time before one of us asks, "How will it play twenty years from now?"

I talk so much about the future that I feel I already live in it. People have said to me, "You're sixty-four years old, Dave, and you have cancer. Do you think you'll live long enough to see Longaberger Homestead?"

"I've already seen it," I tell them. It's true. I have. I've been thinking about it for many years.

Since my illness, I find myself thinking more and more about the future. I feel as though I've done everything I could to keep it on course, and I feel secure that under Tami and Rachel, the company will be in good hands. I feel confident that our visions will happen even if I'm not here to see them.

Knowing that I have cancer, people sometimes ask, "Doesn't it make you sad, Popeye, to think about the wonderful future that lies ahead, and you might not be around to enjoy it?"

"I've had a good life," I answer. What a trip it's been to reach sixty-four and to be able to look back and say, "No complaints, absolutely none."

Sure, I'd like to live longer. But when I think about what we've accomplished, I look at it and say, "I'm so thankful I was able to have made a difference in other people's lives and leave a little behind."

Don't get me wrong. I'm in no hurry to go. But knowing me, I'll probably get excited about going because I've never done that before. When the doctors finally tell me I have, say, a few weeks or so to live, I'll start looking forward to it. To me life has been one new adventure after another, and going to the next world will be still another adventure. So when my time is near, I'll start thinking about being able to sit down with my dad and asking him, "What do you think, Dad? How did I do?"

10

The Gift of Giving

I've worked hard all my life, but I was never really motivated by money. When I was a kid, if I had a dollar, then my three best friends and I all had a dollar. My brother Richie used to say, "Dave's got some money, so let's spend it!" I mostly enjoyed money when I could share it with others.

As an adult, when I made a dollar, I would spend three on my business. That's what money is for—to invest in my business and to give away. Personally, money never excited me.

All my employees know they can walk into my office any time of the day. Whether a problem is work-related or personal, I always listen. If a person needs some money for a daughter's wedding, an alimony payment, or an unexpected car repair, I am what you'd call a soft touch.

"Let me tell the bookkeeper what you need, and she'll make out a check," I'll say. Of course, this isn't charity; it's understood they'll pay me back.

When the restaurant and the grocery store started making decent money, I didn't start living high off the hog. That's not what you do in a small town. Instead, you do things to benefit the community.

I sponsored a lot of local events such as buying uniforms for the Little League and contributing to Fourth of July celebrations. I'd go to the county fair and sit there at steer auctions from six in the morning until midnight. I never sent anyone to do my bidding. Being there in person sent a strong message to everyone. I figured if they could be there all day, so could I. I always overbid, sometimes by as much as a few thousand dollars per steer. But I knew the money was going to the

4-H Club, so I felt good about it. When the fair was over, people always said, "We really appreciate your coming down to support 4-H."

Even during our lean years in the 1980s, we always made what we considered our share of contributions. There were many years when we gave away more than Tami, Rachel, and I earned together. More recently, the millions we have given away far exceed what we have taken out.

Today, Rachel heads The Longaberger Foundation. In this capacity, she makes sure we give money intelligently. As foundation president, she likes to say, "Tami's job is to make the money, and my job is to give it away."

■ IF WE DON'T, NOBODY WILL

For years, Muskingum County was one of Ohio's poorest counties. When coal mining was phased out, unemployment there hit the double digits. Today, it's a different story. With a workforce of almost seven thousand at The Longaberger Company, the local economy has undergone an impressive rejuvenation. Today, Muskingum and surrounding counties are healthy and prosperous. The town of Dresden has not only become a popular tourist destination; it also is a great small town in which to live.

Having been born and raised in the area, my roots are here. It's the only place I've ever called home. When I realize how close our company came to going belly-up in the mid-1980s, I shudder to think what could have happened to this area. Without the money the company and our employees spend here, plus what we pay in local taxes, this area might not have prospered as much.

We've done everything we could to prevent that from happening. We've invested millions of dollars into schools, hospitals, parks, and roads in Dresden and the surrounding areas. Some companies demand—and receive—favorable tax treatment in exchange for operating similar facilities in small towns. We've never sought or received a tax abatement. Against advice that a company of our size should have plant sites in multiple locations around the country, we have remained within our twenty-six-mile Dresden-Newark corridor with the exception of Hartville.

I know the advantages of such diversification. Other communities have offered us no-interest loans and tax breaks in exchange for building a Longaberger plant in their area. But no matter how many offers we have received, we have stayed here. This means we support our community.

I believe every company has an obligation to be a good corporate citizen. In big cities, it's common for large companies to step up to the plate. But out in the boondocks, if we don't cut the check, there's no one else to do it.

In 1993 Tri-Valley High School in Dresden needed funds to build an addition. We told the district that if their voters passed a school levy, we'd kick in another $1 million. The voters let the kids down. The school board came back to us, asking what we would do.

Most companies would have said, "Your voters won't spend the money, so why should we?" But we felt this was so important to the future that we agreed to invest anyway.

When the school district showed me the initial plans, the principal said, "Dave, we'd like to construct the first floor so it will be strong enough to support a second floor later. Could we do it so no rooms will have to be torn down when we're ready to grow into it?"

I told him, "We have the equipment, the construction workers, and the materials here right now. Let's just go ahead and do it."

"Won't that increase the cost?" the principal asked.

"If you can already see the need for a second floor, let's build it now," I said.

The $1 million pledge turned into $2.5 million, but the new two-story wing consisted of thirty-four thousand square feet of additional area, nearly doubling the available classroom space and improving the quality of education.

It didn't take long for the school to grow into the two-story building. Instead of having a single classroom for all foreign languages, each has its own room: a French room, a German room, a Spanish room, and so on, each decorated with posters and souvenirs. In addition to twenty new classrooms, there's also an expanded music room, and the new science labs are state-of-the-art, comparable to those in the best public schools anywhere.

Someone suggested dedicating the school in my honor, but I quickly vetoed that idea. I said I'd like to see it dedicated to Norbert Kurtz, a former school superintendent who was responsible for unifying the school districts. That man devoted his entire career to education. He deserved the honor, not me.

The Bonnie Longaberger Senior Center that we built in Dresden is named after my mother, and the Longaberger Family Center, an on-site day care facility for our employees, bears our name. We also donated $5 million to The Ohio State University, part of which went to the building of the Longaberger Alumni House.

We've donated millions of dollars to Dresden so the town could have facilities that rarely exist in a small rural community. Not many villages of sixteen hundred have a modern fitness center and a swim center. We wanted the people of Dresden to have these things. And if we hadn't built them, the town would never have had them.

■ INTELLIGENT GIVING

I believe giving back to the community is a way to thank people for supporting my business. In this respect, we're not just doing our civic duty. It's the right thing to do.

Simply put, I have always believed in giving back to the community. This is something every business owner should do and should consider a normal part of the cost of doing business. You don't have to own a corporation to support your community. Back in 1961, when I first opened Popeye's, it was a tiny dairy bar with eight stools, two booths, and two tables. Each year, Popeye's served free Christmas meals to the Dresden fire department volunteers. It was my way of thanking them for serving the community. My only motive was showing my gratitude, but those volunteers became regular Popeye's customers.

I could have pleaded poverty, and nobody would have faulted me. Most people didn't expect charity from a business that ran on a shoe-string. But I felt in my heart it was something I should do.

Granted, sponsoring a Little League team or overbidding on a steer is no big deal. Just the same, if every small business supported its community, the combined effort would be meaningful. As my business grew, so did my ability to give, and my contributions increased.

A company can do many wonderful things. But so much is needed by many good causes, and no company can support everything. An organization must turn away some while helping others, and making these decisions wisely requires a game plan. Giving randomly without a strategy is not wise. Sure, it would be far easier simply to set aside a certain sum each year and distribute it on a first-come, first-served basis. This policy would certainly be less time-consuming and less costly.

But when it comes to making annual contributions that run into the millions, we like to think we do it intelligently. This way, we get more bang for the buck. Since our customers and sales consultants are mostly women, we target our giving toward women. We've given millions of dollars to fight breast cancer. And when we were approached to support a shelter for battered women in Zanesville, we had to step forward. It's terrible when a woman and her children must escape from a violent situation and have nowhere to go. We even set up our employee assistance program to make loans to people in desperate straits. She could be a battered woman or an abandoned spouse with six children to support. When people face a crisis of this nature, we'll loan them $500 to make ends meet. We'll even help direct their career path toward a higher-paying job.

Likewise, because many of our customers and consultants are mothers, we support children's causes. The research center at Children's Hospital in Columbus, Ohio, is considered one of the finest in the country, and we support it with major funds. We also support Marburn Academy, a private school in Columbus for children with learning disabilities. As you can see, there are common links among the causes we support. Our contributions directly and indirectly benefit our customers and consultants, and their support and loyalty enable us to give as we do.

We believe there are five ingredients that contribute to the success of a healthy community: employment, education, recreation, roads and housing, and community organizations. If a community excels in these areas, it's a wonderful place to live, and people will want to move there. When the communities where our employees live and work have good schools, hospitals, roads, and recreational facilities, it directly benefits The Longaberger Company. Our employees and sales consultants make it possible for us to give generously.

■ BEING TOLD WE GIVE TOO MUCH

There's a big advantage to being privately owned. We don't have to be concerned about shareholders who think we give away too much money. If we were a public company, shareholders would expect dividends from dollars that we earmarked for charitable contributions.

Just imagine what outside investors would say about the millions we poured into Dresden. We'd have to justify the swim center, the fitness center, the athletic center, and the senior center. Then there are the millions we gave to schools and hospitals in Muskingum and neighboring counties. Somehow I don't think shareholders in New York or California would have had the same sense of joy we had in giving "their" money to this small rural community in Ohio.

On many occasions our bankers were concerned that we were giving away too much! While still building our infrastructure back in the 1980s, we poured millions into the community. The bankers were worried we were wasting our capital. They said the money would serve us better if it was invested in manufacturing and technology. One bank went so far as to place a covenant on a loan, limiting how much we could give away.

"When the debt is substantially reduced," the banker said, "we'll remove the covenant!" That was a new one on me. I never heard of a bank restricting a company's philanthropic activities. But then I don't suppose many companies put community support ahead of capital expenditures.

Superior schools and better recreational facilities lead to a better quality of life for our employees. I have to believe that people with certain advantages and outlets for their energy are more productive workers. But back in the 1980s, we couldn't convince bankers that money invested in the community would give us this kind of a return on the future. As far as the bankers were concerned, such generosity could cause us not to have a future!

But my vision included tens of thousands of future employees at The Longaberger Company. I believed the community's infrastructure had to be shored up right along with the company's infrastructure. It's not enough to provide a wonderful job for people. They have to enjoy life off the job! Given a choice, families will find jobs in an area that will provide them with the means to having a positive lifestyle.

I believe a family-owned business is better able to identify and agree on what causes to support. A company with many owners will have a wide range of interests, some of which may be in direct conflict. A shareholder who wants to hold a benefit to support an art museum is likely to find opposition from a VP whose favorite charity is the humane society. In this respect, family members are more likely to share common values and interests and, in particular, support investing in the hometown community. I take great pride in knowing my daughters Tami and Rachel share my commitment to philanthropic causes.

■ A SENSE OF PRIDE

Our longtime employees talk about the days when I asked them to wait to cash their paychecks. They remember how people used to laugh at the company and made fun of them for working here.

"You know, don't you, that Popeye's company will go out of business," people said. "You're crazy to work there with that leaky roof. And without benefits to boot! Besides, the American public will never buy baskets. It's just a matter of time before the company goes belly-up. You'd be smart to get out while you can."

My employees had faith in me, and they stuck with the company through some hard times. Today, when they see us write checks in six and seven figures for charities and civic causes, they nearly burst with pride.

They tell me, "When folks see what you've done for this town, Dave, they say how lucky I am to have a job with The Longaberger Company."

Once an employee told me, "I used to be embarrassed to tell people I worked for you, Dave, but no more. I can't wait for a stranger to ask me what I do for a living, because I feel so good about telling people I work at this company."

One woman said, "I recently bought a car, and when we talked about financing, the salesman asked what I did for a living. When I said I worked for Longaberger, he said, 'Really? What a great company to work for.' He then went into this long story about how his son had a birth defect and spent two months at Children's Hospital. He knew about the $2 million the company donated to the hospital, and couldn't help praising us."

Employees have told me how much their children enjoy the language room at their school. "What a wonderful thing you did for the kids, Dave. Don't you wish you had a place like it when you were in school?"

"The kind of student I was," I reply, "it wouldn't have helped." And we laugh, but I think what a wonderful thing it is to have given just one child a reason to enjoy school a little more.

What's really interesting is the employees who tell us how proud they are because we built the addition on the school—and they don't even have any children who use it. "It was just a great thing to do for the community," they say.

While we were establishing the family center on the Manufacturing Campus, executives of other companies warned us that it was a high-priced program, considering the small percentage of our own employees it would benefit. With a workforce in the thousands, they said, perhaps only a hundred employees would benefit from it directly.

"In the grand scheme," they said, "you could get a better return for your money in other benefits."

We knew comments of this nature had merit, but some of our employees needed day care in order to work, and in a rural location there were few options. Quite frankly, Rachel was the center's relentless champion. Since the center opened, it's remarkable how many of our employees express their appreciation to us for funding a beautiful building and the excellent programming. Instead of anyone being resentful because it doesn't personally benefit them, we constantly hear remarks such as, "I don't have any children or grandchildren, but whenever I drive by the center, I feel so proud I work for this company."

When I hear such remarks, I think to myself that the center is a testament not only to our company but also to the kind of people who work here.

■ KIDS ARE OUR FUTURE

I'm always looking toward the future, so it's no surprise that I'm interested in kids—what they're thinking, what motivates them, and what they want to do with their lives. This interest has allowed me to find a way to give back to the community. Giving back takes more time than writing a check, but it does more for me and for the kids than any amount of money could do. It's pretty simple. I go talk to students at their schools. I think everyone in business ought to find a way to get personally involved with our schools. Today's students will be your employees in the future. So, it's not only the right thing to do; it's also the smart thing to do.

Over the years, I've been invited to speak to many business groups. While those invitations are flattering, I don't accept very many. However, I can't recall ever turning down a student group. I've actually driven for an hour to talk to five students. Why? Because they asked me.

Now, the teachers, parents, and students who ask me to come to their schools are not usually asking me to talk to their honor roll students. There appear to be plenty of speakers who can motivate them. I seem to do best with students who are facing challenges and don't understand their potential. They seem to connect with a guy who was left back three times in elementary school and who stuttered, had seizures, and struggled with a learning disability. I see lots of eyes light up when I tell them I've been the founder and CEO of a $700 million company, and that I read at the level of a sixth grader.

These young people need a message of hope. They need to hear they are as special as the top students. They need to know they can build a fun and successful life, even if they are struggling with schoolwork. They need to understand the American Dream is their dream, too. I know it takes more than a positive outlook and determination to deal with learning disabilities or physical and mental challenges, but how can we expect young people to try to reach their potential without our encouragement and support? Sometimes, it takes only one person to show us a potential we didn't know we had. Maybe that's why I've never been too busy to visit a school.

■ HOW ABOUT TEN BUCKS?

One time I was asked to speak to more than a hundred high school students. Frankly, I prefer small groups. I was warned they wouldn't pay attention and that I shouldn't expect too much. That was a challenge if I ever heard one.

I went to the bank and got 130 ten-dollar bills. After I was introduced, I pulled out the cash and told the group that I had an important message for them. It was so important that later I was going to ask one of the students to tell me three key words from my talk. If that person got it right, I'd give ten bucks to everyone in the audience. If he or she got it wrong, I'd put the money back in the bank.

When I started to speak, everyone listened. Many took notes, to the amazement of their teachers. No way were they going to cost their friends and classmates ten bucks. I said the three key words—*listen, trust*, and *relationships*—so often I knew whoever I called on would be successful, and he was.

■ LONGER-TERM INCENTIVE

Another time, I was speaking to a group of high school seniors who weren't planning on going to college. Some didn't care about their grades or learning much the rest of the year. Life is too precious to waste that way. I decided to get their attention—not just for my talk, but for the rest of the year. I told them that the five seniors who raised their grade point average the most between that day and the end of the school year would each receive $5,000. Sure, it cost me $25,000, but that senior class was motivated.

■ WHAT CAN BUSINESS DO?

Even a small business can have a tremendous impact on a school and its students. Employee volunteers reading in the classroom, sharing real-world experiences, or tutoring students can make a big difference. Small, targeted gifts to meet the needs of even one classroom are rewarding for the students and the gift givers. Those old computers in your storage closet could be helping students next week.

At The Longaberger Company, we encourage volunteerism and recognize employees for their efforts. Rachel has led several projects in which employees volunteer their time in the schools and with charitable organizations, and I expect her work with The Longaberger Foundation will be reaching lots of students. Ask yourself, is there anything more important than our future?

■ MAKING A DIFFERENCE

When I look back to the early years of this company, what first comes to mind is all those people who believed in me. We had many doubting Thomases who were convinced we'd go under, but they never influenced the loyal employees who stayed with me. They stuck by me, ignoring the awful working conditions. They were willing to accept poor wages with no benefits, believing that someday there would be a bigger payday down the road. I don't see how I could have succeeded without their faith in me. The more they believed in me, the more I had to make our dream come true. They didn't want to let me down, and I didn't want to let them down.

In part, because so many people gave so much to this company, I vowed if I ever were in the position to do so, I'd give a lot more back to them, as well as to the community. The company has prospered, and my personal affluence far exceeds my needs. Material possessions have never motivated me. What keeps me going is being able to reach out and touch the lives of others. If it were about personal wealth, I would have been out of here a long time ago so I could enjoy what some people refer to as "the good life."

The good life is what we're able to do in the way of making a difference in the quality of other people's lives. By opening up a life of opportunities to our employees, I am rewarded every day by watching them grow and succeed. We are in a position to enrich the entire community and reach out to more and more people. This is what I love most about my life. I consider myself to be the luckiest man in the world.

11

Eighteen Management Principles
That I Live By

Over the years, I've developed a list of eighteen principles that I've used throughout my business career. I learned these principles through personal experience and observation.

In the beginning, it was nothing more than telling someone what I thought was a good way to work with people in a given situation. I'd say, "Funny, but the same thing happened to me a couple of months ago. Here's what I did that you might consider trying . . ." Watching how this worked, I took notes on the results so I could pass my ideas on to my employees.

What began as just sharing some of my random ideas eventually evolved into these management principles that are now followed throughout the company. The application of these principles mirrors The Longaberger Company culture. During the past few years, I have conducted lengthy management seminars on these principles, and our instructors at Longaberger University use them in management training programs.

These principles worked when we were a small company with a handful of people, and they're equally effective in running a $700 million company with seven thousand employees. I firmly believe these principles will work for every company. They're written informally because I wanted people at all levels to share my management philosophy. At the same time, I didn't want them to seem rigid. I wanted something to provide direction. Each Longaberger manager has the freedom to improvise according to his or her personality. I don't expect everyone to feel comfortable doing everything the way I do it. We all have our own style. It's not my intention to have a pack of Dave Longaberger clones out there.

The title of each principle consists of three words, and I have included acronyms in parentheses after the title. Each principle is purposely titled so it's easy to remember—and easy to refer to. It takes a while before a new manager does them automatically.

Keep in mind it's the spirit of these eighteen principles that is practiced by our management team. I believe these principles have attributed to our success. They can also enhance your career. After you have read them, you can pick and choose what you think works best for you.

I live by these principles. I may refer to them many times on any given day. They will be familiar when you read them because I have been using them throughout this book. Sometimes I will give examples of how I applied a particular principle. I have also added bits of information to spice things up.

I have divided these principles into two parts. The first ten are the foundation of a good, strong organization. The remaining eight will help you maintain that strong organization.

■ PART I

THE FIRST PRINCIPLE
Personal, Creative, Technical (PCT)

I believe three basic skills are needed to succeed in the workplace. Of the three skills, I believe personal skills are the most important aspect of good management. Here I refer to how you get along with people. How do you treat people? Do you have compassion and empathy?

Personal skills are developed partly through your character, disposition, enthusiasm, and sense of humor. Are you born with these personal skills? Perhaps, to some degree. For the most part, however, you get them through experience. Whatever you've been born with is a blessing, but to enhance your gift you must work at it, and this requires experience. The better you develop these traits, the more people will rally around you. Any manager worth his salt cares about his people. It goes further than your concern about them on the job. You must show an interest in their personal lives. Find out if they have problems, and see what you can do to help them. People know when you care about them, and they respond by caring about you. It shows in their work because they don't want to let you down!

Conversely, employees who have bad feelings will also demonstrate it through mediocre performance, simply going through the motions. Their attitude says, "I'll do what I have to do, and nothing more. Then I'm out of here!"

You have to sell yourself to the people you work with. Remember, they're evaluating you every day. Earn their respect and loyalty, and they will move mountains for you.

The creative skills I refer to are not the innate ability to produce great works of art or music. But then, it's not necessary to be a Michelangelo or a Beethoven to be creative in the workplace. Anyone can be creative on the job. Creative skills stem from one's resourcefulness, imagination, and tenacity. One important way to be creative is to find ways for your people to have fun at their jobs. Another is to gain a better understanding of your people. I believe it takes creativity to figure out ways to get inside people so you can find out how they think. In this respect, everyone can be creative. But first, you must honestly evaluate your strengths and weaknesses—and don't shy away from revealing your faults. You must be totally honest with yourself. When you tally it all up, you'll discover that your pluses far outnumber your minuses. So place the accent on the positive, not the negative.

You must also paint a definite picture in your mind about what you want to be and what you want to do. I tell our people to do this exercise so their life will have some direction. Some of them may want to spend their entire careers with The Longaberger Company, and others may not.

"There will be some of you who want to start your own business," I tell them. "If so, that's great. We hope what you learned from us will contribute to your success. What's important is that you create a picture in your mind about what you want.

"And those of you who plan to be here for the long haul are invited to participate in the exciting ventures that are down the road. We are looking to diversify into other areas that relate to the home. This can be anything from real estate to furniture. For us to do this, you must believe in yourself. We welcome you to come up with better ways for us as a company to achieve our goals."

By believing in yourself, and by helping your employees to believe in themselves, you are taking a big step toward being creative.

The technical skills I refer to are developed strictly on the job. These come from study, training, or experience—or a combination of all three. A physician develops technical skills by going to medical school, completing an internship, and finally practicing on his own. Likewise, a Longaberger weaver spends sixteen weeks in school, works with experienced weavers, and then hones her skills.

In our business, a good manager wins the respect of her workers by demonstrating to them that she has paid her dues. If she has spent time on the floor, they know she's "been there." She has the background to teach them that they also can succeed.

In summary, I believe a good manager should have 50 percent personal skills, 40 percent creative skills, and 10 percent technical skills. What it all boils down to is to know how important it is to work with people. It's difficult to find people with personal skills that exceed their creative and technical skills. Those who do generally listen to their people. This leads us into the second principle.

THE SECOND PRINCIPLE
Listen, Learn, and Lead (the Three L's)

Archaic ways of managing people never included listening or learning. In my youth, I remember hearing old-time coal miners tell about how a foreman would say, "From the second you set foot in this mine, I do your thinking for you. I'll fire anyone who says otherwise."

Foremen on the early automobile assembly lines preached the same message: "Check your brains at the door. You're not authorized to think."

Can you imagine the morale of those workers? They must have despised their jobs, and this certainly was reflected in their workmanship. The cars that came off those assembly lines had dozens of defects.

Today, management is supposed to know better. Good leadership isn't about telling people what to do. It's about listening to what they have to tell you. Your people are a great source of information, but only if you're willing to learn from what they have to say. Notice that I say "willing" to learn. You have to listen with sincerity. If you're listening just to pacify them, they will sense it. Remember: they can read you. You can't fake it because it will show in your body language and facial expressions. Only by listening and learning from your people can you effectively lead them.

Programs such as our incentive plans work because department managers routinely seek advice from their workers. The people who work with the materials day in and day out are the ones who are most likely to see ways to cut out waste. By learning from our people, we're able to realize significant efficiencies. I believe there is no better way to lead people.

Trust, Comfort, and Humor (TCH)

We live in a world where trust cannot be taken for granted; it must be earned. A good manager earns it every day. She walks the talk day in and day out.

I believe every manager should rank *trust* as the most important word in the dictionary. Simply put, if your people don't trust you, it will show in their performance.

I walked the plant floor on a daily basis, sometimes for hours at a time. All the time I was on the floor, the employees watched me. They watched me while they wove baskets, taking in how I treated people. People saw that I was sincerely interested in them. The newer employees scrutinized how I interacted with the old-timers, and they saw that we had close relationships. They observed how these longtime workers felt comfortable with me—and trusted me.

Many of these senior employees were the same ones who I took to lunch or dinner and played my every-time-you-say-basket-it-costs-five-dollars game. It's good times that make people feel comfortable, and also build solid relationships. This is why I never wear a suit and tie when I walk the floor. In our business, a suit and tie has the same effect as a uniform representing authority. Such a uniform would shatter the relaxed atmosphere we've worked hard to create. Consider this: What's the first thing you do when you get home after wearing business attire all day? You change into "comfortable clothes" so you can relax! I want my people to feel comfortable with me, and I encourage this by being one of them.

People who feel comfortable do better work than uptight, stressed-out people. For this reason we incorporate humor into our day at The Longaberger Company. We think work should be fun—at least 25 percent of the day. What better way is there to relax people and make them feel good about coming to work every day? Unfortunately, many managers take the opposite view. They don't think humor belongs in the workplace. Boy, are they missing the boat!

Our "Christmas in July" caper is a good example of how humor and fun relieve tension. The employees knew I cared about them and that I was sorry I couldn't do better for them. They accepted my way of expressing my regrets. Consequently, despite the unbearable heat, they continued working in the plant. Had I made excuses or token apologies, certainly if I had said, "You'll just have to live with it," I would have had a riot on my hands.

THE FOURTH PRINCIPLE
Patience, Time, and Resources (PTR)

Being a good manager requires patience. This is especially true with new employees, who need time to adapt and learn your way of doing things. It's essential to recognize how different people are and to realize that each person moves at her own pace. This takes time. Don't rush anyone to accept your belief system. To her, it may seem foreign. Be patient, and give her time to learn from your example. Eventually, this individual will become a valued employee.

Recognize, too, that it takes time for people to get to know you—and vice versa. A long time ago, I learned to size people up before telling them certain jokes or using a cuss word in their presence. At times I must be on guard to watch my language so I don't offend someone.

Also realize that occasionally neither side will be right. So it takes patience coupled with tolerance to see the other's point of view and work toward a compromise.

Patience is a virtue. But if you allow too much time to pass, opportunity may go with it. In the world of business, timing is crucial. Indecision can result in the loss of a golden opportunity. So be patient, but don't drag your feet. Remember to take an opportunity while it is still an opportunity.

Don't rush things. Add patience to time and you conserve resources. Looking at the big picture, it takes resources to achieve your long-term goals. You must wisely make the best use of these resources and think through each project along the way. As the expression goes, "Rome wasn't built in a day." To realize your twenty-year plan, you must first build a solid foundation. Otherwise, everything could come crumbling down.

If there was any liability in sharing my visions with my people, it was that at times they didn't understand some of my goals would take years to achieve. I had a clear vision of what would eventually happen, but not everybody saw it as vividly as I did. Consequently, they didn't always share my optimism. Oftentimes I'd hear subtle remarks made by older employees to new ones such as, "Popeye likes to come out here and talk about the future as if it's going to happen tomorrow. But it's going to take years for it to happen—if it ever does."

At The Longaberger Company, subordinates evaluate management. Following a series of evaluations, we sit down with our managers and review what their employees think about them. This allows managers to take a good look at themselves and learn about their strengths and weaknesses. By doing this, we are able to improve their managerial skills, thereby enhancing our most valuable resource—our people.

As a person, you are a valuable resource. Learn to pace yourself by using time with patience. I used to think that if I wasn't out there working hard physically, I wasn't being productive. When you're working hard at working hard, you end up spinning your wheels. It took me a while, but I finally discovered there's a lot of value in just sitting down and thinking. This took a lot of patience, but it helped me to organize my thoughts. Had I not done this, I would have drifted without direction. The fifth principle involves a lot of soul-searching and asking yourself some hard questions so you will have direction.

THE FIFTH PRINCIPLE
Do, Doing, and Done (The Three D's)

To understand this principle, you must ask yourself a lot of questions. What do I want to do? What am I doing? Is what I do what I want to do all my life? Is what I do a stepping-stone to enable me to do something else later on? Do I have good labor? Do I have a good P&L? Do I have the commitment? Do I have the desire?

You must address these questions to honestly evaluate yourself. I love to paint mental pictures of what I see down the road. I routinely do these mental exercises. They always start with my asking myself a lot of questions such as the ones just listed, and from there I start my painting. Longaberger people who have been around here a long time will say, "Popeye's got his brush out again."

Damn right. Get your brush out and paint your picture. Every great achievement starts with an idea.

How does this work? Let's say you decide that you want to start a fast-food restaurant chain. You should ask yourself, "What have I done in the past to get me closer to this dream?" Ask yourself what experiences and resources you have that will help you. By analyzing your past, you may decide you need some "grill time." This means getting a job at a fast-food restaurant to learn the nuts and bolts of the business. Go back to the fourth principle. You'll have to be patient. Give yourself enough time to properly learn the business. Understand it will take time and resources to open your first restaurant. Once you've figured out a formula to successfully operate one restaurant, your next step will be to see if you can run a second one. You'll be splitting your time between two locations, so you'll have to recruit and train a manager and delegate responsibilities. Through on-the-job training, you'll eventually acquire the know-how to operate many restaurants. All this takes patience. You can't kick off twenty-five fast-food restaurants without learning the basics. You have to crawl before you can walk!

In summary, you must first decide what you want to do. Second, you must learn how to do it. And third, after you have successfully done it, you can move onward to the next phase of realizing your goal.

When I put together my twenty-year plan, I mapped it out year by year. As a Chinese proverb teaches us, each long journey begins with a single step.

To do anything on a grand scale requires surrounding yourself with good people, which takes us to the sixth principle.

THE SIXTH PRINCIPLE
People, Product, System (PPS)

A company and its people are linked by a common interest. They work as a unit for their mutual benefit. Together, they provide a product or service that is of value to customers. These people are united by a common culture.

Cultures vary from company to company. Our culture at The Longaberger Company has a sense of family; we truly care about each other. And like a family, we set aside time for fun. Almost anyone who has either worked here or been around Longaberger people will pick this up. I believe our culture sets us apart from other companies—more so, perhaps, than the actual products we sell. While we may be identified as a company that manufactures and sells baskets, it's our company culture that binds us together. This is why our people put their heart into their work, and it's what creates mutual trust between management and the workforce.

Every company has a product or a service, and at The Longaberger Company, everything we do is our product. Our product line includes much more than baskets, fabric, and pottery. The landscaping at our buildings and along State Route 16 is also a product. Every stop our guests make is also product. Each part of the Longaberger experience is a part of our Longaberger marketing program.

People are always the most important part of an organization. And every company has a product or service to sell; if not, it wouldn't generate any revenue and would cease to exist. Finally, a company must have a system in order to operate. Our system includes our manufacturing facilities, information technology, and marketing program. Our multilevel sales organization is the distribution arm of our system. Had we sold our products retail, at best, we'd be a $10 million company instead of a $700 million company. And our potential to reach $10 billion by the year 2020 would be limited.

We must never forget that it's the people who run the system; it's never the other way around. So the people always come first. Oftentimes, you'll see a company that sets up an elaborate system and is ultimately consumed by it. The system is so complicated, it dictates to the people what they must do to work within it. Hence, making sure the system keeps working becomes management's top priority. While we value our Information Systems Department, its purpose is to serve our people, not the other way around!

At The Longaberger Company, we constantly remind ourselves that our home office serves every single employee and sales consultant. We thoroughly understand that our people, products, and system are crucial to our success. But so are our customers, which I will discuss in my seventh principle.

Marketing, Merchandising, and Selling (MMS)

It's true we sell the best-quality handmade baskets, but we always remember our product doesn't sell itself. We tried selling our baskets in retail outlets. They sat on the shelves and collected a lot of dust. Only when we started to tell our story face-to-face with customers did our sales take off. People love our baskets because they know the story behind them. Without the story, the baskets wouldn't sell.

Telling the story also involves selling yourself. When I operated my grocery, we spent hours getting the store ready before the doors opened. Everything from the meat counter to the produce was well planned, and we took pride in our lavish presentation. But no matter how impressive it looked, a rude checkout clerk could ruin the entire effect.

Just one surly expression, and all that hard work went down the drain. Even careless handling of the purchase or body language that suggests boredom can cause a customer to walk out the door feeling let down.

It's not just about selling customers. Managers must sell themselves to their people—and here, too, they must tell their story. "Tell your own story," I say to managers, "not mine. Your people already know the Longaberger story. You have to sell them on you."

"What's my story?" you may ask. "I don't have a story."

Everybody has a story. And it's not just making them privy to your personal background. Part of your story is the way you care for your people. It's listening to what they have to say. It's the way you go to bat for them when they have a problem. It's the support you give them, and it's the way you put yourself in their shoes. It's also just being a regular person and a decent human being. Taking a subordinate out to lunch or remembering someone's anniversary is part of your story, too. Telling your story is earning the trust of your people, so they feel comfortable in your presence.

I'm selling myself to the workers in our plant when I walk the floor wearing Levi's, a western shirt, and work boots. People have said, "Popeye, you need to wear a suit because you're chairman of the board." Well, when I did, I felt like I was wearing barbed wire because so few workers approached me. I went back to my casual clothes, and they flocked around me with comments and suggestions. So just like a product, we are constantly marketing, merchandising, and selling ourselves.

THE EIGHTH PRINCIPLE
Labor, Material, and Cost (LMC)

Here's a lesson from Business 101: you must know your costs of labor and material. It's so obvious, you'd think all merchants would know them like the backs of their hands. But few do, and those who don't are generally in a constant battle to make ends meet.

I learned this lesson when I first opened my tiny restaurant. "Keep your labor cost at 20 percent, Popeye, and your food between 25 to 30 percent, and you'll make money," a wise person advised me. I followed that advice, and I always made money in the restaurant business. The same thing was true in the grocery business. The only difference was that percentages fluctuate from business to business. Numbers differ, depending on the industry. But by reviewing these numbers as a matter of course, you develop a series of snapshots of what's coming in and what's going out. This keeps you focused on your bottom line.

It's not just business owners who must pay attention to costs. I am constantly preaching to managers to stay on top of their departmental costs. We teach them to make regular comparisons between current figures and the previous year's numbers. By comparing these numbers, it's possible to spot a trend before things get out of hand. This allows them to adjust and implement cost-cutting procedures.

For years at The Longaberger Company, I've given my people a target to shoot for. I made it our company goal to net 10 percent after taxes. This could be done only by controlling costs and with everybody pitching in. While we haven't reached that goal, profits have increased for many years.

Oftentimes owners of privately owned companies refuse to disclose their sales figures to employees. I've never withheld these numbers. In fact, going back to the early days of my restaurant, I had the employees tally up daily receipts to see if we beat the previous day's figure. Even though people advised me against it, I believed it made more sense to share this information with my employees. It not only gave them ownership but also helped them see how important it is to increase our sales.

Intelligence, Common Sense, and Mistakes (ICM)

Unless you happen to be a nuclear engineer, there are few tasks in life that require tremendous intelligence. If we really make up our minds, we can accomplish just about anything in our chosen fields. What we do need, however, is good old-fashioned common sense and a willingness to learn from our mistakes. Here, intelligence serves us by letting us draw on past experience.

I've learned over the years that being a good manager requires 15 percent intelligence, 35 percent common sense, and 50 percent learning from past mistakes. I'm not knocking a good education, but some people believe the human mind is like a warehouse for storing information. The mind is not a warehouse. It is an instrument to think with. A highly educated person who fills her brain with facts and figures and uses no common sense won't cut it in today's workplace. Anyone with a laptop computer has access to a million times more information in a matter of microseconds.

I don't measure a person's worth by his degrees in business but instead on his degree of experience in managing people. Any success I've had as a manager has resulted from my ability to apply practical judgment through common sense. It's so easy. It doesn't take a genius to know that everyone wants to be appreciated. I know I do, and I am sure you do, too. Treat people the way you want to be treated. This is all you have to do, and you'll be on your way to being a good manager.

Common sense is what tells you to make people feel comfortable. Let's face it, when a person feels comfortable, she'll be more productive than someone who is filled with anxiety and stress! Common sense also guides you to conduct yourself in a manner that induces people to trust you. This makes good sense, doesn't it? After all, would you be more inspired by a trustful or a distrustful manager?

Common sense also dictates that you admit your mistakes. Making mistakes is human nature. A person who never makes mistakes probably never tries anything new. And as they say, "Nothing ventured, nothing gained." Study successful people, and you'll find they've all made their share of mistakes.

Being able to admit your mistakes makes you more human. It shows humility. I've never been bashful about admitting my mistakes. I'm constantly telling people, "If I ever wrote a book on my successes, it would be about this thick," and I hold up two fingers, about a quarter of an inch apart. "But if I were to write a book on stupidity, and all the dumb things I've ever done, it would be this thick," and I move my fingers six inches apart.

There have been thousands of times when I've been on the plant floor and told a worker, "Hey, we all make mistakes, don't sweat it. I can top yours. Let me tell you about the dumbest thing I ever did in my lifetime." Then I rattle off a few of my biggest blunders.

Usually, after I do this, the minute I walk away, that worker tells somebody else, "Do you know what? Popeye came out here and told me about some dumb things he once did. Can you imagine that?"

By letting people know that you know you're human, you become dear to them. You're showing them a side of yourself they can identify with. You're no longer one of those highfalutin' managers who puts himself on a pedestal. You're a real person with your share of flaws like everyone else!

Naturally, your past experiences influence the person you are today. Knowing this, you should take time to find out who you are and what you want to be. Lock yourself in a room, take a walk by yourself in the woods, or go for a stroll on a remote beach. Go someplace where you can be alone and think about your past. This will enable you to understand how much knowledge you've accumulated about people. In the next principle, I'll tell you a good way to do this.

THE TENTH PRINCIPLE
Pictures, Places, and People (The Three P's)

When I was writing my first book, *The Longaberger Story and How We Did It*, it was difficult trying to think about material to use. I wasn't coming up with much, so I decided to rent a cabin at a nearby state park where I could do some serious thinking. I planned to remain there in solitary confinement and rack my brain until I was able to come up with some good stuff.

Days went by, and I wasn't making any progress. Then I had a brainstorm. To help me focus on the past, I gathered hundreds of old photographs, took them to the cabin, and spread them on the floor around me. I had pictures from grade school, my army days, the original Popeye's—my whole life was in front of me. The pictures brought back all kinds of memories, not all good, although most of them were. I started thinking about some of my old buddies. There was Max Hittle. I remembered when we went to Washington, D.C., on our senior class trip, and how the two of us dressed up like girls and walked down Pennsylvania Avenue. We even stuffed our shirts with grapefruits. I thought, boy, people sure would react differently if we did that today!

Photos of some of my old teachers were on the floor. I remembered some who really helped me and some who didn't.

I looked at photos taken of me in the 1940s when I worked at Fred Shoemaker's grocery. Then my mind wandered to some of the other grocery stores where I worked as a kid. I thought about so many things I had learned, both good and bad. I recalled how some grocers would shortchange customers by a few ounces on five-pound bags of flour and sugar.

I remembered all the fun things I did with my brothers and sisters. I realized how much they had given to me—much more than I could ever repay. I thought about how happy we were, even when fourteen of us lived in a small house with a single bathroom. We had few toys. It made me think about how happy people can be even though they don't have a lot of material possessions. So it's not the things you own that give you true happiness. Then I came across some pictures of Mom and Dad. I tried to think of something profound they had said to me, but nothing came to mind. How sad, not to remember anything, I thought. But I realized it's not what people say, it's what they do that matters. They taught us kids by what they did! That's when I understood that my parents were my mentors. So much of who I am today reflects what I learned from them. Prior to this photograph exercise, I never thought I had a mentor, but I had for all those years. And I never realized it until I was in my fifties!

We all have a mentor or two. It could be an aunt or uncle, a neighbor, a teacher, or a boss. Perhaps when you get out your old photos, you'll discover a mentor you never realized you had.

Those photos brought back memories of people and events I hadn't thought about for years. It was the greatest journey of self-discovery of my life. I strongly recommend you do the same thing. You'll revisit places that no longer exist. My photos included buildings that have long since been torn down, places on Main Street in Dresden that have been replaced with new buildings, and some that are now Longaberger properties.

Most important, I thought about what I learned from so many different people. As I looked at the photos, I was almost able to hear what they said to me. I felt strong because I remembered who and what made me the person I am today.

Perhaps the most exciting thing about reviewing these old pictures is that they not only gave me a snapshot of my past but also helped me envision the future.

■ **PART II**

THE ELEVENTH PRINCIPLE
Motivate, Create, and Organize (MCO)

As a manager, you must first know how to motivate yourself before you can motivate others. Admittedly, getting yourself fired up is one of the hardest jobs in the world, especially when it seems as if everything is going against you and everyone is knocking you down. Believe me, there were times when the company was on the verge of going under, but I couldn't let my people know I felt like crawling into a hole somewhere. I had to motivate myself. No matter how beat I felt, I'd walk with a bounce in my step. I talked about the future, even though the present was dismal.

Once you can motivate yourself, you can start motivating others. But you can only do it when you truly understand them. You have to walk side by side with them and find out who they are. Just being among them is a good place to start. You have to know each of your people as an individual. That's because everyone is different. What motivates one person will not turn on someone else. As a manager, you must play the role of a psychologist. Sometimes this means looking at people and knowing what they're thinking. It's like my old high school basketball coach taught me: a good defensive player can look an opponent in the eye and pick up his next moves. It's the same thing in selling and managing people. Look them in the eye; watch their body language. They will telegraph what they are thinking.

You don't have to pressure people to become more productive. In fact, that can work against you. They know when they haven't been productive. Be their friend; you don't have to always talk shop. Ask about their families. Get them on subjects that aren't related to work. Say things such as, "That was a helluva football game the Buckeyes played on Saturday" or "I like that new set of wheels you just bought. Get a deal on it?"

Most managers pooh-pooh small talk and say it's a waste of time in the workplace. Boy, are they mistaken. Letting people know you're okay with who they are motivates them. When they sense you feel good about them, they'll do all they can to make you look good. It's that simple. Managing people isn't hard; don't complicate it.

I'm always amazed at how hard people will study for a test in school, but when it comes to studying their people, managers goof off. This doesn't make sense to me. These people are paying their bills! These same managers who get A's and B's in school enter the workforce thinking they're through learning. Their education is just beginning! Now they have to study their people. How else can they know how to motivate each of them?

One of the most creative ways to motivate people is to make sure they have fun at their work. It astounds me to see how few companies make any attempt to encourage their employees to have fun. Use humor at every opportunity you can. If you're one of those people who just isn't funny, don't worry about it. In any group there's always one person who will make everyone laugh. Give that person some space and let her go. It's great for everyone's morale. Some managers want to discourage the joker, calling him a wise guy or a troublemaker. Good managers, however, recognize laughter in the workplace is healthy, and they do their best to promote it.

Motivated people are more creative. Everyone possesses creativity, and as a manager you have to bring it out in your people. You can do this in a variety of ways. First, you can create opportunity by giving people a sense of freedom. Give them permission to make decisions. Even when they make the wrong decision, praise them for trying. People also get creative when you invite them to participate in your business. This gives them ownership. When my restaurant employees found out we took in $165 at lunch on Monday and $180 on Tuesday, they felt good. They were challenged to do better, and they did! Once when the pie maker didn't show up for work, I asked a waitress to bake pies that day. She insisted she didn't know how, but I coaxed her into trying. Her crusts turned out so hard, I said they would make good ashtrays, and we passed them out to customers. She was a good sport, and we all had a big laugh. Instead of feeling bad about her pies, we had a lot of fun that day. We talked and laughed about it for years!

Managers must create excitement. And boy, when they do, will their people ever respond. A manager's job is to quarterback the team. The workers in the organization are the players. He must get their input, then call the play. Each player has an important responsibility to carry out the play. Once the manager has them organized, they can work as a team. With thirty minds working toward a single goal, it's bound to be better than having everyone wonder what everyone else is doing!

Now, it's one thing to build a team and quite another to maintain it. A big-time college football coach spends months recruiting top players from across the country. Then he must help his players learn how to work together as a team. Remember, just one missed block results in a broken play. The coach must also see that his players are in top physical condition. Once a team is solid and ready to play, a coach needs a different set of talents to maintain a winning team, to keep those players up for each game, always working together, striving to win. The next principle explains how to keep up that winning spirit.

THE TWELFTH PRINCIPLE

Judgment, Attitude, and Relationships (JAR)

Once you have built an organization, its ongoing success depends on the quality of the relationships you have with your employees. Similarly, a manager is only as good as the relationships he has with his people. The same applies to salespeople and their customers. Relationships are the fuel that keeps everything in business running smoothly; without them, people as well as organizations are ineffective.

Each of us has many relationships, and, like motivation, they come from inside. As corny as it might sound, you must have a good relationship with yourself. By this, I mean knowing who you are and liking yourself. In a nutshell, you better get your own head on straight before you start managing other people.

Off-the-job relationships run the gamut: your relationship with God, your family, your spouse, your community, and so on. How well these relationships are working will carry over into your job. Poor personal relationships can affect your business judgment. For instance, if you're stressed out from marital problems, it shows up in your performance at work. I've been known to tell employees, "If your personal relationships are getting you down and you're coming to work in a bad mood, I'd rather you stay home. We don't want you making everyone else miserable, too. We don't want your negative attitude around here."

We think a manager's relationships with his people are so important, we listen carefully to what they say about him. This feedback helps us to appraise a manager's performance. A manager who doesn't foster good relationships isn't likely to have a rosy future with this company. It's a manager's job to make his people feel good. And when they feel good, they'll respond by being more productive. Let me describe an example of how this works. Since our basket makers are paid a piece rate, the more baskets they weave, the more they earn. When a strip of wood has a small flaw, or if say a weaver drops it on the floor, it's faster for the weaver to discard it than to fix it or, for that matter, pick it up. But such waste is costly to the company. Our studies reveal that the weavers who have a good relationship with their supervisors are less likely to be wasteful, and although it slows them up, they'll use that strip of wood. Why? Because they want their boss to do well, and they know his performance is dependent on how well he keeps costs down. As you can see, their relationship with their manager influences their attitude and the judgment they apply to their everyday work.

As I have stressed throughout this book, building relationships with people is what built this company. As we grow, we must always remember we're in the people business.

THE THIRTEENTH PRINCIPLE

Energy, Appearance, and Rest (EAR)

Many companies think their managers are more productive when they work more hours. These people don't receive overtime pay, so senior management thinks they're getting a bargain by giving them assignments that can't possibly be completed in a normal work schedule. That's a big deception. Tired people are ineffective, nonproductive workers. So when five o'clock rolls around at The Longaberger Company, we expect everyone to go home.

If I see somebody who is still working, I'll make a comment such as, "Can't you get your work done on time?" or "You won't score any points by staying here late, because I won't be here to see you." I want them to get enough rest so they'll be energized the following day. When people overwork, they burn themselves out—and it shows in the poor quality of their work. This is why I encourage people who don't get their proper rest to take a sick day and stay home. If they drag themselves to work, they're likely to do more harm than good!

Rarely do you hear any mention of the importance of rest in business schools or management circles. Yet, I've been preaching it for years. How well I know from personal experience that if I don't get my six hours of sleep each night, I'm a dead man at work. I love sports, and I used to stay up past bedtime watching Monday night football. Sometimes a game on the coast would go until 1 A.M. Instead of getting the usual six hours' sleep that I needed, I was getting only four. If the team I was rooting for lost, it didn't affect my income. But the way I felt the next day *was* affecting my income because I was a zombie. My lack of energy caused me to do sloppy work. I lacked my usual zing, and I couldn't concentrate. It's not just TV. Too much of anything can be a waste of time and can sap your energy. It's only a matter of applying a little willpower: turn off the TV, the computer, or the shop lights, and go to bed.

Remember when you played ball in high school? My basketball coach gave us strict instructions to get a good night's sleep. Back then, we understood we'd have better focus during the game, more endurance, and quicker reflexes. Isn't it a shame that when we're old and should know better, we neglect ourselves. Because there's no test in class the next day, we're not smart enough to realize that due to a lack of rest, we miss many opportunities in the workplace. Studies show a good night's rest will enhance your relationships with people, your attitude, and your judgment by as much as 50 percent. It will also increase your creativity. When you're too tired to think of something or to find a solution to a problem, you're apt to procrastinate and put it off until next week, then the following week, and so on. If you're constantly tired, you never get it done.

This is something else your people will pick up by observing you. No matter what, you can't hide your drowsiness and lack of focus. Believe me, your people are watching you, and your appearance will give you away. You got only four hours of sleep last night—and it shows. They will see it in your walk, your posture, and your eyes. It will also be evident in your mood. When you're tired, you're prone to be irritable and cranky. At the worst, a continual lack of sleep can adversely affect your health, a subject to be covered in the following principle.

THE FOURTEENTH PRINCIPLE
Health, Experience, and Opportunity (HEO)

Many people take their health for granted. It's a shame, but only when they lose it do they realize how important it is.

Good health is a blessing. If you have it, cherish it. Like most other things of value, you must maintain it. Remember you're no good to yourself or your company when you're too ill to put in a full day's work. It goes further than not being able to perform physical work. Even with a desk job, health problems sap your energy and cause fatigue and mental lapses.

A friend who's an author once told me that when he's pushing to meet a deadline on a manuscript, he works long hours. To maintain his mental sharpness, he follows a particularly healthy diet and increases his daily exercise routine. "You've heard of a boxer keeping in good shape by getting down to his fighting weight," he told me. "Well, I do the same by getting down to what I call my 'writing weight.' I'm serious about it, Dave. In order for me to sit behind a computer for long periods at a time, I require extra stamina. Otherwise my neck and back ache, and I become drowsy. Even though my work is sedentary, being in good physical shape is essential to my productivity as a writer."

I don't care what kind of work you do, whether you're a construction worker, a veterinarian, or an accountant; when you're under the weather, it affects your productivity.

Obviously, poor health will restrict your capacity for physical work more than nonphysical work. But it will hamper even the most sedentary activities. When your body is ailing, it saps your energy, and, in turn, your mental alertness is impaired. Additionally, fatigue causes stress—and believe me, there's already enough stress in the workplace!

Picture a tree growing in the middle of a field, and another in the midst of a crowded forest. The tree in the field receives plenty of sunlight and rain, and because it is fully exposed to all the elements with plenty of room to grow, its trunk is thick and strong; its branches extend out in all directions. However, the tree in the forest is crowded by other trees. It doesn't get as much sun or rain, so its trunk is spindly. Its branches are weak and deformed. As you can see, one tree grows to its full potential while the other does not. In the same way, you will limit your opportunities for growth in business by neglecting your body.

A word to the wise: take good care of yourself. I won't go into details because you already know what you're supposed to do: exercise, follow a good diet, get sufficient rest, and be sure to get routine physical examinations. Remember: an ounce of prevention is worth a pound of cure. From a selfish point of view, The Longaberger Company has a big investment in our people. They are our most valuable asset—and we want to protect that asset.

There are so many opportunities in America. To take advantage of them, you must stay healthy so you can be strong. You must also draw upon your past experiences. Read the tenth principle again and picture places and people from your past. Let those images guide you to the future. With good health and a full understanding of your experiences, you will find unlimited opportunities.

THE FIFTEENTH PRINCIPLE
Strong, Firm, and Fair (SFF)

Your employees are always watching you to see if you are strong, firm, and fair. You are being measured by your actions, not your words. You must always remember to walk the talk.

The people who work for you put their future in your hands, giving you an awesome responsibility. It's no wonder they're constantly evaluating everything you do. They want to be led by someone who doesn't buckle during the heat of the day. Managers who are indecisive and unpredictable are scary. Nobody wants a weak leader.

A strong leader is unshakably dependable. I tried to live my life in a way that delivers a message to my people: you can depend on me. They need that. I may not always say the right thing, but I have always been able look my people squarely in the eye and let them know I'm dependable. When I speak to them, they know I would die for this company. They clearly understand that this is my life, and it means everything to me.

People follow a leader who is firm. This doesn't imply that you are inflexible, because a strong leader will admit being wrong and will confirm his strength by having the courage to face the challenges that change brings. However, when it comes to matters of principle, a leader must be as steadfast as a rock.

Above all else, a leader must exhibit a sense of fairness. Everyone is treated equally, which means not showing favoritism. I learned this lesson well growing up in a family of fourteen. Mom and Dad treated us equally, never giving special treatment to a "favorite" child. Imagine the chaos in a family with twelve children if there had been a favorite! Because my parents were strong, firm, and fair, my brothers, sisters, and I never got into any trouble away from the family. We respected Mom and Dad so much, we didn't want to do anything to disappoint them. They were wonderful role models, the kind today's children need so badly. We did our best because we wanted to make them proud of us.

When it came to discipline, Dad, in particular, was the epitome of firmness and fairness. We all knew his rules about when to be home if we wanted dinner and when to be home if we didn't. If we broke his rules, he'd paddle us. In hindsight, he never hit us hard enough to hurt us—only to bruise our feelings a little. He was consistent with his punishment, and we knew that as long as we abided by the rules, we'd be just fine. I truly believe children need this discipline because it lets them know their parents care about them. A parent disciplines children out of love. In turn, it makes kids feel secure. Kids without boundaries are the ones most likely to have hang-ups and insecurities. Likewise, as adults in the workplace, people want the same sense of firmness and fairness. It lets them know where they stand with the boss, and that's healthy. This is the kind of relationship you as a manager must develop with your employees.

THE SIXTEENTH PRINCIPLE
Look on the Bank (LOB)

Growing up in Dresden, there was an unwritten rule at the swimming hole: never swim without someone on the bank to watch you. The older boys made sure little kids who couldn't swim never went in the water by themselves. Later, as the younger ones became older, they were responsible for enforcing this rule. There were accidents on the river and at the Trinway gravel pit, but nobody ever drowned at our swimming hole. Even though this was a rule made by kids, it taught me a valuable lesson I have followed throughout my business career.

Everybody needs somebody on the bank to be there in time of need. When I opened my first business, Popeye's, I knew that if it failed, I could always drive a bread truck. And I knew if my grocery business went under, I could always flip hamburgers. Having a fall-back plan assured me that if my enterprise failed, I'd be no worse off. Similarly, when I took early risks in the basket business, I knew if it failed, I could always open a grocery or restaurant. This principle stresses the importance of having a backup plan, or what some refer to as plan B.

My LOB principle also means having someone to give you advice when you have a problem. This can be a mentor or a friend, or simply your employees. In my case, I can fall back on the combined experience of seven thousand employees and fifty thousand sales consultants.

Finally, this principle advocates having a place to where you can escape. Everyone needs a spot of peace and quiet. Being still for just a little while helps you think clearly. It might be in the middle of a shower, on the drive to work, or in a corner of the warehouse where you can find just five minutes to meditate. This slows down your heart, lowers your blood pressure, and helps you keep the proper perspective on things.

THE SEVENTEENTH PRINCIPLE

Past, Present, and Future (PPF)

The past is the present, and the present is the future.

This sounds like a word teaser, but it is just what it says it is. To clarify it, I'll refer to the dictionary, which defines the past as time gone by. The present is defined as what exists now, or what's in progress, and the future is defined as time that will come.

Let me explain. Everything we've done in the past has contributed to the foundation we have in the present. And going forward, we build on this existing foundation in preparation for our future.

First I'll talk about the past. I know some people don't like to dig into the past, but I believe we have to understand our past because it's our foundation. I was reminded of a couple who lost their ten-year-old son to leukemia. They went through much grief.

"How do you cope with it?" I asked the mother.

"It's very difficult, Dave," she replied, "but I have learned that I have to let go in order to hang on."

What a beautiful thought. She taught me a lesson I never forgot. We must hang on to past experiences—the good and the bad—so we may continue with our lives. In the same vein, we must learn from our past mistakes and leave them behind, hoping not to repeat them. Having benefited from past mistakes, we can anticipate a better present and future.

Now and then I look at a 1977 photograph of the old woolen mill. When I bought it, it barely had a roof. Trees were growing inside the building, and every window was broken. It hadn't been occupied for twenty-five or more years. It was such a worthless-looking place, the kids in town made fun of Tami and Rachel. My daughters were teased, "Your dad is the dumbest man in Dresden for buying that old broken-down building."

However, we moved into the building and slowly fixed it up while we made baskets. All the while, mice, rats, and raccoons ran across the rafters. Birds and bats fluttered above and made occasional nosedives toward targets at ground level. Now and then, a woman would shriek that a snake had just slithered over her foot. Cardboard boxes were built around workstations with space heaters where the weavers huddled to keep warm. Snow blew through windows. Those first employees went without paychecks, and in spite of the miserable working conditions, they remained loyal. This is our past, our company heritage. These were truly remarkable people.

Today, our employees work in state-of-the-art conditions. Their compensation and benefits package is the envy of the area. To those first employees, this workplace would be utopia. We must never forget those who built this company's foundation. They resemble our country's early pioneers, who endured enormous hardships. If not for the hardships they withstood, this great nation would have remained a wilderness. America's present and future generations must always pay homage to their forefathers; they are the spirit of our nation. Similarly, it is my hope that present and future Longaberger employees will remember the early pioneers of our company. We must always learn from them, and we must emulate their commitment.

I live for the future. To do so, I use a snapshot of the past and present. This enables me to have a clear picture of what will be. By understanding where we come from, we can identify our strengths and our weaknesses. This knowledge equips us with the foresight and direction toward the future.

The future is filled with opportunity, but you must go after it. Opportunity knocks loudly, but it won't come to you. You must answer the door. You must plan for the future. With each project I undertake in the present, I ask myself, "How will it play in the future?" I consider the future to be the year 2020—and I make today's decisions accordingly. It is not likely I will be here in 2020, but The Longaberger Company surely will.

THE EIGHTEENTH PRINCIPLE
Look, Think, and Do (LTD)

Any success I may have had I credit directly to this final principle: look, think, and do. First, you must look at everything. There are so many opportunities out there. Find out what your options are. This advice applies to every manager and every entrepreneur. Prior to starting my restaurant business, I looked at many small businesses. With an empty bank account and no credit, my best option was to make an offer on Harry's Dairy Bar via a land contract. Had my offer been turned down, I would have continued to look until I found another opportunity. Obviously, buying the restaurant wasn't my only option. There were an infinite number of opportunities, and I had to find only one. Later I bought the grocery store, again on a land contract. Had I not been able to make this transaction, I would have found something else. But only if I looked for something else.

I always look for opportunities. I don't wait for them to come to me. If I did, I'd still be driving a bread truck! You must be proactive. The opportunities are there, but you must seek them out.

When you spend enough time looking, you're bound to come across opportunity. It might be camouflaged, and uncovering it takes vision. Remember the old woolen mill, which sat vacant for more than a quarter of a century. Believe me, it was well camouflaged! But after I looked at it, I gave it some hard thought. I envisioned what it would look like after we fixed it up. When I first looked at Dresden's Main

Street and thought about turning it into a tourist attraction, I saw what nobody else did. I didn't see run-down existing storefronts; they were obvious. Everybody saw them. Instead, I saw dozens of fancy boutiques and quaint restaurants lining both sides of the street. I had driven down Main Street thousands of times before I had this vision. Thousands of other people had driven down the same road as many times as I had, never seeing what I saw.

"Do you ever doubt your visions?" people ask me.

"Of course," I reply. When properly applied, self-doubt is an asset because it makes you think. And it makes you question yourself: "Does it look good? Can I feel it? What's my gut feeling? What are the risks? Can I afford them? If it succeeds, what will it lead to?" The more you question yourself, the more you are prepared to make a smart decision.

Closely related to self-doubt are the questions you ask yourself about the competition. "What are the strengths and weaknesses of the competition? What can I do to be better than my competition?" Competition is healthy because it challenges you—and pushes you to do better. You can also learn from your competition. You can study its mistakes and its successes, then you can pick and choose what lessons you learn from it. I caution you: never shy away from competition. It's what makes our free enterprise system work. Ultimately, your competition will make you better.

Finally, there comes a time when you must do it! You can look and you can think, but eventually you have to put your money where your mouth is. The greatest intentions are meaningless unless they are put into action. You have to walk the talk. I could have come up with a million excuses for why I shouldn't have gone into the basket business. I still could. But anyone can make excuses. I wanted to do it. So I did, and I did it my way!

I recommend you read these eighteen principles several times and think about what you've read before applying them. You don't have to apply all eighteen at the same time. Practice one or two at a time, and then go on to others. You've gotten this far in your life without them, so a temporary delay won't rock your boat.

In summary, I emphasize you can only look good when your people feel good. I believe this statement encompasses all of my eighteen principles.

Only in America

The Longaberger Company is proof that the American Dream is alive and well. The odds are we couldn't have done what we did anywhere else in the world. And ours is not an unusual story in this country. You'll find other stories like ours, spread out from coast to coast.

Out of Earth's 6 billion people, are we ever lucky to be one of the 270 million Americans. No other country's government is based on the concept that its citizens have the right to life, liberty, and the pursuit of happiness. Imagine the wisdom of Thomas Jefferson when he wrote those words. Our nation was founded with the goal of an equal opportunity for all. The commitment to every American having a fair chance to develop his or her talents to the fullest is central to the American Dream. This doctrine has deep roots in our history and culture. While being born rich is certainly an advantage in this country, everyone has the opportunity to become a member of America's elite.

I believe all Americans have many opportunities to succeed during their lifetime. Often they simply don't recognize opportunity when it stares them in the face.

Am I lucky? Sure, luck plays a role. I was lucky to be born in America. I wouldn't have had the same opportunity in a place like Afghanistan or Cuba. Even in America, social origins and family background make a difference. Not each of us begins the race at the same starting line. The kind of family into which a child is born has a major influence on his or her adult success, perhaps more than any other measurable factor. I was blessed to be born into a wonderful family. I was lucky to have Mom and Dad as my parents, who taught me good values and a strong work ethic. I was also lucky my father made baskets. I could go on and on about how luck has contributed to what I have been able to achieve.

Sometimes we can influence our luck by the decisions we make. You may be "at the right place at the right time," but you may have to change your mind along the way. This means being open to opportunities that come from out of nowhere. Remember: at The Longaberger Company, everything is subject to change. You can't make long-term plans by simply mapping out your future and then meekly moving from point A to point B. You cannot ignore external factors. In the real world, we must expect the unexpected. Someone once described the future by saying it will be more of the same, only much different.

You must remain flexible and be willing to change your goals and aspirations, even your career, when the right opportunity presents itself.

As Americans, we should give thanks for the freedom our country guarantees every one of us. I truly feel we should make Thanksgiving the biggest of our celebrations to thank God for everything. We are blessed to have a political and economic system that allows us to believe in ourselves and seek out opportunities. This is the American way. The American Dream exists, and it's available to all. I know because I've experienced it beyond anything I ever imagined. Keep pursuing your dreams, and may your dreams come true.

What better way can I end this book than by saying, "God bless America."

Important Dates in Longaberger History

1902	J. W. Longaberger is born in Dresden, Ohio
1908	Bonnie Gist Longaberger is born in Trinway, Ohio
1927	J.W. and Bonnie are married
1934	Dave Longaberger is born in Dresden, Ohio
1936	J.W. and Bonnie purchase the Dresden Basket Factory on Tenth Street
1940	Dave begins first grade
1955	Dave graduates from high school
1955	Dave works as a Fuller Brush salesman for six months
1956	Dave starts work as a route man for Cannon's Bakery
1959	Dave becomes a route man for Nickles Bakery
1961–62	Dave serves in U.S. Army

1961	Tami Longaberger is born
1963	Dave purchases Harry's Dairy Bar and everyone calls it "Popeye's"
1967	Rachel Longaberger is born
1968	Dave purchases the old A&P grocery store in Dresden. Name is changed to Dresden IGA
1972	J.W. makes ten dozen baskets, which Dave sells to retail shops
1973	J. W. Longaberger passes away
1974	Dave attempts different ways to sell baskets at malls, department stores, and other retail outlets but without success
1976	J. W. Longaberger Handwoven Basket shop opens at Third and Main Streets in Dresden
1977	J. W. Longaberger Handwoven Basket shop moves to 95 Chestnut Street
1978	Charleen Cuckovich joins company and has first basket show; the same year, Dave establishes a direct sales organization
1980	Longaberger employees construct the world's largest basket
1981	First Basket Bee is held in Dresden with 150 in attendance
1981	Dave sells Popeye's restaurant
1983	Dave sells Dresden IGA

1983	The J. W. Longaberger Collection is introduced. The J. W. Market Basket, the collection's first edition, exceeds 6,000 in sales
1983	Dave agrees to purchase the Asplin Basket Company, a veneering plant in Hartville, Ohio
1983	Hartville plant has devastating fire
1983	Dave purchases old paper mill on lower Main Street
1984–90	The corporate office is located in Zanesville, Ohio
1984	Tami Longaberger graduates from Ohio State University and begins career with the company
1986	Company has severe financial problems, and 500 workers (50 percent of the workforce) are laid off; product line is also drastically reduced
1987	Rachel Longaberger begins her career with the company
1987	The Bee moves from Dresden to the Convention Center in Columbus
1988	Company opens its first retail shop, the Village Etc. Shop in Dresden
1988	Dresden Senior Center opens
1988	*The Longaberger Story and How We Did It* is published
1989	First basket tours are conducted
1990	Kenny Wolford Park opens
1990	Pottery products are introduced by the company

1990	Company name is changed to The Longaberger Company
1990	Manufacturing Building A opens
1990	Popeye's Soda Shop opens in Dresden
1990–97	Corporate office is located in Dresden, Ohio
1991	Employee health clinic opens
1992	Manufacturing Building C opens
1992	The J. W. Longaberger Collection's Cake Basket has sales in excess of 98,000
1993	Two Basket Bees are held back-to-back
1993	Manufacturing Building B opens
1993	Dresden Swim Center opens
1993	Dedication ceremony for Tri-Valley High School addition
1994	Dave, Tami, and Rachel form The Longaberger Company's board of directors
1994	Tami is named president
1994	Dave's old elementary school is renovated and reopens as Longaberger University
1994	Company sales hit $350 million mark
1995	The millionth guest visits the factory
1995	Groundbreaking for the new corporate office building in Newark, Ohio

1995	Family Center opens
1995	Hartville Employee and Guest Center opens
1995	Manufacturing Building E opens
1995	An estimated 400,000 visitors come to Dresden
1996	Company sales reach $500 million
1996	Company has a million shows
1996	*Forbes* lists company as number 497 of top privately owned companies in America
1996	The Product Gallery at the Manufacturing Campus opens
1997	The Place Off the Square (the hotel) opens in Newark, Ohio
1997	Corporate employees move into new office building (the Basket)
1998	Three Bees are held back-to-back
1998	The Crawford Barn raising occurs
1998	Tami Longaberger named CEO and president
1998	Senior Center renamed the Bonnie Longaberger Senior Center
1998	Annual sales exceed $700 million
1998	Rachel Longaberger named president of the Longaberger Foundation
1999	The sales organization has 52,000 sales consultants

1999   First two non-family members, Bob Beam and Stephanie
                Imhoff, named to serve on company board of directors

1999   Dave Longaberger passes away

1999   Longaberger Golf Club, an eighteen-hole championship
                golf course, opens

1999   Longaberger Homestead, a retail, entertainment, and
                dining complex, opens

INDEX